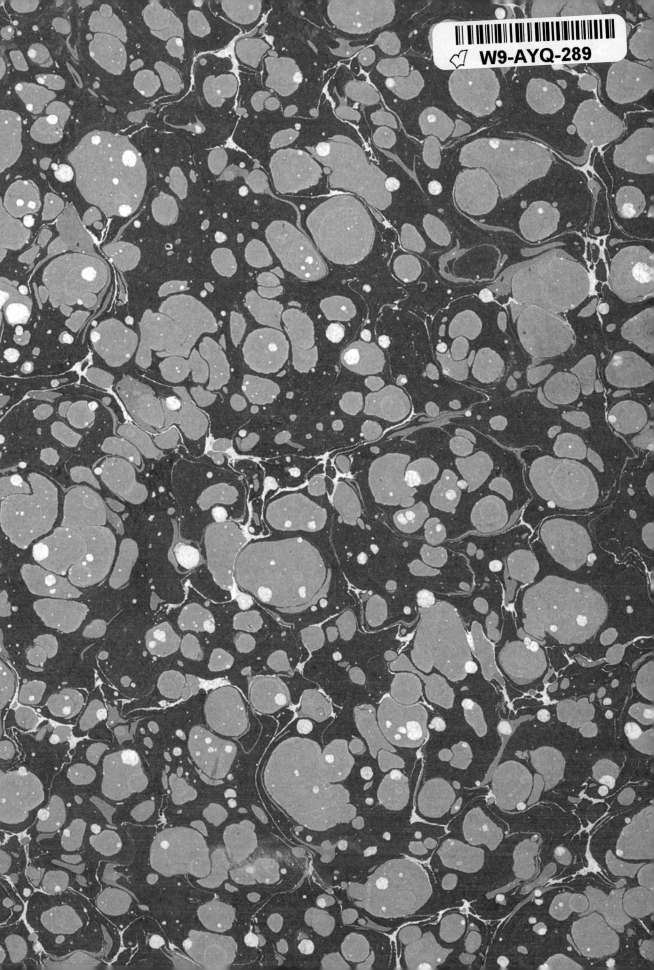

BOOKS AS HISTORY

"Li interrogo e mi rispondono. E parlano
e cantano per me." –
Francesco Petrarca, on books
Aprile 2010

BOOKS AS HISTORY

The importance of books beyond their texts

DAVID PEARSON

THE BRITISH LIBRARY & OAK KNOLL PRESS 2008

First published 2008 by
The British Library
96 Euston Road
London NW1 2DB
and
Oak Knoll Press
310 Delaware Street
New Castle
DE 19720

A CIP record for this book is
available from The British Library
and the Library of Congress

ISBN 978 0 7123 4923 9 (BL)
ISBN 978 1 58456 233 7 (OKP)

Designed and typeset by
Phil Cleaver and Emily Berry
of etal-design.com
Printed in Hong Kong by Paramount Printing Company Ltd.

CONTENTS

IC
XC

CHAPTER ONE

BOOKS IN HISTORY

For many centuries, books have been emblems of our culture and regarded as one of the defining characteristics of developed civilisations. They have been symbolically central to many religions and they have been identified with learning and sound moral virtues. They have been signs, or even manifestations, of power and magic: Shakespeare's Prospero, whose library was 'dukedom large enough', was to be overthrown by seizing and destroying his books; Marlowe's Faustus would burn his books as a last desperate measure to save himself from damnation. The need to control the dangerous potential of this key medium of communication and information has exercised the minds of many political rulers, who have supported the approach taken in Ray Bradbury's *Fahrenheit 451*; contentious books should be suppressed or destroyed. The coming of the book, and its subsequent spread to mass markets, has brought entertainment, education, political change, and spiritual or intellectual development to millions of people over the centuries. An eleventh-century mosaic (opposite) still surviving on the walls of St Sophia in Istanbul, depicting Christ flanked by the Emperor Constantine IX and his wife, nicely summarises the veneration and respect in which the book, and the idea of the book, has been held over many ages. The Emperor holds a bag of money, while Christ holds a book.

Books are also tremendously familiar objects, and easy to find. New ones are being produced all the time, and our libraries and bookshops are full of them, providing access to information, knowledge and cultural heritage. As historical artefacts go, they are still relatively cheap to acquire and abundant in supply. A nineteenth-century book, or even a seventeenth-century one, in sound contemporary condition, can often be bought for a fraction of the price which might be sought for a clock, or a picture, or some other household object of comparable date. It is not hard to obtain permission within our extensive networks of research and historic libraries to be able to hold, examine and study books of all periods.

Books have always been an essential part of the equipment of wizards and magicians, who are often represented with books—Prospero's books were the source of his magic, while Faustus summoned the devil with book in hand

The burning of books is an emotive cultural image. The Nazis are notorious as book-burners, and the images of their book bonfires of the 1930s are well known (overleaf), but the idea has a much longer history. The first Chinese Emperor, Qin Shi Huang, is remembered not only for the Great Wall of China and the terracotta army, but also as the first great ruler to try to control the thinking of his people by burning books. Ray Bradbury's Fahrenheit 451 *has entered the canon of classic 20th-century fiction for its portrayal of a society in which the reading or keeping of books is a crime, and in which firemen are employed to burn books*

The Future of the Book in the Digital Age
Edited by Bill Cope and Angus Phillips
CP CHANDOS PUBLISHING

Talks

Digitise or Die: What Is the Future of the Book?

The roll-out of e-books could result in the availability of a plethora of material currently out of print, but will it also leave the book trade experiencing the same copyright problems as the movie and music industries? And whither the relationship between an author and a publisher when writers can publish their own work cheaply? These and other pertinent questions are pondered by a London Book Fair panel that includes Margaret Atwood (*below*), Andrew O'Hagan, Erica Wagner and Stephen Page, the chief executive of Faber & Faber. *QEH, London SE1 (08703 800 400) Tue* **Stuart Price**

Despite all this, we are now living through a time of great change in which the status and future of the book is increasingly questioned. The death of the book has been in the air for some time, as a consequence of the communications revolution brought about by new technology. The advent of the Internet is widely and rightly identified as one of those great watersheds, like the invention of printing or the mechanisation of industry, which affect the way people live and think. Other new communication media, like radio and television, have come along and established a comfortable co-existence alongside books, but the Internet has greater potential to supplant, rather than supplement, the primacy of print on paper as the preferred method of transmitting texts from one person to another, whether it be for work or pleasure.

Will books die? Much speculation takes place against a background of fast-moving change. We are currently too close to the first wave of that change process to be able to forecast all the consequences, or their precise chronology, but we can make some predictions and try to pick our way through some of the conflicting opinions which abound. The death of the book is resisted and denied at least as much as it is forecast, partly on the grounds of empirical observation and partly on more sentimental ones. People *like* books and many current users of such a familiar and trusted part of the fabric of life are instinctively hostile to the notion that they may become less necessary. More concretely, it is rightly observed that we are still seeing a steady increase in the numbers of books published and purchased year on year, that e-books of today are poor and clumsy substitutes, and that the long-term stability of electronic media has yet to be proven. The death of the book could be like the paperless office, a false prophecy which will not come to be.

We should be wary of such observations; the technology is in its infancy and there are already some arenas, like the world of scientific journals, in which electronic communication has all but taken over from traditional formats. Scientists and biomedical researchers, who need immediate access to the outputs of the global research network, rely primarily on Internet-enabled electronic

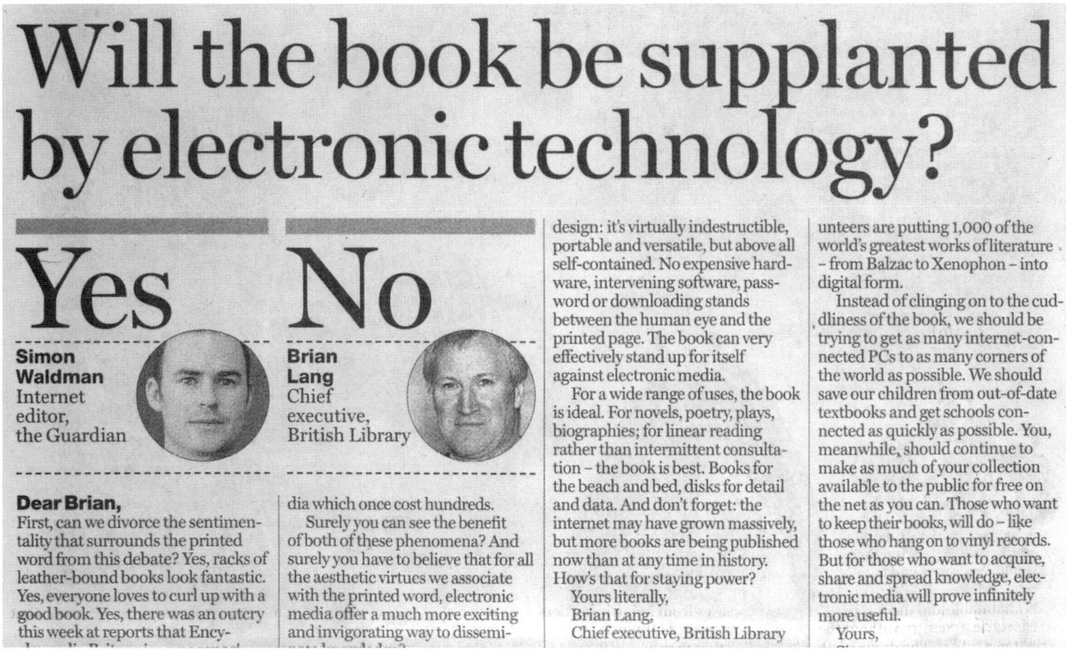

Will the book be supplanted by electronic technology?

Yes

Simon Waldman
Internet editor, the Guardian

No

Brian Lang
Chief executive, British Library

Dear Brian,
First, can we divorce the sentimentality that surrounds the printed word from this debate? Yes, racks of leather-bound books look fantastic. Yes, everyone loves to curl up with a good book. Yes, there was an outcry this week at reports that Ency-

dia which once cost hundreds.

Surely you can see the benefit of both of these phenomena? And surely you have to believe that for all the aesthetic virtues we associate with the printed word, electronic media offer a much more exciting and invigorating way to dissemi-

design: it's virtually indestructible, portable and versatile, but above all self-contained. No expensive hardware, intervening software, password or downloading stands between the human eye and the printed page. The book can very effectively stand up for itself against electronic media.

For a wide range of uses, the book is ideal. For novels, poetry, plays, biographies; for linear reading rather than intermittent consultation – the book is best. Books for the beach and bed, disks for detail and data. And don't forget: the internet may have grown massively, but more books are being published now than at any time in history. How's that for staying power?

Yours literally,
Brian Lang,
Chief executive, British Library

unteers are putting 1,000 of the world's greatest works of literature – from Balzac to Xenophon – into digital form.

Instead of clinging on to the cuddliness of the book, we should be trying to get as many internet-connected PCs to as many corners of the world as possible. We should save our children from out-of-date textbooks and get schools connected as quickly as possible. You, meanwhile, should continue to make as much of your collection available to the public for free on the net as you can. Those who want to keep their books, will do – like those who hang on to vinyl records. But for those who want to acquire, share and spread knowledge, electronic media will prove infinitely more useful.

Yours,

The future of the book, and its survival (or not) in a digital age, is much discussed and debated

publishing mechanisms to disseminate their findings and discover those of their peers. In 2004, the pharmaceutical company GlaxoSmithKline announced that it would be closing its fourteen libraries and replacing them with an entirely electronic network to meet the documentation and information needs of its staff. Humanities scholars are gradually catching up with their scientific colleagues by recognising the potential of the Internet to go beyond mere access to textual sources, to the creation of interactive frameworks within which subjects can be explored, and knowledge shared, in new ways. Universities are increasingly complementing – or replacing – their traditional-style libraries (centred around the storing and providing of books) with learning resource centres or information commons, where students can access electronic media without losing the element of social space which libraries have always provided. These changes can happen very quickly once all the necessary strands of a new technology come together; consider the speed with which vinyl records were overtaken by CDs.

This celebration of the function of a printer was compiled by Beatrice Warde in 1932. The digital age makes the whole notion of a printing house, and its importance, as obsolete as the hand-operated common press shown in this 19th-century illustration below. Words and ideas will continue to be produced, but the way of publishing and storing them will be radically different

This is a printing office

Crossroads of Civilization;
Refuge of all the Arts
against the ravages of time:
Armoury of fearless truth
against whispering rumour;
Incessant trumpet of trade!

From this place words may fly abroad—
not to perish on waves of sound,
not to vary with the writer's hand,
but fixed in time,
having been verified in proof.

Friend, you stand on sacred ground...
This is a printing office

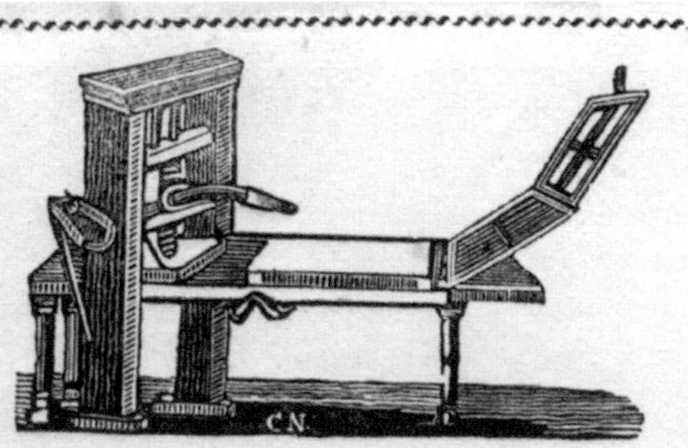

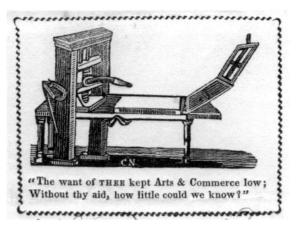

"The want of THEE kept Arts & Commerce low;
Without thy aid, how little could we know?"

The observation that other media have developed in the past in parallel is sometimes used to challenge the idea that books, as we know them, will vanish – other competitors for the attention of readers, like radio or television, have come along, and books have continued to thrive. This is a false line of reasoning. A film of *Pride and Prejudice* is not the same thing as Austen's text, and it is widely appreciated that people will want to experience both, as they are each rewarding in their own way. The threat, or promise, of the e-book is that it will replace the physical format of the book by becoming a completely acceptable, or improved, surrogate, without changing the communicative experience in any significant way (although it may also offer the opportunity to write new kinds of books). As J. Yellowlees Douglas put it in *The end of books* (published in 2000), 'in the entertainment industry, killer technologies generally make only equipment obsolete: the compact disc destroyed the market for turntables and vinyl alike but did not alter so much as a single musical genre'. The physical format of the book, in this context, is the equipment.

OVERLEAF
Will the library of the future be like the Jedi Archive in Star Wars, *where the books are all containers of electronic data, to be read with a computer?*

One of the *Star Wars* films contains a scene in a library, where Obi-Wan Kenobi goes to find some information which was captured and recorded in the past. The library looks spatially familiar – it is strikingly reminiscent of the famous Long Room at Trinity College, Dublin – but the 'books' are capsules of electronically-stored information and they are read on a computer. If our world of books is to be completely transformed in this way, a number of things will have to come together. Most obviously, the contents of books – the texts – will need to be available digitally rather than as words on paper. Books published today invariably exist in some kind of electronic format before going to print and making the transition to genuinely electronic publication depends essentially on commercial viability and user acceptance; the world of electronic journals shows how it can work.

We also have an enormous heritage of the printed and written word, bequeathed to us over countless generations. Until recently, most pundits would have predicted that the prospect of comprehensive retrospective digitisation of this vast collective store of world culture was far-fetched and implausible; now we may be less sure. Towards the end of 2004 Google made the headlines with its

At the end of 2004, Google announced the start of a huge digitisation initiative, to convert the holdings of a number of major libraries to digital forms; it was rightly recognised as a milestone project, of global significance. Not everyone is happy about these developments; the publishing industry has expressed concern about where Google is going, and on a perceived threat to commercial and copyright interests

Google to put books from great libraries on internet

announcement of a huge digitisation programme, working with major libraries in England and the USA, to make the full-text contents of millions of books freely available on the Internet. Given the myriad other initiatives which have been moving forward in recent years to retroconvert books, manuscripts, images and every other kind of documentary heritage to digital format, the day draws ever closer when there is an electronic option available for most of the texts that people want to read, for whatever purpose.

Google's competitors have been swift to join the digitisation race: in 2006, for example, Microsoft signed a major deal with the British Library

The world of digital content is arguably developing faster than the hardware we use to read it. Most people still find a book a far more comfortable option for reading a text than a desktop or handheld computer screen, and we typically print our electronically-transmitted texts out onto to paper to read them. We are still waiting for the e-book, with its e-paper, which is genuinely as convenient to read as the paperback we read on our lap, on the train, or in the bath. A number of major players in global technology are actively working on this challenge and new products are gradually being introduced to the marketplace. Once the really successful model comes along – which it surely will? – a step change will take

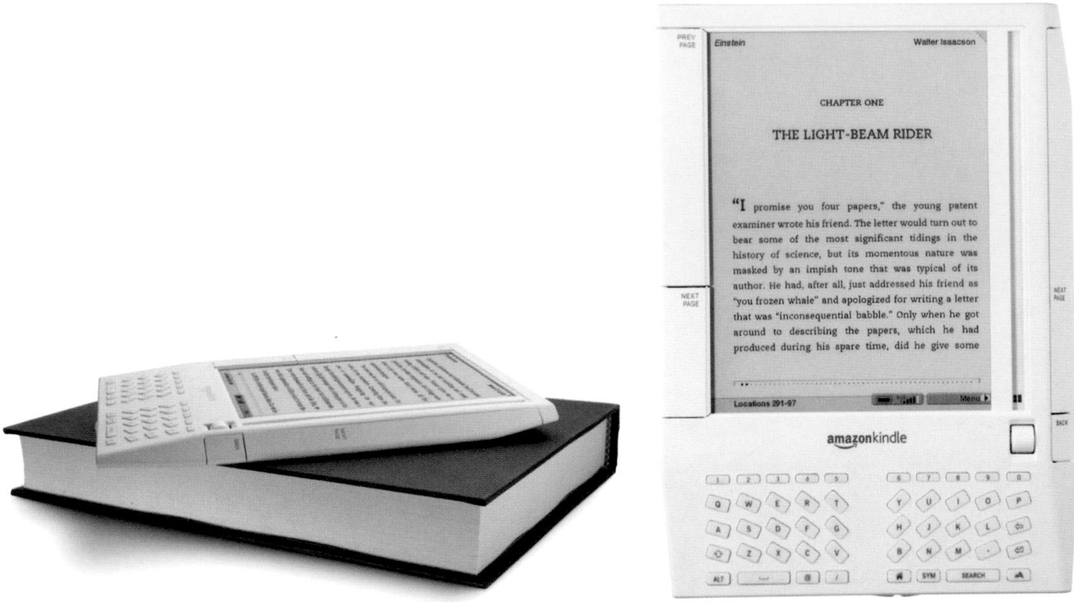

How long will it be before you can read this book as satisfactorily on a hand-held e-book as you can read it as a printed book? At the end of 2007, the Internet bookseller Amazon announced the launch of the latest generation of e-book readers, the Kindle

place in the transformation process. We also have some serious issues to address over copyright, not only for new material but also in the context of moving the published output of the twentieth century onto digital platforms, but the music industry, which is ahead in this game, is showing that these issues can be resolved, albeit with some bumpy rides along the way.

The other big question mark over digital media concerns their long-term sustainability. People rightly observe that a book, or a clay tablet, is a more stable format than a digital file on a hard disc or a CD-ROM. The former will last for hundreds, or thousands, of years whereas the latter may become unreadable within a decade. The prevalence and importance of electronic media is too great for this problem to remain unsolved and it seems likely that the considerable efforts now being devoted to digital preservation will generate the answers.

Once this is done, all the essential building blocks will be in place to allow that full-scale shift in the world's reading habits to take place. Texts will be freed from the bondage of printed books; a Shakespeare sonnet, or a cookery book, will exist and be used as happily in cyberspace as it does on paper. In that form, it has a physical reality as a short sequence of electronic code which can be stored on computers and swiftly transmitted from one to

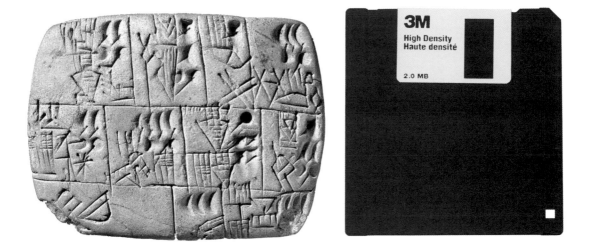

another, but it is essentially an intangible one. Not marble, nor the gilded monuments of princes, shall outlive this powerful rhyme (as Shakespeare put it in his sonnet 55), but books as physical objects may no longer be needed to ensure that.

This book is not primarily about these technological changes, but is rather about our perception of books, and the things that matter about books, against this transformational backdrop. The changes on the horizon are likely to affect not only the ways in which we transmit and read the kind of information which was traditionally contained in books, but also our whole framework of values around them. They will affect our relationships with books individually, and collectively in libraries.

A clay tablet, one of mankind's earliest means for long-term recording of information, can hold only a few sentences but can last for thousands of years and remain readable (as long as you know the language). A floppy disc can hold hundreds of thousands of words but is already yesterday's technology and may become unreadable as computing moves on. Much work is now being done on digital preservation, to ensure the long-term saving of electronic media, and to solve the challenges posed by the pace at which the technology develops

A NEW SET OF VALUES

The main purpose of this book lies in challenging the notion that books are interesting only as gateways to texts, and in demonstrating that they have much more to offer as cultural and historic artefacts. If their rationale is purely textual, their obsolescence seems guaranteed: the key point is that it is not, and that we are collectively in danger of making bad decisions about what should and should not be preserved for posterity if we overlook this.

We may end up with some adjusted values about books, and the features of books, which really matter, but they will be considered ones which are founded on the world we now live in, rather than the inherited and insufficiently questioned values of the past.

Separating books from texts presents some intellectual challenges as we are so used to using the terms synonymously. Much of the veneration with which books have been surrounded for so long is to do with texts and ideas, and their transmission, rather than with the books as objects. When Milton spoke of a good book as 'the precious life-blood of a master spirit, embalmed and treasured up on purpose to a life beyond life', or when Thomas Jefferson said 'I cannot live without books', they were really praising the ability of words, put together as text, to do all those things that texts can do: inform, inspire, educate, move. Books have been the containers, the hardware, the conduits which have been so essential to take the texts from authors to consumers, and to preserve those texts for posterity.

They have not been passive conduits. Books have, in their three-dimensional formats, physical characteristics which have both affected the ways in which their contents have been received, and been exploited for their artefactual potential. The pioneering thinking of the late twentieth-century bibliographer Don McKenzie on what he came to call the sociology of texts – how the material form in which texts are transmitted influences their meaning – has focused the attention of many contemporary scholars onto the importance of the whole book, and not just the words on the page. The book as a text is something which is open to various kinds of surrogacy, but the book as an object is something for which there is no complete substitute. The qualities they have as objects are not only part of the history of communication, but also of the history of art and design.

Books, down the ages, have not been lifeless intermediaries in between authors and readers; their physical reality has been fully exploited for the opportunity for interaction between texts and their recipients. Here is a real difference between the world of books and the world of cybertexts, where the latter is the poorer. A book can be written in, defaced, altered, beautified or cherished, to produce a preservable object with an individual history. A true e-book, or a computer which is used to display texts garnered from a web-accessible databank, does not have those qualities. Someone reading this text, as a book, may scribble comments in the margins, or put it in a new binding, and create an object with qualities of lasting individuality which the PC on which it was written will never have. The developing web world of wikis and blogs may one day produce e-books in which the cumulative reactions of everyone who reads them are recorded, but the model is not quite the same.

For many centuries, until the introduction of mechanisation in the printing and publishing industries in the nineteenth century, all books were unique handcrafted objects. The texts were set by hand, each copy produced represented a series of separate pulls on the printing press, and the resulting printed sheets were gathered, folded, sewn and bound by hand. No two copies of a book of this period, even before they leave the bookseller's shop, can be truly identical; the printing process could introduce no end of slight variance between one copy and another, and the binding process yet more. The idea of uniform edition binding, with which we are familiar today, is a relatively modern one; locate twenty copies of an eighteenth-century book and the chances are that the bindings will all be different. Binding was just the beginning of a customisation cycle that developed as books passed from hand to hand and were owned by successive generations, each of whom might leave some mark: inscriptions, annotations, bookplates, new bindings, armorial stamps, defacements. Nineteenth- and twentieth-century books display less variety resulting from their production techniques, but are equally susceptible to being marked or written in by their owners.

Books develop their own individual histories which become part of our wider historical heritage. They can provide a direct interface between readers and authors; we know which books were published in the seventeenth century but we learn a lot more about their contemporary influence and reckoned worth when we have copies which have been through the hands of owners of the time. We have a series of values in our minds about the relative worth of authors of the past, influenced by the standards of our own age and layers imposed by previous generations; if we wish to truly understand their influence and standing among their contemporar-

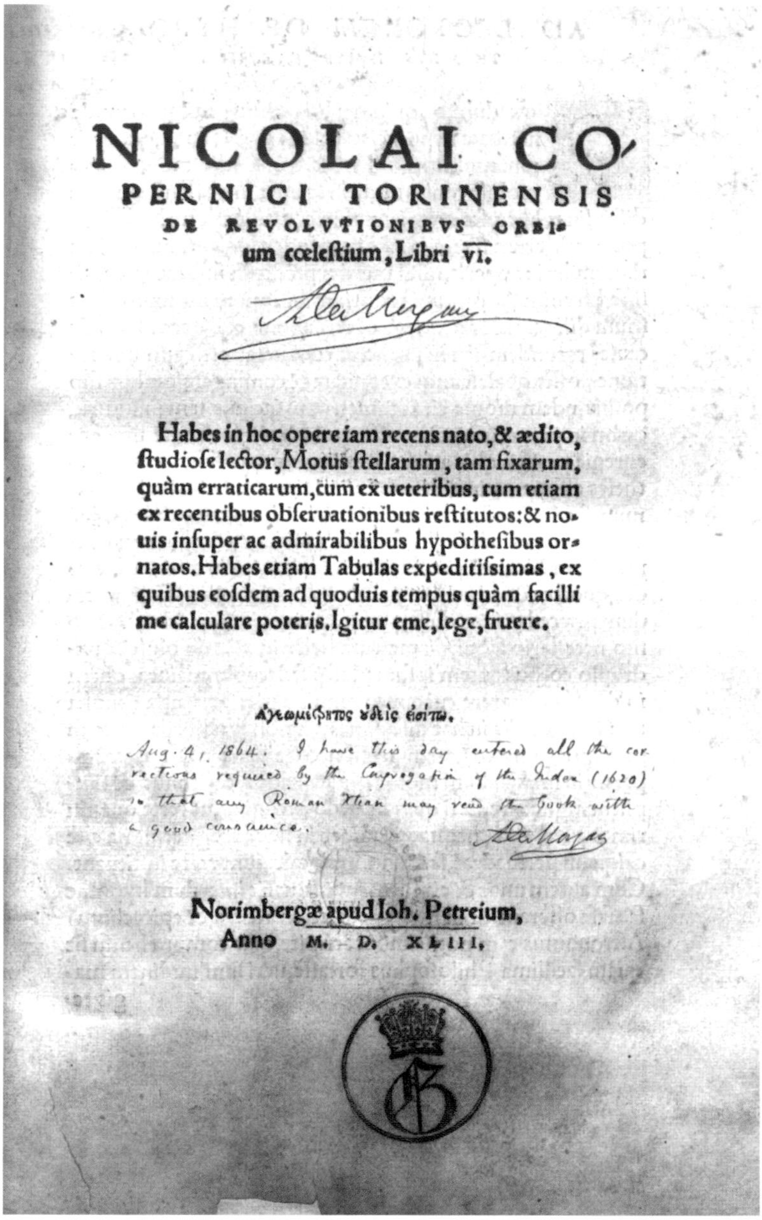
NICOLAI CO-
PERNICI TORINENSIS
DE REVOLVTIONIBVS ORBI-
um cœleſtium, Libri VI.

A De Morgan

Habes in hoc opere iam recens nato, & ædito, ſtudioſe lector, Motus ſtellarum, tam fixarum, quàm erraticarum, cum ex ueteribus, tum etiam ex recentibus obſeruationibus reſtitutos: & nouis inſuper ac admirabilibus hypotheſibus ornatos. Habes etiam Tabulas expeditiſsimas, ex quibus eoſdem ad quoduis tempus quàm facillime calculare poteris. Igitur eme, lege, fruere.

Ἀγεωμέτρητος οὐδεὶς εἰσίτω.

Aug. 4, 1864. I have this day entered all the corrections required by the Congregation of the Index (1620) so that any Roman Xtian may read the book with a good conscience.
A De Morgan

Norimbergæ apud Ioh. Petreium,
Anno M. D. XLIII.

A study of every surviving copy of early editions of Copernicus's De revolutionibus*—the book which first explained that the earth circles the sun—was able to demonstrate, from the evidence of ownership and the notes in the books, how Copernicus's ideas spread, how contemporary scientists regarded them, and how they networked with one another* ies, we should look at the ways in which their books were treated at the time.

The possibilities of this approach to books has been demonstrated by Owen Gingerich, who carried out a detailed survey of all known surviving copies of the first two editions of Copernicus's *De revolutionibus*. By recording the ownership, annotations and other physical features of over 600 copies, spread around the world, Gingerich was able to show how quickly the book was acquired by sixteenth-century astronomers across Europe, how that network of experts shared and communicated ideas, and how receptive (or otherwise) those first generations of readers were to Copernicus's heliocentric theories. There is now a growing industry in this kind of scholarship, looking closely at various kinds of copy-specific evidence in books to gain a better understanding of their impact on early readers. Kevin Sharpe has analysed the annotated books of one particular mid seventeenth-century country gentleman, Sir William Drake, to get behind his political ideas and developing thoughts, while Eamon Duffy has looked at the annotations of individual owners in a number of fifteenth-and sixteenth-century liturgical books to gain insights into devotional practice around the time of the Reformation at a personal level.

Of course, texts remain central to the values and purposes associated with books, and will continue to do so; the word will be at the end as it is at the beginning. But the status of books as essential mediators in the process is likely to change, and this book will further explore and illustrate the ways in which they matter instead as objects, and as historical artefacts, beyond their initial purposes as containers and conveyers of texts. It will, by extension, imply the importance of selectively preserving them and the evidence they contain, even though their primary textual function may come to be fulfilled by other media. The examples included here of the different kinds of historical meaning which books can convey are only examples chosen from the almost endless supply which can be found in our libraries, bookshops and private collections. 'Books as history' may seem to be a phrase with sinister overtones but let us increasingly recognise that books may be history in an entirely positive sense, as unique objects in our inheritance from the past, with a wealth of meaning worth preserving and interpreting.

A puissant noble et excellent prince Jehan filz du Roy de france duc de berry et dauuergne. Conte de poitou. destampes. de bouloingne et dauuergne. Laurens de premier fait clerc et vostre moins digne secretaire et serf de bonne foy toute obeissance et subjection deue. comme a mon tresredoubte seigneur et bienfaitteur et act

ttrablement recevoir le labeur de mon estude et benignement excuser la petitece de mon engin au regard de la grant besongne de vre commandement ja pieca entreprise et nouvellement finee. Combien que par vostre especial mandemet Jaye soubz la confiance de vostre naturele benignite et en espoir de vostre gracieux ayde et confort. entreprins le dangereux et long traueil de la transflation dun tres seu

CHAPTER TWO

BOOKS BEYOND TEXTS

THE IMAGE OF THE BOOK AND THE BOOK AS IMAGE

The Duc de Berry receives a newly-completed work from the translator, Laurens du Premierfait, as depicted in a late 15th century manuscript

The book is a hugely pervasive image in western culture. Books are found everywhere; not only the real things in libraries and bookshops, but representations of books in pictures, in architectural decoration, in memorial sculpture, in signs and symbols. An image of writers and scholars presenting their books to rulers and saints, conveying a sense of completion of worthwhile work and the transfer of wisdom, was an enduring one throughout the medieval and early modern period (as in the example opposite). Countless saints, statesmen, clerics and writers have had their portraits painted with books in their hands or in the background; many universities include books within their coats of arms. A lawyer's office will be full of books not just because they are working tools, but because they create a desired image. Politicians, when interviewed on television, regularly choose to do so with shelves of books as a backdrop. People like to be represented in association with books; it lends them an air of seriousness and knowledge.

Of course, as has already been observed, the imagery in most of these cases is primarily a reference to texts, to those sequences of words which contain the knowledge, art, or message of salvation which the creator of the image wishes to conjure up in the mind of the viewer. The book as an object, as a three-dimensional device to contain those texts and make them accessible, is merely incidental in that context. Or is it? How important is that physical manifestation? What do books offer us, beyond words, and how do their physical formats and design characteristics contribute to their overall impact? Where do we draw the line between the book as a text and the book as an object, something which cannot be entirely replicated by transferring the content to another medium? This chapter will seek to explore some of these questions by considering ways in which books as objects have properties which

Saints, statesmen, kings, scholars, doctors, clergymen and many others have had their portraits drawn, down the ages, with books in their hands or in the background: here are St Jerome, Henry VIII, the 17th-century oriental scholar Edmund Castell, the 17th-century owner of Charlecote Park (Richard Lucy), and the 18th-century doctor Giovanni Morgagni

It was the worst year of her life when Trisha Goddard, queen of daytime TV, lost her mother and her close friend. Now she's through it, and ready to tackle other people's problems once again

BY RACHEL COOKE

IN A Soho hotel, Trisha Goddard, doyenne of the television bear pit that is daytime chat, sips peppermint tea. Staying healthy — which includes avoiding caffeine — is one way she "manages" her mental health. "I'm not taking any risks with it again," she says, as if it were a recalcitrant child.

In 2004, Goddard lost both her mother, Agnes (to cancer of the brain) and her personal trainer, Darryl, a close friend (he died after a run-of-the-mill bang to his head led to severe complications).

Thanks to the beady eye she keeps on both her stress levels and the alcohol she consumes, Trisha survived. "I know shit happens, but I've got enough in my arsenal to be able to get through. Last year was crap.

Politicians (like Richard Nixon, shown here)—and other kinds of celebrities—like to be depicted against a background of books; they help to support the image they wish to project

"Isn't this a bit excessive, Dad? We're not even sure if I failed yet."

Books lend an air of seriousness to a situation

University coats of arms regularly include books, the containers of the knowledge that is used and created by their members (here are Leeds, and Harvard); books regularly feature as symbols or representations of learning, as in the Times Higher *award logo (below, right)*

The image of the book, symbolising wisdom, worthwhile pursuits, and lasting achievement is familiar from all kinds of sources. The device of the Elizabethan printer John Wight, showing him carrying the Book of Knowledge (Scientia), urged readers to welcome the bringer of such material

The monumental visual impact of massed ranks of books is captured in different ways by Thomas Bodley's memorial in Merton College Chapel, Oxford—where he is encased within a frame of books—and by Anselm Kiefer's sculpture The High Priestess *(overleaf), with its rows of lead volumes of mysterious, or impenetrable, content*

Euphrat

make them special in their own right, beyond the verbal content of their texts.

THE MEDIUM AND THE MESSAGE : THE IMPACT OF DESIGN ON COMMUNICATION

Books have a diverse potential for expression and communication. A Shakespeare sonnet is something which you can hold in your mind; you can memorise the words, repeat them in your head, and appreciate the authorial art independently of any printed representation. The epic poems of Homer, *The Iliad* and *The Odyssey*, were experienced only in the mind, via recitation, for several centuries before they were ever written down. Many people would agree, though, that this is not quite the same as reading them on a page, where what the eye takes in is a not insignificant part of the total experience. You can read Shakespeare in any number of editions printed over four centuries; you can read him in an economically produced compact version, or a generously laid out private press edition with carefully chosen typeface and handmade paper. You can read him as words on a page and nothing else, or you can choose an edition where the words are supplemented by decoration or illustration. Is the experience the same? Different readers will prefer different things, but most will agree that there are subtle distinctions between the various reading experiences, to do with the visual and tactile characteristics of the different books. Modern literary scholars have increasingly recognised, and become interested in, the influence which presentation has on the way a text is perceived by a reader. The meaning or interpretation of a text is not something absolute, but is endlessly recreated through the experiences of successive readers; typography, layout, physical format and everything surrounding the words themselves all contribute to the framework within which meaning is constructed.

The book, in its physical manifestation with which we are so familiar, is a highly functional piece of design which is pleasing to use and to look at, to hold in the hand and to turn the pages. The idea of putting text onto double sided pages, and sewing leaves together – the codex format, the shape of the book as we know it – emerged in the Near East in the first few centuries AD and the

The text of Shakespeare's sonnet 106, from its 1609 printing, from a 20th-century edition, and from a handwritten one: is the reading experience identical in every case? How do the orthography, type, design layout and other features impact on the reader?

SONNETS.

106

WHen in the Chronicle of waſted time,
I ſee diſcriptions of the faireſt wights,
And beautie making beautifull old rime,
In praiſe of Ladies dead,and louely Knights,
Then in the blazon of ſweet beauties beſt,
Of hand,of foote,of lip,of eye,of brow,
I ſee their antique Pen would haue expreſt,
Euen ſuch a beauty as you maiſter now.
So all their praiſes are but propheſies
Of this our time,all you prefiguring,
And for they look'd but with deuining eyes,
They had not ſtill enough your worth to ſing:
For we which now behold theſe preſent dayes,
Haue eyes to wonder,but lack toungs to praiſe.

When in the chronicle of wasted time
I see descriptions of the fairest wights,
And beauty making beautiful old rhyme,
In praise of ladies dead, and lovely knights,
Then in the blazon of sweet beauty's best,
Of hand, of foot, of lip, of eye, of brow,
I see their antique pen would have expressed
Even such a beauty as you master now.
So all their praises are but prophecies
Of this our time, all you prefiguring,
And for they looked but with divining eyes,
They had not skill enough your worth to sing:
For we, which now behold these present days,
Have eyes to wonder, but lack tongues to praise.

One Hundred Six

When in the chronicle of wasted time
I see descriptions of the fairest wights,
And beauty making beautiful old rime,
In praise of ladies dead and lovely knights,
Then, in the blazon of sweet beauty's best,
Of hand, of foot, of lip, of eye, of brow,
I see their antique pen would have express'd
Even such a beauty as you master now.
So all their praises are but prophecies
Of this our time, all you prefiguring;
And, for they look'd but with divining eyes,
They had not skill enough your worth to sing:
For we, which now behold these present days,
Have eyes to wonder, but lack tongues to praise.

THE VALLEY OF UNREST

Once it smiled a silent dell
Where the people did not dwell;
They had gone unto the wars,
Trusting to the mild-eyed stars,
Nightly, from their azure towers,
To keep watch above the flowers,
In the midst of which all day
The red sun-light lazily lay.
Now each visitor shall confess
The sad valley's restlessness.
Nothing there is motionless—
Nothing save the airs that brood
Over the magic solitude.
Ah, by no wind are stirred those trees
That palpitate like the chill seas
Around the misty Hebrides!
Ah, by no wind those clouds are driven
That rustle through the unquiet Heaven
Uneasily, from morn till even,
Over the violets there that lie
In Myriad types of the human eye
Over the lilies there that wave
And weep above a nameless grave!
They wave:—from out their fragrant tops
Eternal dews come down in drops.
They weep:—from off their delicate stems
Perennial tears descend in gems.

BRIDAL BALLAD

The ring is on my hand,
  And the wreath is on my brow;
Satins and jewels grand
Are all at my command,
  And I am happy now.

And my lord he loves me well;
  But, when first he breathed his vow,
I felt my bosom swell—
For the words rang as a knell,
And the voice seemed *his* who fell

The Valley of Unrest

ONCE it smiled a silent dell
Where the people did not dwell;
They had gone unto the wars,
Trusting to the mild-eyed stars,
Nightly from their azure towers,
To keep watch above the flowers,
In the midst of which all day
The red sunlight lazily lay.
Now each visitor shall confess
The sad valley's restlessness.
Nothing there is motionless,
Nothing save the airs that brood
Over the magic solitude.
Ah, by no wind are stirred those trees
That palpitate like the chill seas

THE VALLEY OF UNREST.

ONCE it smiled a silent dell
  Where the people did not dwell:
They had gone unto the wars,
Trusting to the mild-eyed stars,
Nightly from their azure towers
To keep watch above the flowers,
In the midst of which all day
The red sunlight lazily lay.

Three settings of Edgar Allen Poe's poem The Valley of Unrest, from editions of 1870, 1908 and 1952, with and without illustrations: again, what differences do the presentational and design factors make to the impact on the reader? Does a picture enhance, or interfere with, the reader's envisaging of the scene? Which page layout permits the optimal appreciation of the poem?

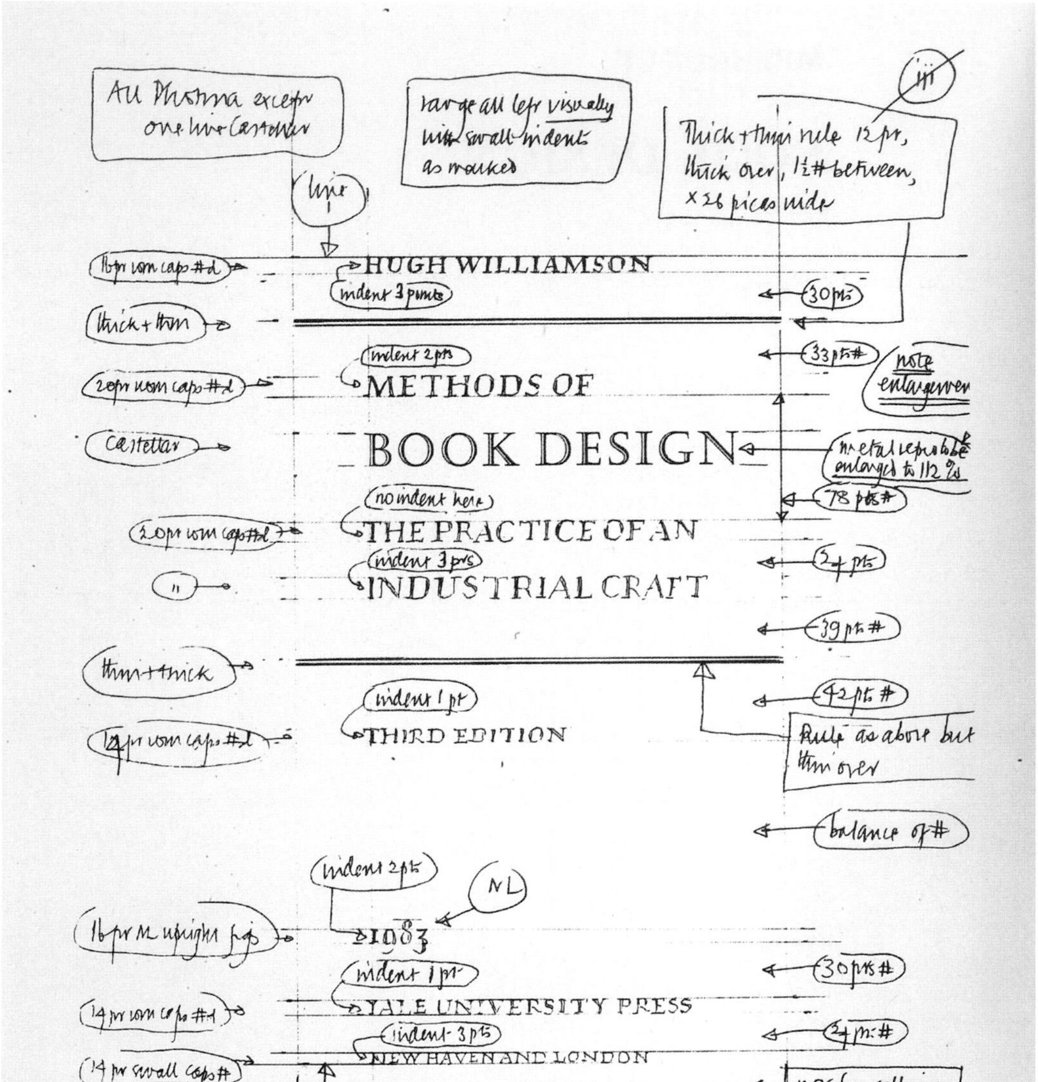
HUGH WILLIAMSON

METHODS OF

BOOK DESIGN

THE PRACTICE OF AN

INDUSTRIAL CRAFT

THIRD EDITION

1983

YALE UNIVERSITY PRESS

NEW HAVEN AND LONDON

1983

DELHI

OXFORD UNIVERSITY PRESS

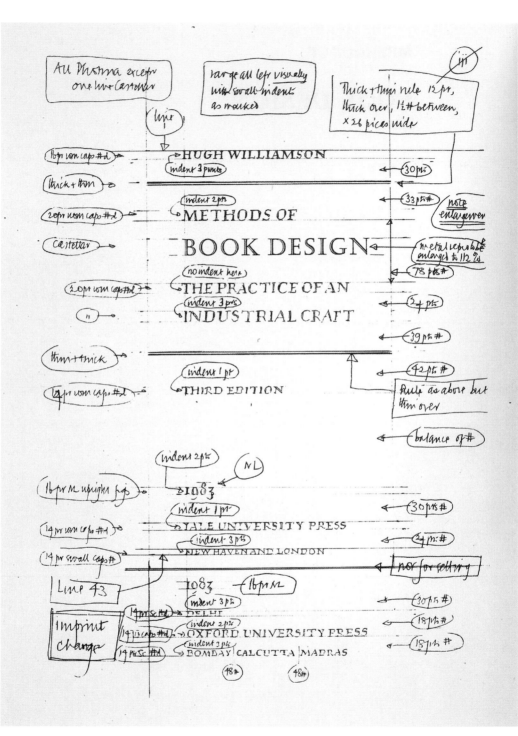

BOMBAY CALCUTTA MADRAS

subsequent longevity of the design, which has yet to be superseded by anything that can match it for portability and all-round usability, testifies to its success. Books are effective, as well as satisfying, objects.

The importance of paying attention to the look and feel of books has a long history rooted in sound commercial sense – those who produce books wish to make things that people want to buy. A successful book must have a combination of design factors working in harmony. The typeface must be legible, the layout of the pages and the interrelationship of the various parts of the text must be pleasing on the eye, and the finished product must be of a size and shape which opens easily and handles comfortably. Understanding the history of books, and of the communication of ideas through books, needs to take into account the impact of their physical forms, and of the ways in which these may have influenced the perceptions and expectations of the readers.

Form, and format, may subtly affect the way in which the content of a book is approached, in ways which make it difficult for the text to be read entirely objectively. The issue is not dissimilar to the debate around the way in which the quality of academic research outputs may be unfairly assessed depending on the journals in which they are published, rather than on their actual content. A brilliant piece of work published in an obscure journal may not have the impact it deserves, compared with a less original piece in a highly respected journal, not just because the obscure journal may have a smaller reader base but because people come to that journal with lower expectations. The way in which a text is physically presented to its readers preconditions them, to some extent, before a word is read; someone opening a handsomely produced book is likely to have some innate expectations about its content, influenced by the form and design, which will be subtly different from the expectations generated by opening a cheap, unattractively produced one. The packaging of a text at any particular point in time is a part of its (and our) history.

Book design is a subtle skill – as Richard Hendel put it, writing *On Book Design* in 1998, 'if printing is the black art, book design may be the invisible one'. Like much of the most effective design, it is most successful when the user of the object does not stop to think

OPPOSITE
Successful book design involves careful attention to each individual component of a page, as well as to its layout and overall visual impact: the example opposite shows the meticulous care given by Hugh Williamson to the title page of his classic text on the subject

OVERLEAF
The effective design of the Everyman series, like many other 20th-century publishing ventures which reached wide audiences, was a significant element of its success

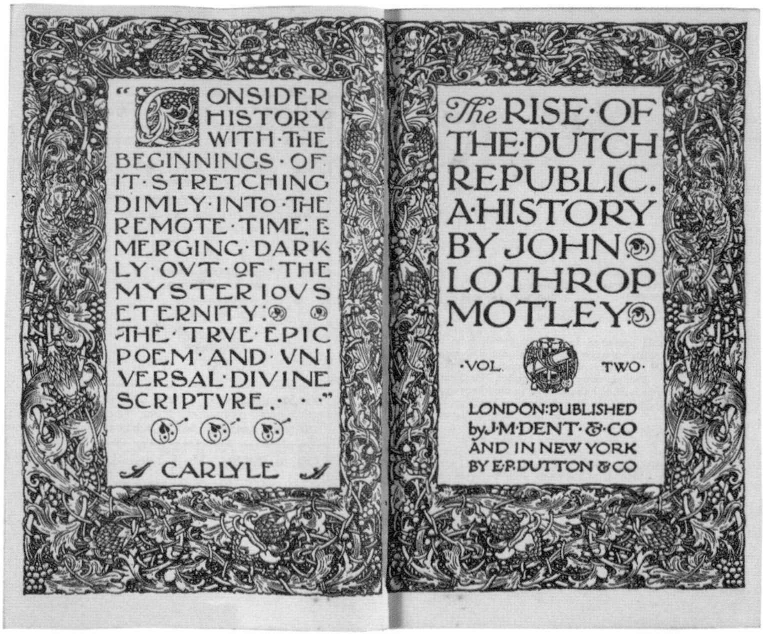
"CONSIDER HISTORY WITH·THE BEGINNINGS·OF IT·STRETCHING DIMLY·INTO·THE REMOTE·TIME; EMERGING·DARKLY·OVT·OF·THE MYSTERIOVS ETERNITY: THE·TRVE·EPIC POEM·AND·VNIVERSAL·DIVINE SCRIPTVRE . . ."

CARLYLE

The RISE·OF THE·DUTCH REPUBLIC. A·HISTORY BY JOHN LOTHROP MOTLEY

·VOL. TWO·

LONDON: PUBLISHED by J·M·DENT·&·CO AND IN NEW YORK BY E.P. DUTTON & CO

about what makes it work; it just does. Many grand books have been produced over the centuries which were intended to impress, to appeal to aesthetes and collectors; they have an obvious beauty and continue to be treasured in libraries, but they were not necessarily read as extensively as more ordinary-looking books have been. Relatively cheap and humble books have had more impact on more people, through their accessibility and effectiveness in communicating, than grand and imposing ones. The devising of a new small format for publishing classical texts by Aldus Manutius at the end of the fifteenth century is well known not only as an example of sound business sense, but also as a milestone in spreading the impact and acceptance of print culture in Europe.

The Everyman series, which began publishing at the beginning of the twentieth century, was hugely successful in bringing a wide range of literature to big audiences, not only because the books were affordable but also because they were strikingly well designed. The early Everyman titlepages, with their Arts and Crafts flavour, succeeded in bringing William Morris's aesthetics and ideas about

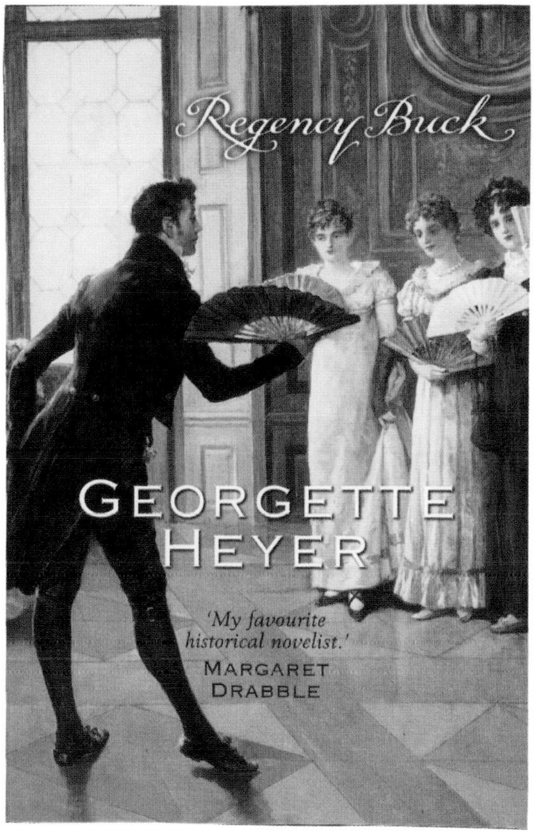

craftsmanship in an accessible way to millions, in a way that his expensive and exclusive Kelmscott Press productions could never achieve. The success of Penguin Books, founded in 1935, and the subsequent widespread popular acceptance of the paperback format, was not just to do with cost but also with smart design.

Books become part of, and testify to, the aesthetics and values of their time. This is perhaps most immediately noticeable in books produced since the middle of the nineteenth century, when changes in the organisation of publishing and in the manufacture of books led to the exploitation of book covers for marketing and representing what lay inside. This began with the use of decorated

In 2004, Arrow Books began reissuing the novels of Georgette Heyer (typically perceived as rather middle-brow historic romances) with new covers, suggesting a more sophisticated, Jane Austen-like flavour; sales improved markedly

WON
AT LAST

THE ENGLISH
COTTAGE
BRIAN COOK

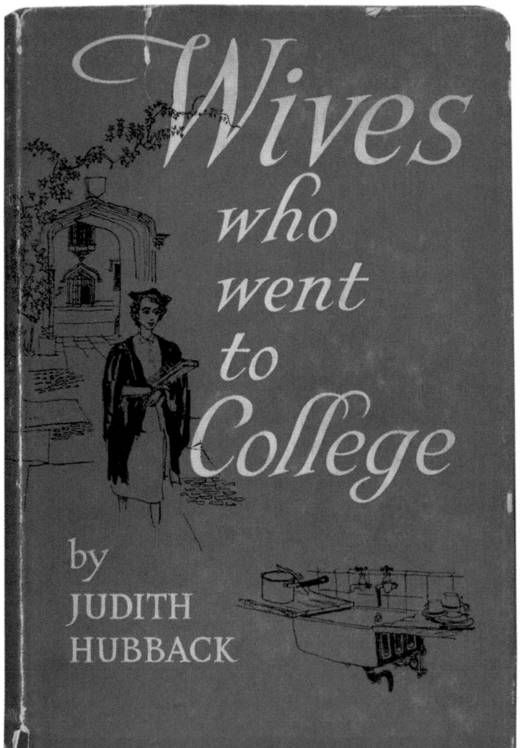
Wives
who
went
to
College
by
JUDITH
HUBBACK

Elaine Showalter
HYSTORIES
Hysterical Epidemics
and Modern Culture

cloth covers, before the evolution of the dust jacket in the late nineteenth and early twentieth century led to the full range of pictorial possibilities for the outsides of books that we are familiar with today. The historical importance of dust jackets has only slowly been recognised, and they can be hard to find in libraries which typically operate on the basis that dust jackets are trivial things, whose preservation does not merit much thought or attention. A Victorian decorated book cover, or one from the interwar years of the twentieth century, can speak just as eloquently for the spirit of its times as any other contemporary artefact. A chronological succession of the book covers used for a particular text can similarly provide a snapshot of changing cultural values or attitudes towards authors and their works. Publishers today invest heavily in cover design, recognising the importance of capturing the interest of potential buyers with striking, amusing or intriguing imagery, and in using their covers to enforce their brand and identity. Classic texts are regularly republished with new pictures on their covers, aimed at capturing new generations of readers with imagery that will appeal to them. 'Never judge a book by its cover' is an adage more related to advice than practice.

Book covers can speak eloquently not only about the subject of the text, but also about the aesthetic and cultural values of their age. Here are four book covers from 1892, 1938, 1957 and 1997 which clearly belong to their time in a way we can readily recognise—to put it another way, these covers have a contribution to make to documentary and artistic history

TYPE AND LETTER FORMS

The look and layout of the lettering in a book is an important aspect of that invisible design skill, something we rarely stop to think about but which contributes significantly to the impact and character of the finished product. Type design is a subtle art in which a combination of factors to do with the thickness, proportion and balance of the lines and curves which make up the letters determine the success of the end product. The letter shapes and type fonts we use today, which derive ultimately from Roman capitals and the uncial book hands which developed in the post-Roman era, were first perfected for printing in the late fifteenth century in Italy, most notably by the Venetian printers Nicolaus Jenson and Aldus Manutius. The very first printed books used typefaces which replicated the gothic, black letter hands which were then used for the manuscripts which this new technology was deliberately copying. Early 'Roman' typefaces were inspired

Alice's Adventures
In Wonderland

ALICE IN WONDERLAND
CENTENARY EDITION

PENGUIN CLASSICS
LEWIS CARROLL
ALICE'S ADVENTURES IN WONDERLAND AND THROUGH THE LOOKING-GLASS
CENTENARY EDITION

LEWIS CARROLL
ALICE'S
adventures in
WONDERLAND
LYNX
ILLUSTRATED BY JUSTIN TODD

A selection of examples showing how book cover designers have approached a particular text over time can be illuminating both as design history and as an insight into the perceptions and expectations of those texts down the generations.

What is the mental picture of Alice which the reader develops, reading the text, and how might the cover image precondition or influence that? Is Alice a tender (and possibly vulnerable) innocent, or a teasing minx?

These examples date from 1888 to 1999

The development of Nicolaus Jenson's Roman typeface, first used in his 1470 edition of Eusebius, has long been hailed as a milestone in western type design, and it has been widely copied in later centuries. Its clarity, good proportions and clean lines make for elegant and legible pages of text

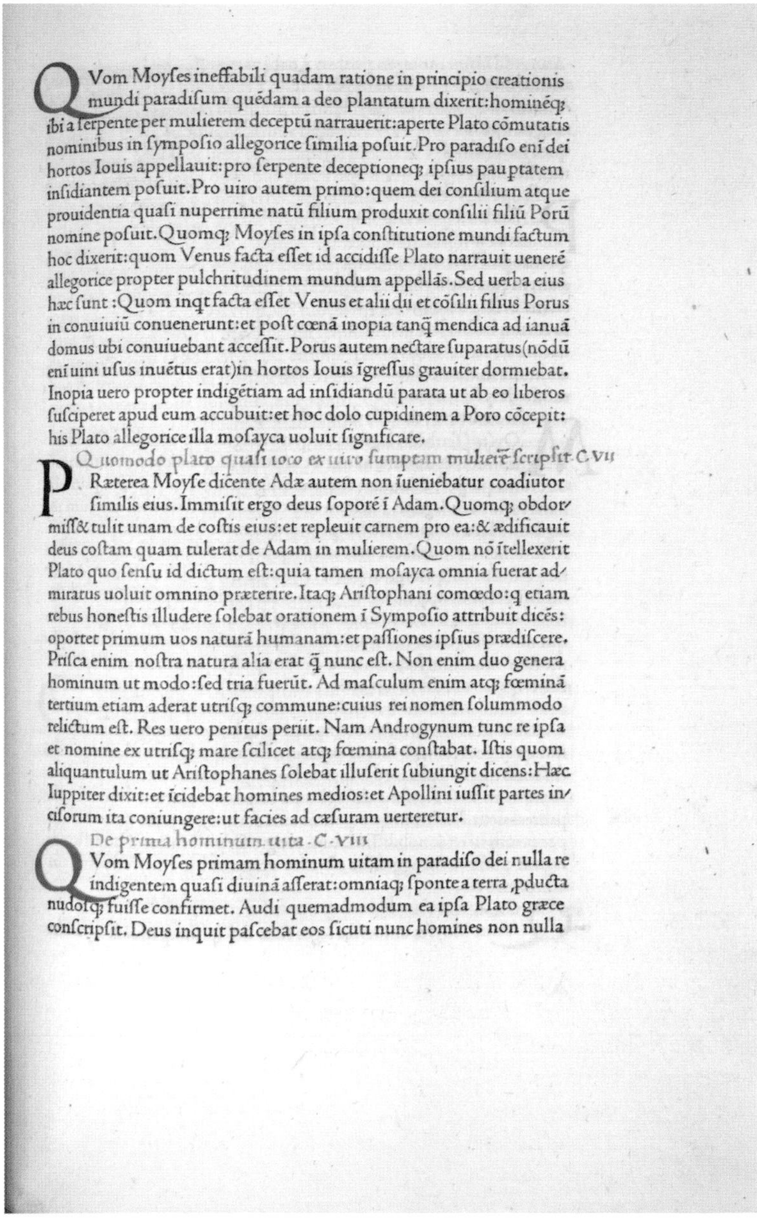

QVom Moyses ineffabili quadam ratione in principio creationis mundi paradisum quẽdam a deo plantatum dixerit: hominéq; ibi a serpente per mulierem deceptũ narrauerit: aperte Plato cõmutatis nominibus in symposio allegorice similia posuit. Pro paradiso enĩ dei hortos Iouis appellauit: pro serpente deceptioneq; ipsius pauptatem insidiantem posuit. Pro uiro autem primo: quem dei consilium atque prouidentia quasi nuperrime natũ filium produxit consilii filiũ Porũ nomine posuit. Quomq; Moyses in ipsa constitutione mundi factum hoc dixerit: quom Venus facta esset id accidisse Plato narrauit uenerẽ allegorice propter pulchritudinem mundum appellãs. Sed uerba eius hæc sunt: Quom inqt facta esset Venus et alii dii et cõsilii filius Porus in conuiuiũ conuenerunt: et post cœnã inopia tanq̃ mendica ad ianuã domus ubi conuiuebant accessit. Porus autem nectare superatus (nõdũ enĩ uini usus inuẽtus erat) in hortos Iouis ĩgressus grauiter dormiebat. Inopia uero propter indigẽtiam ad insidiandũ parata ut ab eo liberos susciperet apud eum accubuit: et hoc dolo cupidinem a Poro cõcepit: his Plato allegorice illa mosayca uoluit significare.

Quomodo plato quasi loco ex uiro sumptam mulierẽ scripsit · C VII

PRæterea Moyse dicente Adæ autem non ĩueniebatur coadiutor similis eius. Immisit ergo deus soporẽ ĩ Adam. Quomq; obdormiss& tulit unam de costis eius: et repleuit carnem pro ea: & ædificauit deus costam quam tulerat de Adam in mulierem. Quom nõ ĩtellexerit Plato quo sensu id dictum est: quia tamen mosayca omnia fuerat admiratus uoluit omnino prætereire. Itaq; Aristophani comœdo: q etiam rebus honestis illudere solebat orationem ĩ Symposio attribuit dicẽs: oportet primum uos naturã humanam: et passiones ipsius prædiscere. Prisca enim nostra natura alia erat q̃ nunc est. Non enim duo genera hominum ut modo: sed tria fuerũt. Ad masculum enim atq; fœminã tertium etiam aderat utrisq; commune: cuius rei nomen solummodo relictum est. Res uero penitus periit. Nam Androgynum tunc re ipsa et nomine ex utrisq; mare scilicet atq; fœmina constabat. Istis quom aliquantulum ut Aristophanes solebat illuserit subiungit dicens: Hæc Iuppiter dixit: et ĩcidebat homines medios: et Apollini iussit partes incisorum ita coniungere: ut facies ad cæsuram uerteretur.

De prima hominum uita · C · VIII

QVom Moyses primam hominum uitam in paradiso dei nulla re indigentem quasi diuinã asserat: omniaq; sponte a terra ꝑducta nudosq; fuisse confirmet. Audi quemadmodum ea ipsa Plato græce conscripsit. Deus inquit pascebat eos sicuti nunc homines non nulla

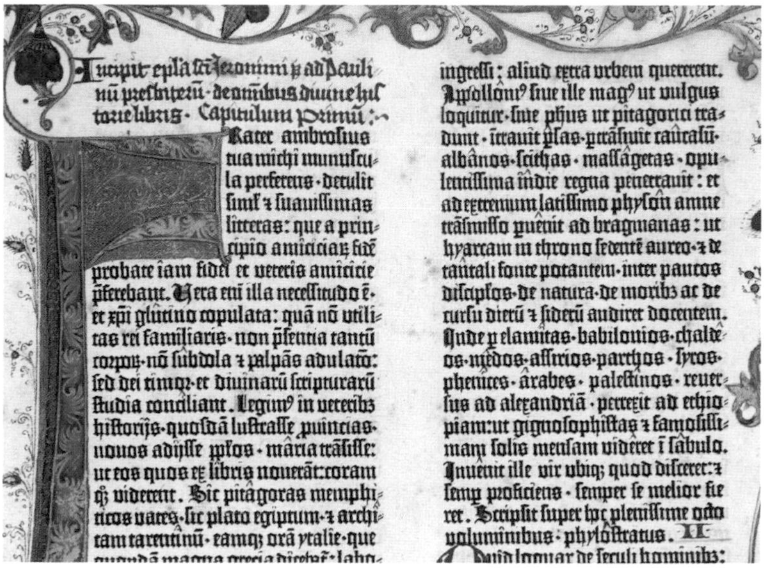
Incipit epl̃a sc̃i ieronimi ad paulinũ presbiterũ de omnibus diuine hiſtorie libris. Capitulum primũ.
Frater ambroſius tua michi munuſcula perferens detulit ſimul ⁊ ſuauiſſimas litteras: que a principio amiciciarũ fidẽ probate iam fidei et veteris amicicie preferebant. Vera enim illa neceſſitudo ē. et xp̄i glutino copulata: quã nõ utilitas rei familiaris. non pñtia tantũ corporũ. nõ ſubdola ⁊ palpãs adulacio: ſed dei timor. et diuinarũ ſcripturarũ ſtudia conciliant. Legimus in veteribus hiſtoriis. quoſdã luſtraſſe prouincias. nouos adiiſſe ꝑplos. maria traſiſſe: ut eos quos ex libris nouerãt: coram q̃ viderent. Sic pitagoras memphiticos vates. ſic plato egiptum. ⁊ archytam tarentinũ. eamq̃ orã ytalie. que
ingreſſi: aliud extra urbem querent. Apollonius ſiue ille mag9 ut vulgus loquitur. ſiue phus ut pitagorici tradunt. intrauit pſas. ptranſiuit caucaſũ. albanos. ſcithas. maſſagetas. opulentiſſima indie regna penetrauit: et ad extremum latiſſimo phyſon amne tranſmiſſo puenit ad bragmanas: ut hyarcam in throno ſedentẽ aureo. ⁊ de tantali fonte potantem. inter paucos diſcipulos. de natura. de moribꝫ ac de curſu dierũ ⁊ ſiderũ audiret docentem. Inde p elamitas. babilonios. chaldeos. medos. aſſirios. parthos. ſyros. phenices. arabes. paleſtinos. reuerſus ad alexandriã. perrexit ad ethiopiam: ut gignoſophiſtas ⁊ famoſiſſimam ſolis menſam videret ĩ ſabulo. Inuenit ille vir ubiq; quod diſceret: ⁊ ſemp proficiens. ſemper ſe melior fieret. Scripſit ſuper hoc pleniſſime octo voluminibus. phyloſtratus. II
Quid loquar de ſeculi hominibꝫ:

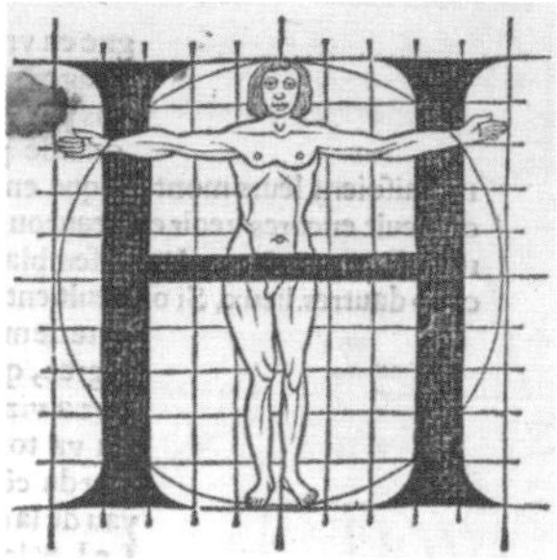

LEFT
The very first printed books, like Gutenberg's Bible, used typefaces based on the gothic handwriting favoured in manuscript books of the time, which the new technology was deliberately imitating

ABOVE
Geofrey Tory's Champ Fleury (1529) set out ideas for constructing ideal letter forms, based on ancient Roman styles, using a grid mapping the letter shapes against the form of the human body

by Renaissance calligraphy, and the rediscovery of classical letter forms, a movement that began in early fifteenth-century Florence. Jenson's type, first used in 1470, was not the first Roman font to be developed but was widely admired in its day and has been both revered and copied in later centuries.

Type, like cover design, belongs to its time and the distinctive look of a book of a particular period owes much to the changing fashions in typefaces. The history of type design over the last five hundred years has been marked by milestones when new craftsmen and printers have brought fresh ideas or sought to raise standards. Although the handpress era has a pantheon of well-known names on this roll call – Garamont and Granjon in the sixteenth century, van Dijck and Grandjean in the seventeenth, Baskerville and Bodoni in the eighteenth – the modern age of mechanised printing has seen more initiatives in this area than ever before. The numerous flamboyant and more experimental fonts that were created in the nineteenth century have a visual quality which both contributes to our mental picture of that age, and readily demonstrates the effect that type design can have on the impact of a text. The typefaces in widespread use today in the English-speaking world are

Changing type designs over time not only demonstrate the subtle connection between letter forms and communication, but also help to create our mental image of periods of history. Just as we see a manuscript in gothic black letter hand and think 'medieval', so we see a handbill like this and think 'nineteenth century'. The exuberance and energy of the design evoke, and belong to, the entrepreneurial spirit of the industrial revolution

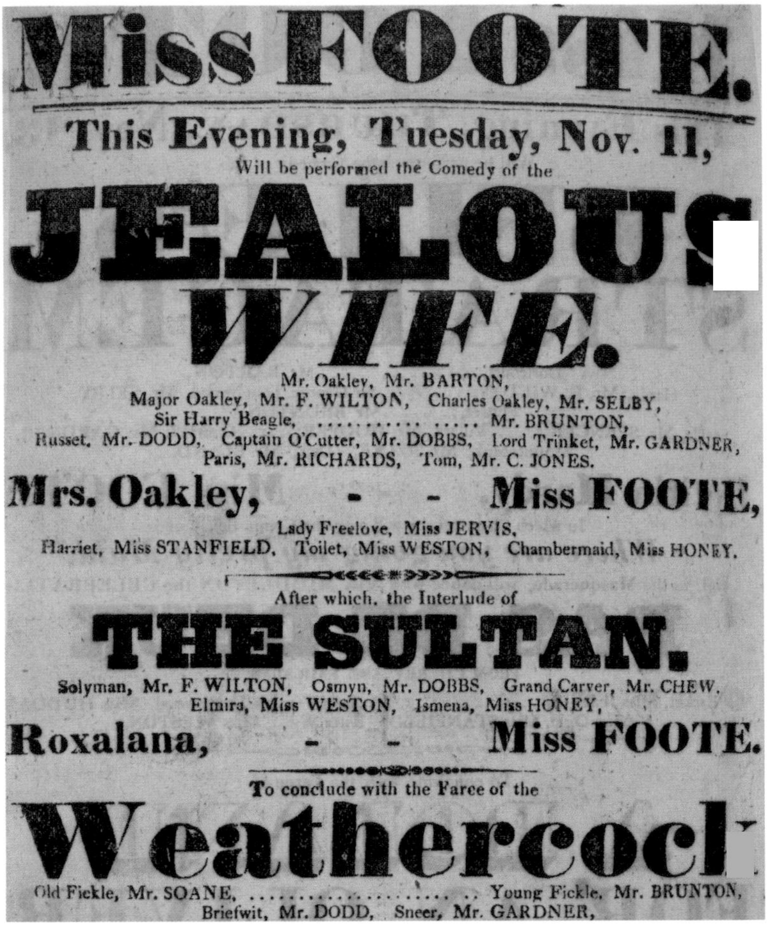

Miss FOOTE.

This Evening, Tuesday, Nov. 11,

Will be performed the Comedy of the

JEALOUS

WIFE.

Mr. Oakley, Mr. BARTON,
Major Oakley, Mr. F. WILTON, Charles Oakley, Mr. SELBY,
Sir Harry Beagle, ... Mr. BRUNTON,
Russet, Mr. DODD, Captain O'Cutter, Mr. DOBBS, Lord Trinket, Mr. GARDNER,
Paris, Mr. RICHARDS, Tom, Mr. C. JONES.

Mrs. Oakley, - - Miss FOOTE,

Lady Freelove, Miss JERVIS,
Harriet, Miss STANFIELD, Toilet, Miss WESTON, Chambermaid, Miss HONEY.

After which, the Interlude of

THE SULTAN.

Solyman, Mr. F. WILTON, Osmyn, Mr. DOBBS, Grand Carver, Mr. CHEW,
Elmira, Miss WESTON, Ismena, Miss HONEY,

Roxalana, - - Miss FOOTE.

To conclude with the Farce of the

Weathercock

Old Fickle, Mr. SOANE, ... Young Fickle, Mr. BRUNTON,
Briefwit, Mr. DODD, Sneer, Mr. GARDNER,

Stanley Morison's Times New Roman typeface, designed specifically for the newspaper in 1932, has been a pervading influence not only in newspapers but also in book design and document styles throughout the later 20th century

DIEU ET MON DROIT

TIMES

LONDON MONDAY OCTOBER 3 1932

PERSONAL

"WISDOM is the principal thing; therefore get wisdom: and with all thy getting get understanding. Exalt her, and she shall promote thee; she shall bring thee to honour, when thou dost embrace her."—Prov. iv., 7, 8.

£5 NOTE GRATEFULLY RECEIVED from an ANONYMOUS DONOR, who writes:—" May I ask you, in His Name, to accept this with the hope that it may be used in the good work you are endeavouring to do. . . . Trusting it may help yet another TIRED and NEEDY LIFE to have the PRIVILEGE and BENEFIT of a REST at 'THE RETREAT,' MALDON." FUNDS, VERY GREATLY NEEDED, will be thankfully acknowledged by the Secretary, ST. GILES' CHRISTIAN MISSION and WHEATLEY'S HOMES, 15, Gray's Inn Road, London, W.C.1.

BANK of ENGLAND.—RECLAIMED REDEMPTION MONEY and DIVIDENDS. No. 17043/4.—APPLICATION having been made to the Governor of the Bank of England to direct the PAYMENT of the REDEMPTION MONEY in respect of the sums of £50 Registered £5 per Cent. National War Bonds, 1927, and £50 Registered £5 per Cent. National War Bonds, 1928, Second Series, formerly in the name of MARIA ESTHER BADGER SIMPSON of Defford Road, Pershore, Worcestershire, Spinster, which Redemption Money was paid over to the Commissioners for the Reduction of the National Debt in consequence of having remained unreceived. Notice is hereby given that, on the expiration of three months from this date (October 3, 1932) the said Redemption Money and the unpaid dividends will be PAID to HERBERT BASIL HARRISON, Solicitor, and ARTHUR WILLIAM SMITH, Chemist, both of Pershore, Worcestershire, Administrators de bonis non of the estate of the said MARIA ESTHER BADGER SIMPSON, now deceased, they having claimed the same, unless some other claim thereto shall in the meantime be made and sustained.

SIR PHILIP BEN GREET can arrange performances of Shakespearean Plays and Old English Comedies at schools, &c., during autumn and winter. Pastoral Plays in the summer.—Address care of 40, Chandos Street, Strand, W.C.2.

"READING THE TIMES."—An Illustrated Guide to the Contents and Make-up of the Paper for those who are not yet regular readers free and post free on application to the Publisher, Printing House Square, E.C.4.

WHEN YOUR SON LEAVES SCHOOL send him out to South Africa without wasting time. Give him a fine, free life as a farmer. Three years' training given gratis ; then moderate capital buys his own land.—Apply 1820 Memorial Settlers' Association, Dept. T.O.3, 199, Piccadilly, W.1.

DANCING SCHOOL.—Lady wishes to SELL her well-established SCHOOL of DANCING in a fashionable South Coast Town. Long lease, splendid ballroom, and spacious accommodation. Price £1,000 (part might remain).—Write Box "Principal," care of Davies and

PERSONAL

HOME TIES, and many difficulties keep me. Can never forget.

TO LET or SELL.—Beautifully FURNISHED Country COTTAGE; 50 yards from lovely golf: private road. Five bed rooms, three reception, four lavatories, three bath rooms; radiators every room; lovely garden, views, veranda, lawn; 18 miles London, 60ft. above sea level.—Box A.580, The Times, E.C.4.

TO be LET, FURNISHED HOUSE, cosy, economical, newly decorated throughout; convenient for Charing Cross, &c. HAMPSTEAD GARDEN SUBURB, near Heath. Four bed, three sitting, good offices, bath room, two w.c.s, loggia, garden, garage, telephone. Electric light, power throughout; gas cooker, fires, and hot water; range and open fires available. Four guineas.—Write Box A.579, The Times, E.C.4.

THE VICAR of TEDDINGTON having to move wishes to SELL his HOUSE cheaply to a Catholic who would value. St. Albans, Teddington.

BEFORE SHOPPING READ the ADVERTISEMENTS of the following firms in to-day's issue:—Marshall and Snelgrove, page seven; Debenham and Freebody, pages 10 and 17; Selfridge's, page 10; Harvey Nichols, page 11; National Fur Company, page 12; Bradleys, page 13; Peter Robinson, page 17; Burberrys, page 18; Smartwear, page 18; Harrods, page 19; Dickins and Jones, page 21; Robinson and Cleaver, page 21.

COUNTESS RECEIVES GUESTS in VIENNA; central position; opportunity learning German; young society, music, skating, introduction society, dancing; moderate terms.—Write Box Y.1625, The Times, E.C.4.

INVALID LADY, unable to walk, would greatly APPRECIATE little HELP to purchase artificial leg, or gift of few books.—Write Box Y.1624, The Times, E.C.4.

MOULDS or MATRICES of Periodicals, Books, &c., required for Overseas printing; subjects must be non-dated.—Details or proofs to be sent to Box K.1435, The Times, E.C.4.

MENTALLY BACKWARD.—Few young gentlemen received.—Mr. and Mrs. Loveless, Woburn Sands, Bucks.

TOBACCO.—Nine years' administrative Manufacturing experience, Belgium, Denmark, Far East, Public School, age 28, desires position with good prospects; any branch tobacco business.—Write Box Y.1657, The Times, E.C.4.

HOLIDAYS are over. Make a Winter hobby of knowing London with the London Rambling Society. 'Phone 1733 Langham.

MAKE YOUR CHOICE OF A CAR from the selection offered under "Motor-cars," &c., on page two.

SIR REGINALD KENNEDY COX urgently APPEALS for JUMBLE badly needed by Dockland for winter work.—Do please send clothes, furniture, any-

BUSINESS OFFERS

3 *lines* 15*s*. (*minimum*)

FIFTY-FOUR YEARS IN FLEET STREET.—An u equalled series of advertising successes, including t development of many famous businesses from sma beginnings to National status by sound economical a vertising, continually adapted to ever-changing con tions. Proved experience combined with a modern ou look, the wisdom of age combined with the inspirati of youth. Full evidence willingly submitted at an inte view, without obligation.—Apply Principal Direct Smiths' Advertising Agency, Ltd., 100, Fleet Stre London, E.C.4.

AN OPPORTUNITY to JOIN First-class BUSINE is offered to gentleman of good education; exce tional prospects with salaried position and assur profits. Qualification £3,000 (secured and returnabl Full particulars at interview only to principals.—Wr Box K.1411, The Times, E.C.4.

SUBSTANTIAL NET INCOMES up to and ov £1,000 p.a. are being made by owners of a new a much-needed public utility service, the British BURTO requiring only ordinary business ability and a mod capital of about £1,000. This proposition is ideal eith as an investment or as a business, and opportuniti exist in all towns of 10,000 or over.—For full particula and terms apply to James Armstrong and Co., Lt 151, Queen Victoria Street, London, E.C.4.

START A POSTAL BUSINESS of your own. Ve profitable. Send 1½d. stamp for particulars. H £14 made £1,720 in one year.—(B) Hand and Co., 2 High Holborn, London, W.C.1.

A1 INVESTMENT OPPORTUNITY.—Sums up £50,000 (with or without active participatio can be safely employed to acquire interests relative to important industrial development and rationalizati scheme. Unquestionably one of the finest opportunit for consistent profit-making and capital appreciation England. Particulars sent on request and inspecti invited.—Write Box W.928, The Times, E.C.4.

CONGENIAL HEALTHY OCCUPATION w assured future offered to several energetic YOUN MEN able INVEST £2,500 and over by large Brit Farming Company of national importance now expan ing to take full advantage of new tariffs; no spec knowledge necessary provided willing work hard a progress.—Write Box A.410, The Times, E.C.4.

OPPORTUNITY for MANUFACTURERS.—Owing business expansion firm desires to dispose of man facturing rights and COMPLETE TOOLS for manuf ture of ATTRACTIVE NOVELTY, made entirely sheet metal stampings. Absolutely unique. Ra seller at all stores and tobacconists at 17s. 6d. ret Supplied to many foremost stores. Excellent line wi out competition. Tools complete ready for use o £475.—Write Box K.1434, The Times, E.C.4.

UNIQUE OPPORTUNITY for INVESTMENT occ in sound county weekly newspapers paying 7½ much influenced by the work of Stanley Morison (1889-1967), who not only designed the Times New Roman face for *The Times* newspaper in 1932, but also helped to introduce a range of new faces in the 1920s and 30s which continue to shape our expectations of what letters on a page, or a screen, should look like.

THINGS BEYOND WORDS – ILLUSTRATION AND DECORATION

Books have had their verbal content supplemented by various kinds of visual imagery for as long as they have existed; the realisation that pictures can complement texts in all kinds of ways to emphasise, illuminate or enliven their message has always been obvious. Illustrated papyrus rolls survive from ancient Egypt, as early as the 12th century BC, which are arguably the world's oldest extant books with pictures. Aristotle refers to accompanying pictures in some of his texts, although no contemporary examples have come down to us. This book is itself an exemplar of the long tradition of combining images with text to make something which would be less effective with only one of those elements in place.

The Vatican Library preserves two fifth-century manuscripts of Virgil's poems, with painted pictures interspersed with the text. These are among the earliest western instances of illustrated books, in which the images are representations of the scenes or activities mentioned in the text, inserted in order to help the reader visualise what the text is describing. Since then, the illustrated books which have been produced, right down to the present time, are too obviously numerous to count; pictures in books is one of those things that we take for granted. They may be factual, conceptual, or diagrammatic; they may be grand or simple; they may be art in their own right.

Pictures began to appear in printed books almost as soon as printing began – the earliest example dates from 1461, just a few years after Gutenberg's Bible – and since then a range of technologies has been employed to make it possible to mass-produce images within the confines of the pages of books. The use of engraved wood blocks, the main technique used for fifteenth-century book illustrations, was superseded by engraved metal plates during the

wie der man · Reit und lest den jungē gan · Liesz er
den knabē reitē · Und lief dem knaben pei der seiten

Daran thet er vil pasz · Do der alt erhoret das · Dō
dem esel sasz er do · Der jung sasz auff und was fro
Der ein zu dem andern sprach · Do er den knaben
reitē sach · wart getreuer geselle meȳ · Der alt mag
wol ein narre sein · Das er lest reiten den knaben ·
Der solt laufen und trabē · Und solt der alt reiten ·
Vil kaum mocht er gepeiten · Das der alt auff den
esel kam · zu dem knaben und reiten hin dan ·

FAR LEFT
Ulrich Boner's Edelstein, *printed in 1461 (just a few years after Gutenberg first established printing) is the first illustrated printed book*

LEFT
5th-century manuscripts of Virgil's Aeneid, *now in the Vatican Library, are among the earliest known examples of books illustrated with pictures which represent the contents of the text*

century that followed, making it possible to produce pictures of much greater subtlety and sophistication.

Medieval manuscripts, individually made, could be illustrated in colour, a possibility that was beyond the capabilities of the handpress era as far as mass production was concerned. Printed books before the nineteenth century were sometimes available with coloured illustrations, but this depended on individual hand-colouring of plates originally printed in black and white (the *Edelstein* illustrated here is an example of this). The nineteenth century saw this revolutionised with the invention of a series of new production methods which made it both possible and cost-effective to publish books with full colour pictures. The invention of photography, around the same time, soon led to the photographically illustrated book. Book production techniques have evolved continuously since then to make book illustration simpler, cheaper, and more sophisticated, so that we now take for granted the wide range of juxtapositions of images and text with which we are so familiar.

Visual enhancement of books does not need to be so directly representational. The creators of the so-called Insular manuscripts

Von achtung des gestirns
Der ist ein narr der me verheißt
Dann er in seym vermögen weisszt
Oder dann er zu thun het mut
Verheyssen ist den ertzten gut
Aber eyn narr verheisszt ein tag
Me dann all welt geleysten mag.
Auff kunfftig ding man yetz vast lendt
Was das gestyrn vnd firmament
Vnd der planeten lauff vns sag

By the end of the 15th century, the illustration of printed books, using wood engraving, was well established: a page from Sebastian Brandt's Narrenschiff, *1494*

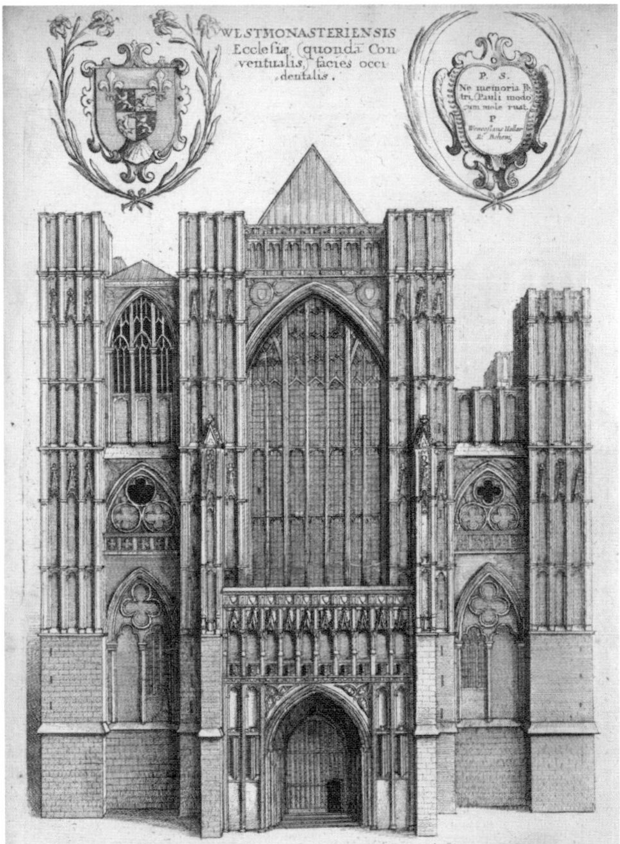

The introduction of metal engraving from the 16th century onwards made it possible to create book illustrations with greater subtlety and detail than was typically possible with wood. This mid 17th-century example is from a collection of engravings of cathedrals by Daniel King

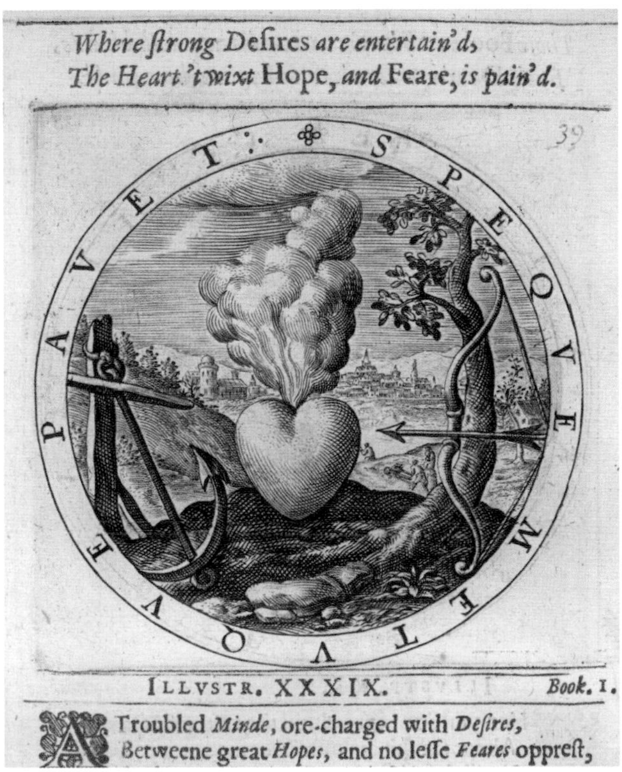

Emblem books became a popular format for a particular kind of juxtaposition of image and text during the 16th and 17th centuries: a text with a moral was much enhanced with a picture whose imagery helped to underscore the message

OVERLEAF

*The invention of chromolithography in the 1840s made it possible to produce books in full colour in ways not previously feasible. Victorian publishers and illustrators made the most of the new technique. (*The Miracles of our Lord*, illuminated by H. Noel Humphreys, 1848)*

still, and commanded him to be called. And they called the blind man saying unto him, Be of good comfort, arise; he calleth thee. And he, casting away his garment, rose, and came to Jesus. And Jesus answered and said unto him, What wilt thou that I should do unto thee? The blind man said unto him, Lord, that I might receive my sight. And Jesus said unto him, Go thy way; thy faith hath made thee whole. And immediately he received his sight, and followed Jesus in the way.

Luke xiii. 11 17.

A Woman of eighteen years Infirmity cured.

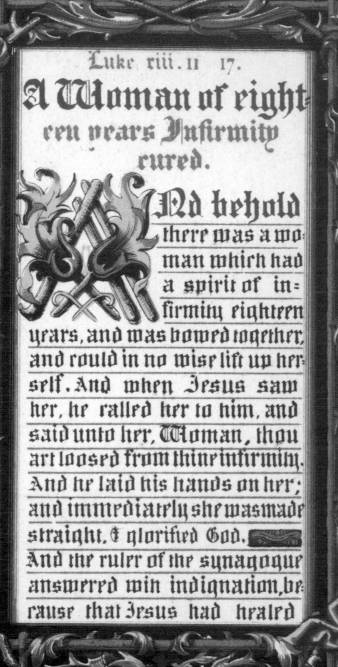

AND behold there was a woman which had a spirit of infirmity eighteen years, and was bowed together, and could in no wise lift up herself. And when Jesus saw her, he called her to him, and said unto her, Woman, thou art loosed from thine infirmity. And he laid his hands on her; and immediately she wasmade straight, & glorified God. And the ruler of the synagogue answered with indignation, because that Jesus had healed

William Fox Talbot's Pencil of Nature, *published in 1844, was one of the first books to be illustrated with photographs*

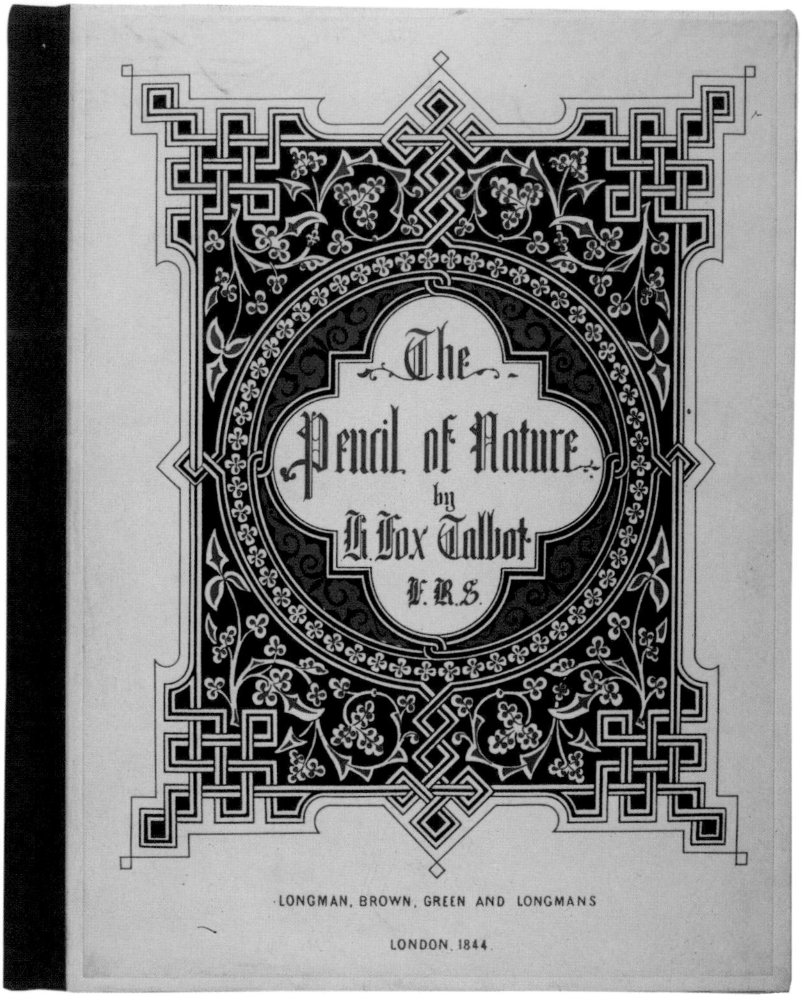

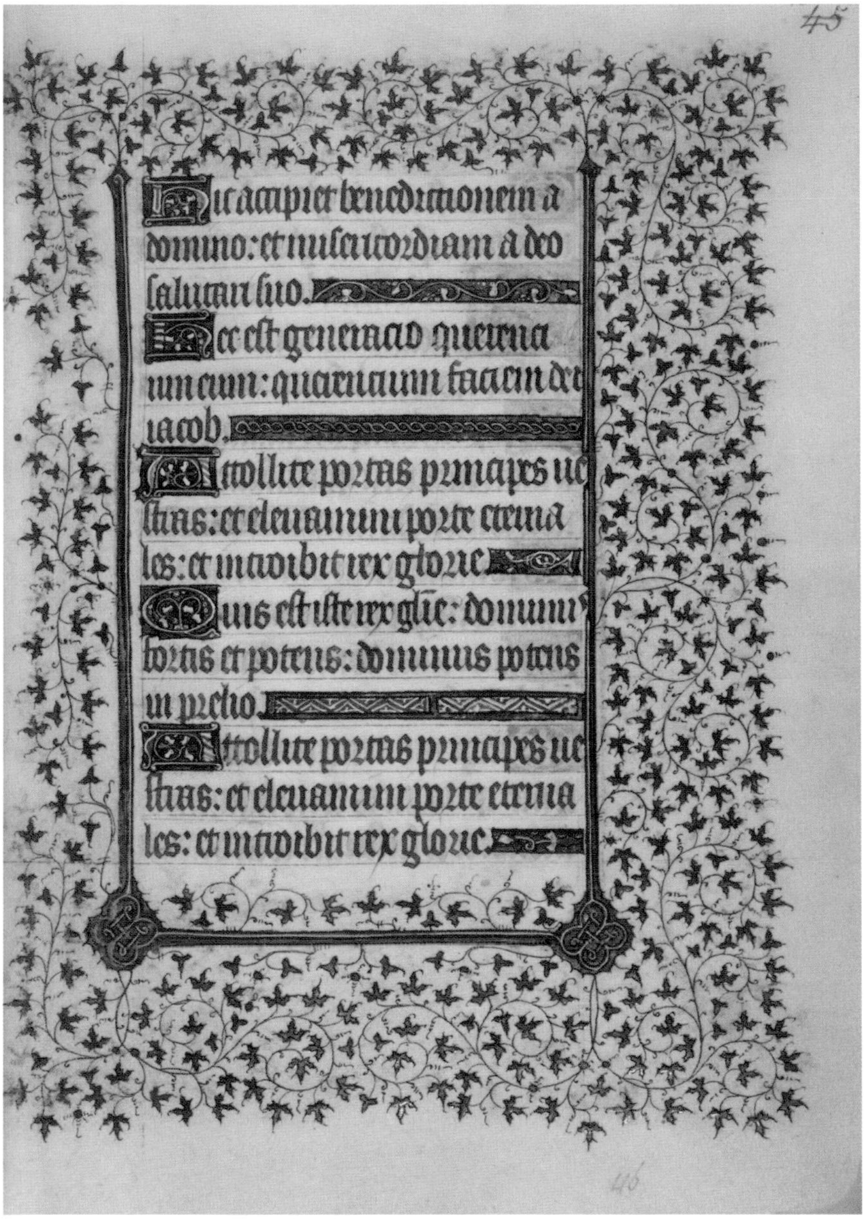

Enhancing the impact of the page and its text through decoration is a tradition going back many centuries; many medieval manuscripts were embellished with page borders and decorated initial letters.

COnuerte nos deus ſa=
lutaris noſter.
Et auerte iram tuam
à nobis.
Deus in adiutorium
meum intende.
Domine ad adiuuandum me feſtina.
Gloria patri,& filio,& ſpiritui ſancto.
Sicut erat in principio,& nunc,& ſem
per:& in ſecula ſeculorum. Amen.
Hallelu ia. Pſalmus.

SAEpe expugnauerũt me à iuuen=
tute mea,dicat nunc Iſrael,
Sæpe expugnauerunt me à iuuentute
mea,etenim non potuerunt mihi.
Supra dorſum meum fabricauerunt
peccatores,prolongauerunt iniquita=
tem ſuam.
Dominus iuſtus cõcidet ceruices pec=
catorum: confundantur, & conuertã=

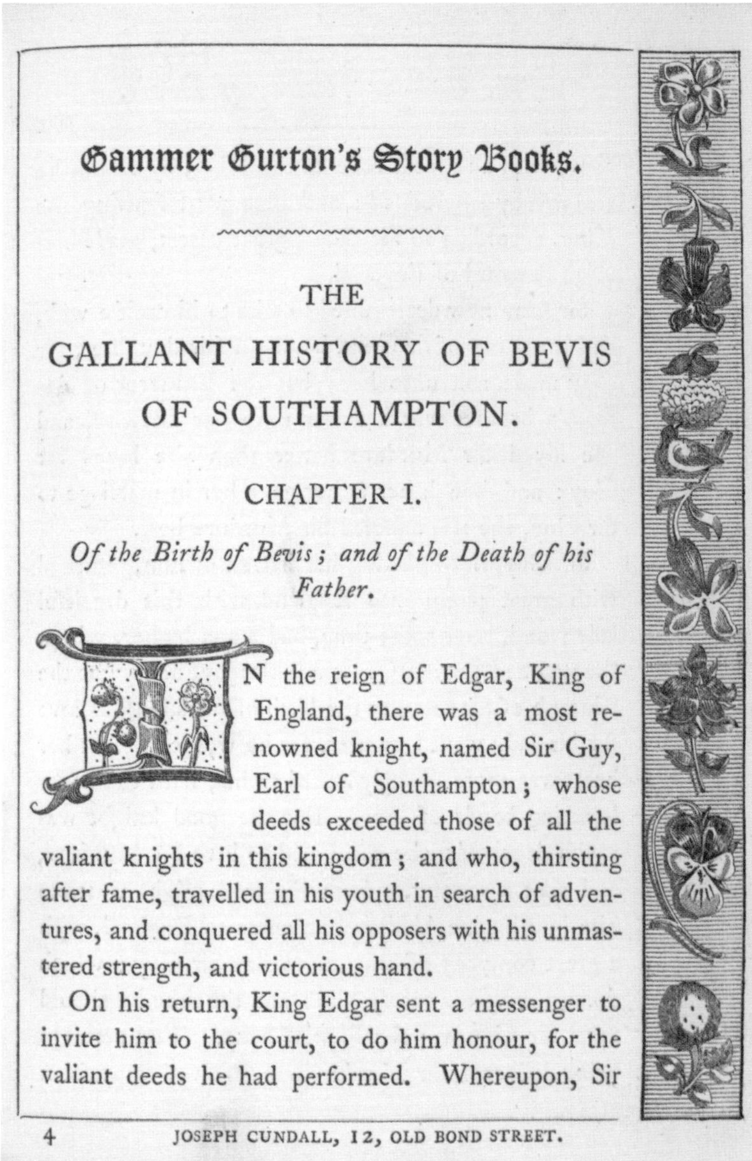

Gammer Gurton's Story Books.

THE

GALLANT HISTORY OF BEVIS OF SOUTHAMPTON.

CHAPTER I.

Of the Birth of Bevis; and of the Death of his Father.

IN the reign of Edgar, King of England, there was a most renowned knight, named Sir Guy, Earl of Southampton; whose deeds exceeded those of all the valiant knights in this kingdom; and who, thirsting after fame, travelled in his youth in search of adventures, and conquered all his opposers with his unmastered strength, and victorious hand.

On his return, King Edgar sent a messenger to invite him to the court, to do him honour, for the valiant deeds he had performed. Whereupon, Sir

4 JOSEPH CUNDALL, 12, OLD BOND STREET.

The use of decorative borders, decorated initials and type ornaments to add to the visual impact of the page flourished throughout the handpress period, and into the 19th century; it is less common today, when book designers rely more on illustration than decoration for visual impact. Here is a mid 16th-century book (opposite) and a mid 19th-century one, decorated in this way

William Hamilton's book on the eruption of Vesuvius, lavishly illustrated with spectacular hand coloured plates, is arguably as much a work of art as a text

in pre-Norman Britain, the tradition which gave us the Lindisfarne Gospels and the Book of Kells, well understood the power of abstract decoration to augment the effectiveness of a page of text. The idea of enhancing a page not so much with separate pictures but with elaborately decorative borders and initial letters is well known from the medieval period, and these practices were carried through into printed books. The use of type ornaments, page borders and decorative letters was common throughout the handpress era and was used to both striking and subtle effect; this kind of decoration is used more sparingly in modern books but the idea remained popular well into the nineteenth century.

OVERLEAF
Throughout the 20th century, numerous private presses have maintained the idea of the book beautiful by producing hand-printed books with the highest standards of craftsmanship applied to design, paper, and presswork: Samuel Johnson's The Vanity of Human Wishes, *printed by the Rampant Lions Press in 1984*

BOOKS AS ART

A beautifully produced book, or a splendidly illustrated one, will often be readily regarded as a work of art in its own right; books like William Hamilton's *Campi Phlegraei*, published in 1779 with hand-coloured plates and vignettes showing the recent eruption of

LET Observation with extensive View,
Survey Mankind, from *China* to *Peru*;
Remark each anxious Toil, each eager Strife,
And watch the busy Scenes of crouded Life;
Then say how Hope and Fear, Desire and Hate,
O'erspread with Snares the clouded Maze of Fate,
Where wav'ring Man, betray'd by vent'rous Pride,
To tread the dreary Paths without a Guide,
As treach'rous Phantoms in the Mist delude,
Shuns fancied Ills, or chases airy Good;
How rarely Reason guides the stubborn Choice,
Rules the bold Hand, or prompts the suppliant Voice;
How Nations sink, by darling Schemes oppress'd,
When Vengeance listens to the Fool's Request.
Fate wings with ev'ry Wish th'afflictive Dart,
Each Gift of Nature, and each Grace of Art,
With fatal Heat impetuous Courage glows,
With fatal Sweetness Elocution flows,
Impeachment stops the Speaker's pow'rful Breath,
And restless Fire precipitates on Death.

But scarce observ'd, the Knowing and the Bold
Fall in the gen'ral Massacre of Gold;
Wide-wasting pest! that rages unconfin'd,
And crouds with Crimes the Records of Mankind;
For Gold his Sword the Hireling Ruffian draws,
For Gold the hireling Judge distorts the Laws;
Wealth heap'd on Wealth, nor Truth nor Safety buys,
The Dangers gather as the Treasures rise.

Let Hist'ry tell where rival Kings command,
And dubious Title shakes the madded Land,
When Statutes glean the Refuse of the Sword,
How much more safe the Vassal than the Lord;
Low skulks the Hind beneath the Rage of Pow'r,
And leaves the *wealthy Traytor* in the *Tow'r*,
Untouch'd his Cottage, and his Slumbers sound,
Tho' Confiscation's Vulturs hover round.

The needy Traveller, secure and gay,
Walks the wild Heath, and sings his Toil away,
Does Envy seize thee? crush th'upbraiding Joy,

of Jesus, which said unto him, Before the cock crow, thou shalt deny me thrice. And he went out, and wept bitterly.

THE MORNING WAS COME, ALL THE CHIEF PRIESTS and elders of the people took counsel against Jesus to put him to death: And when they had bound him, they led him away, and delivered him to Pontius Pilate the governor. ❦ Then Judas, which had betrayed him, when he saw that he was condemned, repented himself, and brought again the thirty pieces of silver to the chief priests and elders, Saying, I have sinned in that I have betrayed the innocent blood. And they said, What is that to us? see thou to that. And he cast down the pieces of silver in the temple, and departed, and went and hanged himself. And the chief priests took the silver pieces, and said, It is not lawful for to put them into the treasury, because it is the price of blood. And they took counsel, and bought with them the potter's field, to bury strangers in. Wherefore that field was called, The field of blood, unto this day. Then was fulfilled that which was spoken by Jeremy the prophet, saying, And they took the thirty pieces of silver, the price of him that was valued, whom they of the children of Israel did value; And gave them for the potter's field, as the Lord appointed me.

Vesuvius, come to mind. The private press movement, which began in the late nineteenth century as a reaction against the perceived mediocrity of machine-made books and which has flourished since, has produced many books which are appreciated for their craftsmanship and overall aesthetic qualities.

The potential of books as forms of art goes beyond the juxtaposition of text and pictures, or the use of pleasing typography in good layouts; people have sought to apply a creative vision to all the various elements that make up a book, to achieve a genuine fusion of words, images and design in a synthesis that relies partly on the physical format of the book for its effectiveness. The Kelmscott Chaucer, a collaboration between William Morris and Edward Burne-Jones, brings together all these things, and leafing through this book is an experience to which all its constituent parts are intended to make an indivisible contribution. Eric Gill's *Four Gospels* for the Golden Cockerel Press is another example; the images, the typeface and the layout were all designed by Gill to make a cohesive whole.

There is a long history of more imaginative experimentation with what can be done within the form and layout of a book. George Herbert's angel wing poems, with their words laid out to represent the shape of wings, appeared in print in 1633, but the idea goes back much further than this; the first known examples of this kind of figured verse were written by the ancient Greek poet Simmias of Rhodes, before 300 BC. A number of early medieval examples survive, such as an early ninth-century manuscript of Cicero's translation of Aratus including representations of the constellations using shaped text. The interplay of words and pictures to help communicate with, and educate, children, similarly has a long history; the Hieroglyphick Bibles of the late eighteenth century are a nice example. Playful use of typography has been more radically experimented with in the twentieth century, as in the *Bezette stad* of Paul van Ostaijen, whose visbly fragmented text reflects the content of the poetic text about the German occupation of Antwerp in the First World War. Often called concrete poetry, these kinds of texts are also sometimes termed calligrams, after a celebrated set by Guillaume Apollinaire, entitled *Calligrammes*, published shortly after his death in 1918.

OPPOSITE & OVERLEAF
Eric Gill's Golden Cockerel Press Gospels *(1931) (opposite)and the Kelmscott Press Chaucer (1896) (overleaf) are both examples of books designed with the intention that text, type and illustration all fuse together to make a whole which is greater than the sum of the parts*

feithful, and ful of stabilite.
Good-Hope alwey kepe by thy syde,
And Swete-Thought make eek abyde,
Swete-Loking and Swete-Speche;
Of alle thyn harmes they shal be leche.
Of every thou shalt have greet plesaunce;
If thou canst byde in sufferaunce,
And serve wel without feyntyse,
Thou shalt be quit of thyn empryse,
With more guerdoun, if that thou live;
But al this tyme this I thee yive.

THE God of Love whan al the day
Had taught me, as ye have herd say,
And enfourmed compendiously,
He vanished awey al sodeynly,
And I alone lefte, al sole,
So ful of compleynt and of dole,
For I saw no man ther me by.
My woundes me greved wondirly;
Me for to curen nothing I knew,
Save the botoun bright of hew,
Wheron was set hoolly my thought;
Of other comfort knew I nought,
But it were through the God of Love;
I knew nat elles to my bihove
That might me ese or comfort gete,
But if he wolde him entermete.

THE roser was, withoute doute,
Closed with an hegge withoute,
As ye toforn have herd me seyn;
And fast I bisied, and wolde fayn
Have passed the haye, if I might
Have geten in by any slight
Unto the botoun so fair to see.
But ever I dradde blamed to be,
If men wolde have suspeccioun
That I wolde of entencioun
Have stole the roses that ther were;
Therfore to entre I was in fere.
But at the last, as I bithought
Whether I sholde passe or nought,
I saw come with a gladde chere
To me, a lusty bachelere,
Of good stature, and of good hight,
And Bialacoil forsothe he hight. Bialac
Sone he was to Curtesy,
And he me graunted ful gladly
The passage of the outer hay,
And seide: Sir, how that ye may
Passe, if it your wille be,
The fresshe roser for to see,
And ye the swete savour fele.
Your warrant may I be right wele;

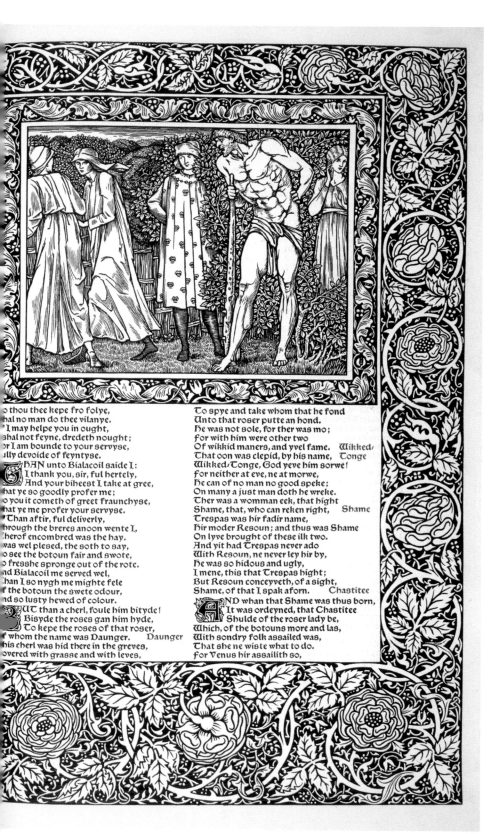

o thou thee kepe fro folye,
hal no man do thee vilanye.
'I may helpe you in ought,
shal not feyne, dredeth nought;
or I am bounde to your servyse,
ully devoide of feyntyse.
THAN unto Bialacoil saide I:
I thank you, sir, ful hertely,
And your biheest I take at gree,
hat ye so goodly profer me;
o you it cometh of greet fraunchyse,
hat ye me profer your servyse.
'Than aftir, ful deliverly,
hrough the breres anoon wente I,
herof encombred was the hay.
was wel plesed, the soth to say,
o see the botoun fair and swote,
o fresshe spronge out of the rote.
nd Bialacoil me served wel,
han I so nygh me mighte fele
f the botoun the swete odour,
nd so lusty hewed of colour.
BUT than a cherl, foule him bityde!
Bisyde the roses gan him hyde,
To kepe the roses of that roser,
f whom the name was Daunger. Daunger
his cherl was hid there in the greves,
overed with grasse and with leves,
To spye and take whom that he fond
Unto that roser putte an hond.
He was not sole, for ther was mo;
For with him were other two
Of wikkid maners, and yvel fame. Wikked-
That oon was clepid, by his name, Tonge
Wikked-Tonge, God yeve him sorwe!
For neither at eve, ne at morwe,
He can of no man no good speke;
On many a just man doth he wreke.
Ther was a womman eek, that hight
Shame, that, who can reken right, Shame
Trespas was hir fadir name,
Hir moder Resoun; and thus was Shame
On lyve brought of these ilk two.
And yit had Trespas never ado
With Resoun, ne never ley hir by,
He was so hidous and ugly,
I mene, this that Trespas hight;
But Resoun conceyveth, of a sight,
Shame, of that I spak aforn. Chastitee
AND whan that Shame was thus born,
It was ordeyned, that Chastitee
Shulde of the roser lady be,
Which, of the botouns more and las,
With sondry folk assailed was,
That she ne wiste what to do.
For Venus hir assailith so,

George Herbert was an early experimenter with the layout of type to produce a text whose shape on the page reflects the content (his poem Easter Wings, *right); Paul van Ostaijen's poems (below) are a more recent and radical example. The dog (below, right) shows an early example of the idea of playful layout of words, to make a visual impact, from a 9th-century manuscript of Aratus. The Hieroglyphick Bible of the late 18th century (top, right) blended words and pictures to create an appealing learning tool for children*

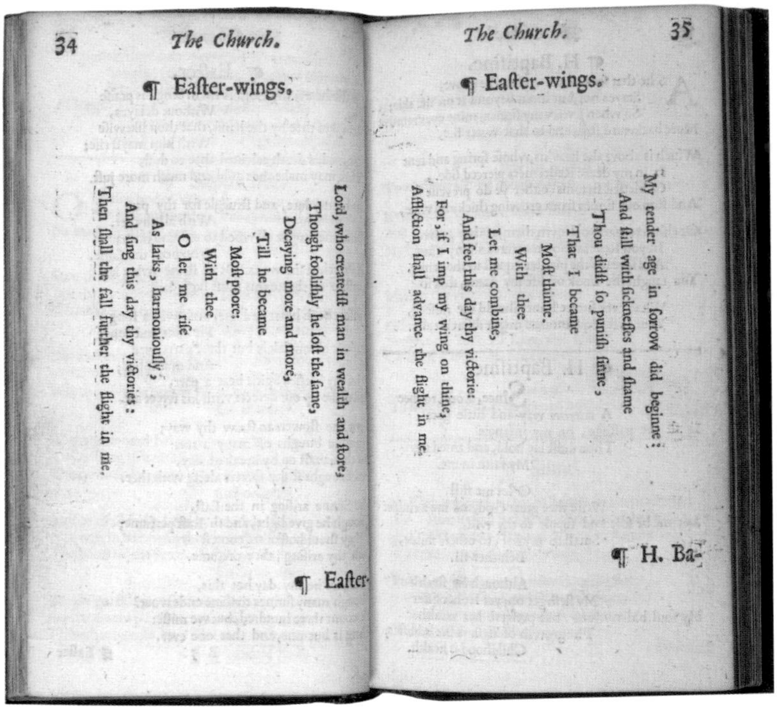

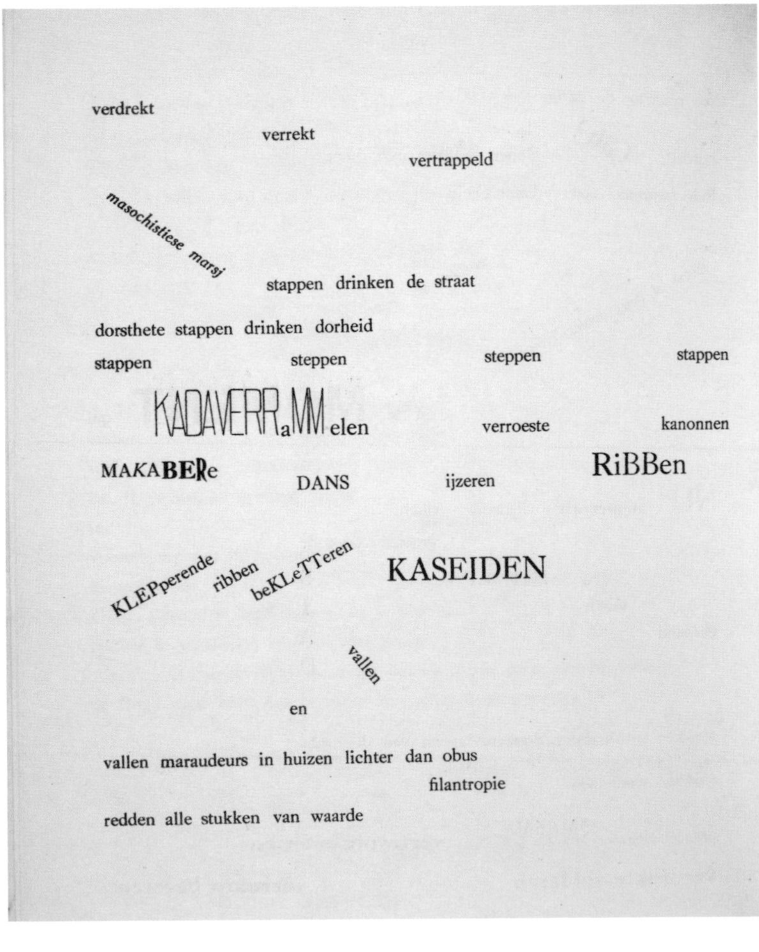

He that formed the [mountains] and createth the [wind] and declareth unto [man] what is his Thought: The LORD [יְהוָה] of Hosts is his Name.

He that formed the *Mountains*, and createth the *Wind*, and declareth unto *Man* what is his Thought: The Lord *God* of Hosts is his Name.

The Pride of thine [heart] hath deceived thee: Thou that dwellest in the Clefts of the Rock, whose [habitation] is high, that saith in his Heart, Who shall bring me down to the Ground? Though thou exalt thyself as the [eagle] and make thy [nest] among the [stars] thence will I bring thee down, saith the LORD.

The Pride of thine *Heart* hath deceived thee: Thou that dwellest in the Clefts of the Rock, whose *Habitation* is high, that saith in his Heart, Who shall bring me down to the Ground? Though thou exalt thyself as the *Eagle*, and make thy *Nest* among the *Stars*, thence will I bring thee down, saith the Lord.

Namque pedes subter rutilo cum lumine clare
fervidus ille canis stellarum luce refulgens
Hunc tegit obscurus subter praecordia uesper·
Et uero toto spirans de corpore flammam·
Aestifero sandidis erumpit flatibus ignes·
Totus ab ore micans iacitur mortalibus ardor·
Hic ubi se pariter cum sole in lumina caeli
Extulit haud patitur foliorum tegmine frustra
Suspensos animos arbusta ornata tenere·

NICANOR PARRA
ANTIPOEMS
THE ANTI - LAZARUS
WHATEVER YOU DO DON'T RISE UP FROM THE GRAVE
WHY SHOULD YOU BE NERVOUS
LIKE THE POET ONCE SAID
YOU HAVE YOUR WHOLE DEATH IN FRONT OF YOU.
PIANO SOLO
I WANT MY SOUL TO FIND ITS PROPER BODY.
I WISH TO MAKE A NOISE WITH MY FEET
PUSSYKATTEN
WHITE WITH ASHES HIS SPINE
SHOWS HE'S A CAT
WHOSE PLACE IS BEYOND GOOD OR EVIL.

The *Livre d'artiste*, the Artist's Book, is a concept generally agreed to have begun in France around the beginning of the twentieth century, with the creation of works like the Vollard edition of Verlaine's *Parallelement* (1900, overleaf), bringing graphic artists and creative writers together in order to produce something which is meant to transcend a mere illustrated book. It is in the later twentieth century that more imaginative book art has really flourished, as artists have sought to begin not so much with the idea of words and images, as with the physical form of the book itself, and create works that spring at least as much from the concept of book as that of text. *Aunt Sallie's Lament* by Margaret Kaufman is, at one level, a poem about making quilts; it is presented on multishaped pages, reflecting a patchwork quilt, that can be opened in different sequences to present various combinations of words. In this case the impact of the words on their own, without the physical form in which they are presented, would be much diminished. Nicanor Parra's *Antibook* comprises a series of short poems which in codex format presents snatches of text in erratic patterns; the pages have to be taken apart and folded into a 3-D polyhedron in order to see the text complete, and joined up. Perhaps the ultimate step along this road is the creation of works like Keith Smith's *String Book*, which has textless blank pages with varying numbers of holes, through which string is passed; turning the pages produces an experience which is visual, tactile and aural. It is an artwork which depends primarily on the physical form of the book for its effectiveness and concentrates the mind on the book as an object. Can a book be a book without words?

OPPOSITE
Nicanor Parra's Antibook *only reveals its text when turned from a codex into a 3-dimensional structure*

OVERLEAF
Ambroise Vollard's edition of Verlaine's poems, Parallelement, *with lithographs by Paul Bonnard which blend into and around the text to help bring the sensual content to life, is often acknowledged as the first true livre d'artiste*

«Elle a, ta chair, le charme sombre
Des maturités estivales,
Elle en a l'ambre, elle en a l'ombre;

«Ta voix tonne dans les rafales,
Et ta chevelure sanglante
Fuit brusquement dans la nuit lente.»

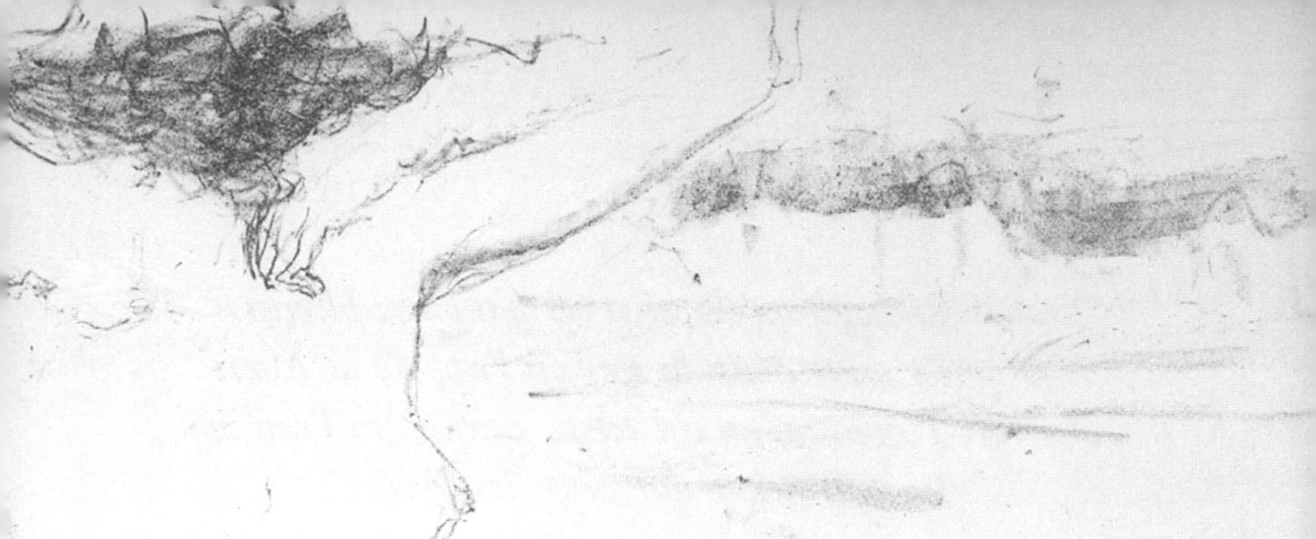

SAPPHO.

Furieuſe, les yeux caves & les seins roides,
Sappho, que la langueur de son déſir irrite,
Comme une louve court le long des grèves froides;

Elle songe à Phaon, oublieuſe du Rite,
Et, voyant à ce point ses larmes dédaignées,
Arrache ses cheveux immenſes par poignées;

Puis elle évoque, en des remords sans accalmies,
Ces temps où rayonnait, pure, la jeune gloire
De ses amours chantés en vers que la mémoire
De l'âme va redire aux vierges endormies :

Aunt Sallie's lament *plays with words and format to produce a book which represents its subject by more than just text*

Keith Smith's String book *dispenses with text altogether, to create something which is essentially a sensory experience based around the physical attributes of books*

Contemporary artists have experimented with the form and idea of the book in all kinds of ways, pushing it to its limits; they have made 'books' of mirrors or grass, without any words, and they have made book-shaped sculptural objects which do have words. People will debate whether a piece of 'book art' is a book, or art, or neither, but these works make us think about what you can do with the form and concept of the book

牛津
OXFORD
高阶英汉
双解词典
ADVANCED LEARNER'S
English-Chinese Dictionary
第6版

CHAPTER THREE

INDIVIDUALITY WITHIN MASS PRODUCTION

Workers at the Xinhua Printing Press produce Chinese-English dictionaries. The company, one of the largest printers in China, produces books and magazines for the domestic and international markets

Printed books – the physical artefacts we hold in our hands – are manufactured objects. At the broadest and simplest theoretical level we can think of their creation as a production line that starts with raw materials and churns out multiple copies of essentially identical artefacts. Multiplicity, and uniform identity, are important concepts here; this is what the invention of printing brought about, the ability to mass produce lots of copies of a particular text, set in metal type and impressed onto paper, so that many readers can have the same thing all at once. It is an important distinguishing feature between printed books and manuscript books, written by hand, which are obviously unique; even if the same scribe writes a text out twice, there are likely to be differences which are readily perceptible, and if two different scribes write it out, in separate places, the products will be distinctly individual.

VARIETY THROUGH PRINTING

There are in fact all kinds of reasons as to why this generalisation may be an oversimplification, as things can happen either deliberately or accidentally during the manufacturing process to introduce variety. Theoretically, every copy of this edition of this book should be exactly the same when it leaves the end of its production chain. The publisher instructs a book printing firm to create a certain number of copies of it and they should all be the same. If you stand in a shop with more than one copy on its shelves, thinking of buying it, there should be no differences between the copies, to make you choose one rather than the other. If, however, one of them has suffered some fault in the manufacturing process – a page has not been inked very well, or a page corner has not been cut properly – there will be visible differences that distinguish particular copies.

THE PROCESS OF PRINTING

Before the introduction of mechanisation in the nineteenth century, printing (like all other aspects of book production) was a handcrafted process. The artisans who worked in the printing house were trained to produce uniform multiple copies of the books they printed, but the process inevitably incorporated greater opportunities for variety and error than the mass production techniques of today.

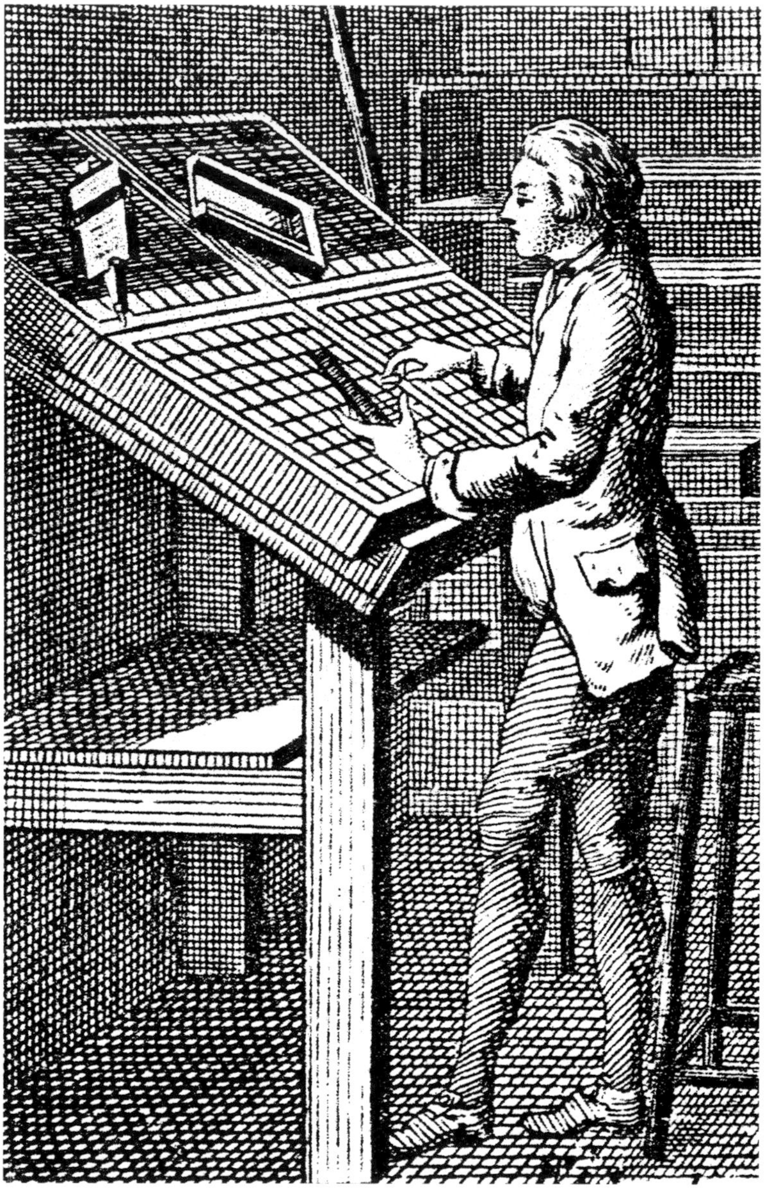

The first step in creating a printed book was the putting together of the type—a compositor would select each individual letter of metal type and put them together in the right order, to make up complete pages which were locked up in a frame ready for printing

The pages of type, on the bed of the printing press, were inked using handheld inked pads. Sheets of paper were placed in a special frame (the tympan and frisket) which was folded over the type when ready for printing. Each sheet of paper would comprise multiple leaves of the finished book, and had to be passed through the press twice so as to produce two pages on each side of each leaf

The last step in the process was the rolling of the sandwich of paper and inked type under the centre of the press so that the platen could be pressed down, using a screw mechanism, to create an inked impression on the paper. The sheets were then pegged up to dry before being folded and assembled in the right order. Each individual sheet of each book had to be produced in this way; the basic techniques, and the design of the equipment, remained unchanged for centuries

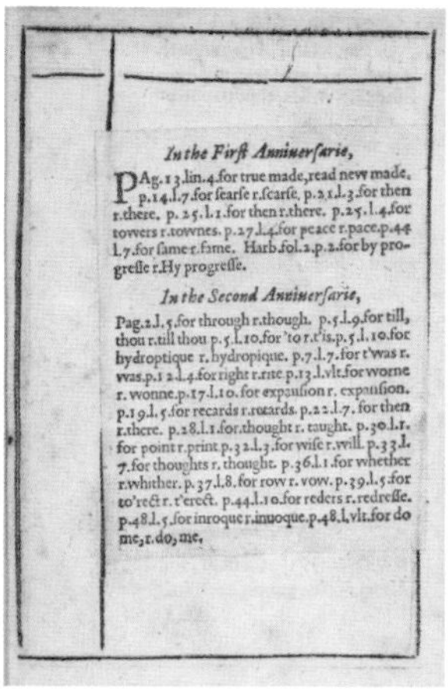

In the First Anniversarie,

PAg.13.lin.4.for true made,read new made. p.14.l.7.for searse r.scarse. p.21.l.3.for then r.there. p.25.l.1.for then r.there. p.25.l.4.for towers r.townes. p.27.l.4.for peace r.pace.p.44 l.7.for same r.fame. Harb.fol.2.p.2.for by progresse r.Hy progresse.

In the Second Anniversarie,

Pag.2.l.5.for through r.though. p.5.l.9.for till, thou r.till thou p.5.l.10.for 'to r.t'is.p.5.l.10.for hydroptique r.hydropique. p.7.l.7.for t'was r. was.p.12.l.4.for right r.rite p.13.l.vlt.for worne r. wonne.p.17.l.10.for expausion r. expansion. p.19.l.5.for recards r.rueards. p.22.l.7.for then r.there. p.28.l.1.for.thought r. taught. p.30.l.1. for point r.print p.32.l.3.for wise r.will. p.33.l. 7.for thoughts r. thought. p.36.l.1.for whether r.whither. p.37.l.8.for row r. vow. p.39.l.5.for to'rect r.t'erect. p.44.l.10.for reders r.redresse. p.48.l.5.for inroque r.inuoque.p.48.l.vlt.for do me, r.do, me.

A printed errata slip pasted into John Donne's Anniversaries *(1612); only one copy of the book is known containing this*

In modern book making, the technology is such that these kinds of errors have been largely smoothed out, although anyone who has attended sales of modern publishers' damaged stock will know that they still happen. In earlier centuries, when every part of the process was done by hand, when manufacture was literally *manu facere*, to make by hand, the opportunities for this kind of variety to creep in were much greater. This should be evident from the pictorial summary of the various stages of printing on the preceding pages. When every letter of the text was set from individual pieces of type, locked up in a frame, and page impressions were made by pressing sheets of paper down onto that type, suitably inked, all kinds of things could go wrong. Some pages or letters could be imperfectly inked, letters could fall out or be damaged, changes could be made deliberately in the middle of the printing operation if mistakes were noticed. The printing of a book was a time-consuming process which could take weeks or more to complete, with ample opportunities for variations to appear between the first and the last set of impressions of any particular sheet. Proof-readers checked sheets of text as they came from the press and if problems were spotted, the work could be halted and the words or spelling corrected before proceeding.

Mistakes that were felt to be unacceptable could be dealt with by printing small errata slips with the correct reading, to be pasted over the offending passage, or by printing whole new leaves of text which would be substituted for the originals when the book came to be bound up. These leaves, known as cancels, are usually readily detectable by the stubs left when single sheets are inserted into the folded gatherings of a book. Again, these features are recipes for variety; within a group of copies of a particular edition there may be ones which did or did not have their correction slips or cancel leaves inserted, or copies in which both cancels and the leaves that were intended to be removed have been bound up together.

These are all manifestations of variety which result from things that happen in the printing process. Some of them are trivial, others less so; it may be argued that the interest to be found in the kinds of variations introduced by poorly inked letters or minor press corrections are akin to those of stamps with one perforation too many, the territory of bibliographical trainspotters. Cancelled text can be more significant, by revealing authorial intentions or changes that had to be made in the light of contemporary political sensitivities. Dryden's *Annus Mirabilis*, a poem celebrating English victories against the Dutch first published in 1667, was originally printed with a line considered excessively critical of one of the English admirals, and a new leaf was printed and substituted in most copies. The first printing of Samuel Johnson's *Journey to the Western Isles* (1775) contained a paragraph criticising the Dean and Chapter of Lichfield, who planned to sell the lead from their Cathedral roof; it was suppressed before publication, and a toned-down piece of text was printed on a cancel leaf which is now found in all known copies, bar one. This kind of thing happens with modern books as well as old ones, which may have to be changed at the last minute for legal reasons; Graham Greene's *Stamboul Train* (1932) is an example.

Bibliographers developed the concept of 'ideal copy' to try to get an intellectual handle on the vagaries of book production processes. It rests on the idea that for every edition of every book that was printed as a distinct project within a printing house, there is a perfect version which represents what the author and the printer intended to produce. An edition is defined as all the copies of a book printed from one particular setting of type, without distributing it and putting it back together again, or significantly altering it. It is common for texts to change and develop between editions, through authorial intention or otherwise, and the charting of editions and the variation between them is a key part of textual bibliography. In recent years, the validity of ideal copy has increasingly been questioned, as people recognise that texts, and the way they were perceived by early readers, were more fluid things than can be encompassed in such a theory. Within an edition – which might be several hundred or even several thousand sets of printed sheets of the complete work, depending on the print run – there may be numerous variant states which differ from the ideal copy by containing the kinds of mistakes or corrections just mentioned, and there may be discrete subsets of the edition which can be identified as having been published or distributed as distinct units. If several hundred sets of sheets of a book were run off and then sold via different retail outlets, separate title leaves might be printed for the

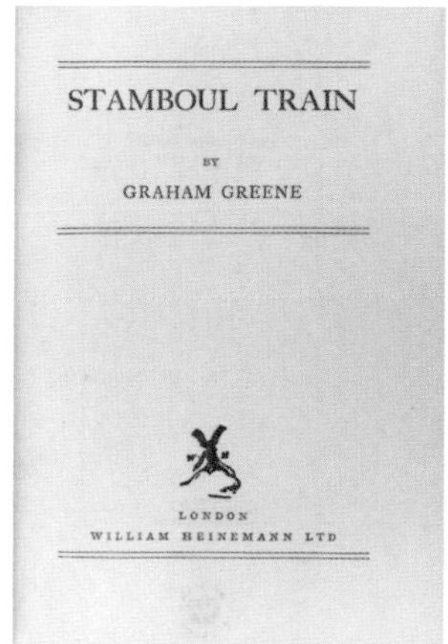

When Graham Greene's novel Stamboul Train *was first published by Heinemann in 1932, it came to the notice of J. B. Priestley (who saw an advance copy) that he had been satirised in one of the book's characters. The threat of libel action from Priestley – then a bigger Heinemann author than Greene – led to Greene revising his text, the original issue of the book being suppressed, and it being hastily reissued in changed form. Only a small number of copies of the first version survive today, which command high prices in dealers' catalogues*

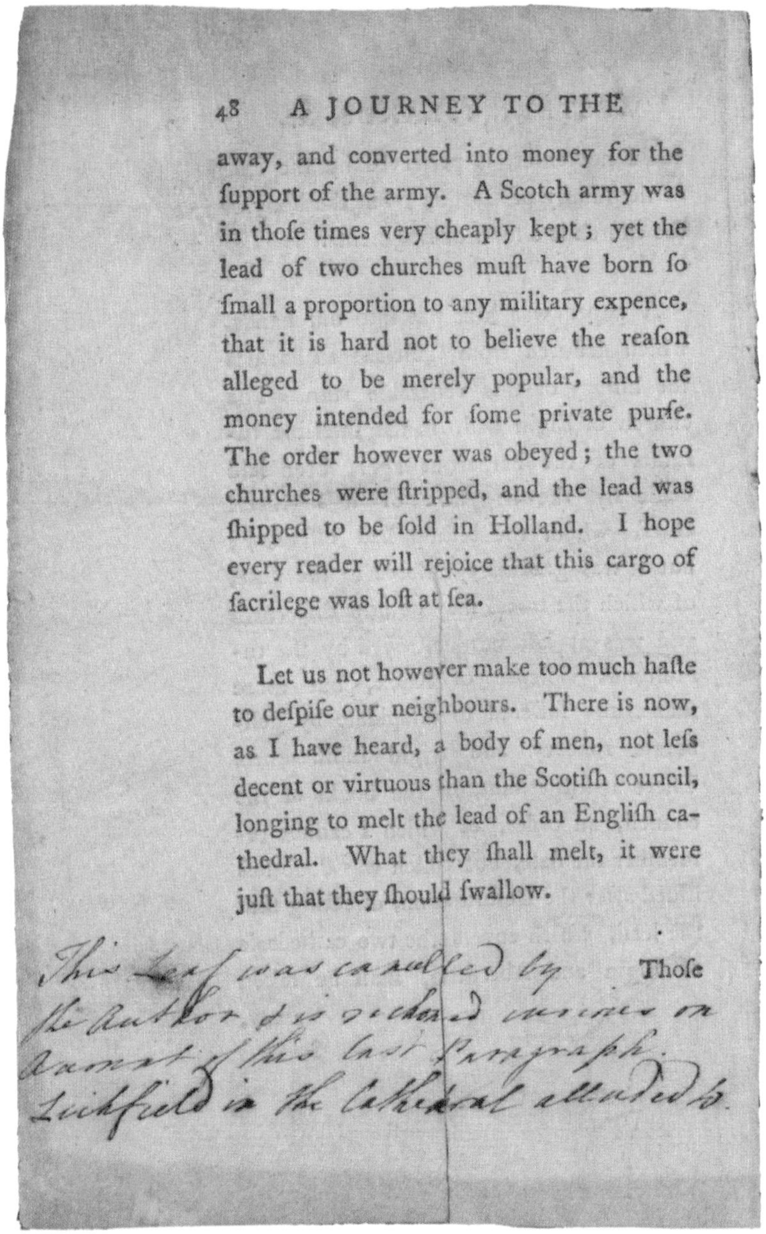

48 A JOURNEY TO THE

away, and converted into money for the ſupport of the army. A Scotch army was in thoſe times very cheaply kept; yet the lead of two churches muſt have born ſo ſmall a proportion to any military expence, that it is hard not to believe the reaſon alleged to be merely popular, and the money intended for ſome private purſe. The order however was obeyed; the two churches were ſtripped, and the lead was ſhipped to be ſold in Holland. I hope every reader will rejoice that this cargo of ſacrilege was loſt at ſea.

Let us not however make too much haſte to deſpiſe our neighbours. There is now, as I have heard, a body of men, not leſs decent or virtuous than the Scotiſh council, longing to melt the lead of an Engliſh cathedral. What they ſhall melt, it were juſt that they ſhould ſwallow.

Thoſe

This Leaf was cancelled by the Author & is reckoned curious on account of this last Paragraph. Lichfield is the Cathedral alluded to.

RIGHT
The original leaf from Samuel Johnson's Journey to the Western Isles *(1775), before the author thought better of his suggestion that the clergy of Lichfield Cathedral should drink molten lead; nearly all known copies contain a substituted leaf, inserted after this one was cancelled, with more moderate text*

OPPOSITE
John Randall's Introduction to ... arts and sciences *was first published in London in 1765 (the titlepage is not dated) but a stock of unsold sheets was still available more than 20 years later, when an attempt to shift them was made by printing a new title page, with a completely different title, and omitting the author's name. From the title leaf onwards, the two books are the same, using the sheets from the original print run*

A N

INTRODUCTION

To ſo much of the

ARTS and SCIENCES,

More immediately concerned in an

Excellent Education for Trade

In its lower Scenes and more genteel Profeſſions,

AND FOR

Preparing YOUNG GENTLEMEN in Grammar Schools to attend LECTURES in the UNIVERSITIES.

In FOUR PARTS.

PART I.

The Theory and diffuſive Practice of ARITHMETIC, VULGAR and DECIMAL; the *Arithmetic* of ALGEBRA by Tranſpoſition introduced, as it gives Rules to the Accomptant; Annuities for Time; the Principles of Mr. *De Moivre*, Mr. *Simpſon*, and of the AUTHOR, in eſtimating Annuities for Single Lives, conſider'd from the Equity in ſinking Money. Digeſted into Syſtems, as Trade, young Ladies, or the Concerns of the Gentry may require.

PART II.

An extenſive Courſe of GEOMETRY; Menſuration; an Introduction to Gauging and Surveying; Plain Trigonometry applied to the Merchant's and Surveyor's Uſe; the Aſtronomical Principles of Geography; the Conſtruction and Uſe of Maps; the Menſuration of the Globes of the Solar Syſtem, and of their Orbits; the Eſtimations of Artificers; and the Debates of the Globes concerning the Earth's two Motions, to effect the Seaſons, *&c.*

Expreſly deſigned to remove that general Complaint of not effectually inſtructing YOUTH, while at School, in what may be of Importance in their future Stations, and enlarging their narrow Conceptions and ſcanty Views of Nature.

The various Subjects are ſo digeſted and expreſſed, as to *aſſiſt* the *Maſter*, and to ground, forward, and encourage the *Scholar*, and to make him of immediate Uſe when he is put to the Teſt.

With Eight COPPER-PLATES.

To which is prefix'd a LETTER on EDUCATION.

By J. RANDALL,

Formerly Maſter of the Academy at Heath *near* Wakefield, *but now at* York.

LONDON: Sold by W. NICOLL, in St. *Paul's* Church-Yard.

[Price bound Three Shillings and Sixpence.]

THE NEW

BOOK of KNOWLEDGE;

OR,

YOUNG MAN's BEST INSTRUCTOR

IN THE

ARTS and SCIENCES.

PART I.

The Theory and Practice of ARITHMETIC, VULGAR and DECIMAL; the *Arithmetic* of ALGEBRA by Tranſpoſition introduced, as it gives Rules to the Accomptant; Annuities for Time; the Principles of Mr. *De Moivre*, Mr. *Simpſon*, and of the AUTHOR, in eſtimating Annuities for Single Lives, conſidered from the Equity in ſinking Money. Digeſted into Syſtems.

PART II.

An extenſive Courſe of GEOMETRY; Menſuration; an Introduction to Gauging and Surveying; Plain Trigonometry; the Aſtronomical Principles of Geography; the Conſtruction and Uſe of Maps; the Menſuration of the Globes of the Solar Syſtem, and of their Orbits; the Eſtimations of Artificers; and the Debates of the Globes concerning the Earth's two Motions to effect the Seaſons, *&c.*

Expreſly deſigned to remove that general Complaint of not effectually inſtructing YOUTH, while at School, in what may be of Importance in their future Stations, and enlarging their narrow Conceptions and ſcanty Views of Nature.

The various Subjects are ſo digeſted and expreſſed as to *aſſiſt* the *Maſter*, and to ground, forward, and encourage the *Scholar*, and to make him of immediate Uſe when he is put to the Teſt.

WITH EIGHT COPPER-PLATES.

TO WHICH IS PREFIXED,

A LETTER ON EDUCATION.

LONDON:

Printed for A. MILLAR, W. LAW, and R. CATER.

MDCCLXXXVII.

[Price bound Three Shillings and Sixpence.]

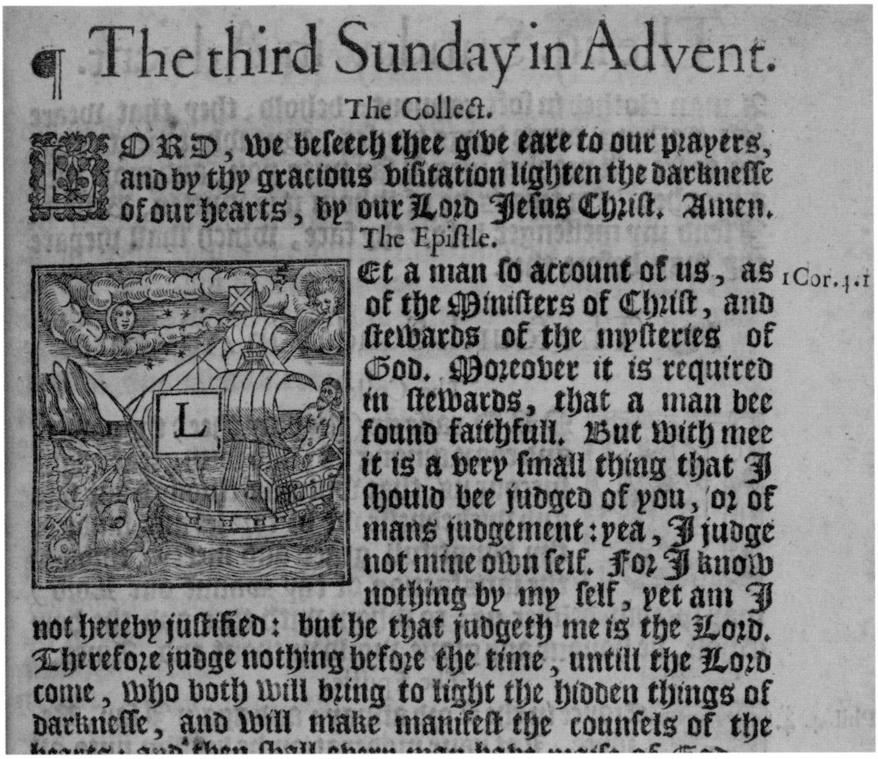

¶ The third Sunday in Advent.

The Collect.

LORD, we beſeech thee give eare to our prayers, and by thy gracious viſitation lighten the darkneſſe of our hearts, by our Lord Jeſus Chriſt. Amen.

The Epiſtle.

Let a man ſo account of us, as of the Miniſters of Chriſt, and ſtewards of the myſteries of God. Moreover it is required in ſtewards, that a man bee found faithfull. But with mee it is a very ſmall thing that I ſhould bee judged of you, or of mans judgement: yea, I judge not mine own ſelf. For I know nothing by my ſelf, yet am I not hereby juſtified: but he that judgeth me is the Lord. Therefore judge nothing before the time, untill the Lord come, who both will bring to light the hidden things of darkneſſe, and will make manifeſt the counſels of the 1 Cor. 4. 1

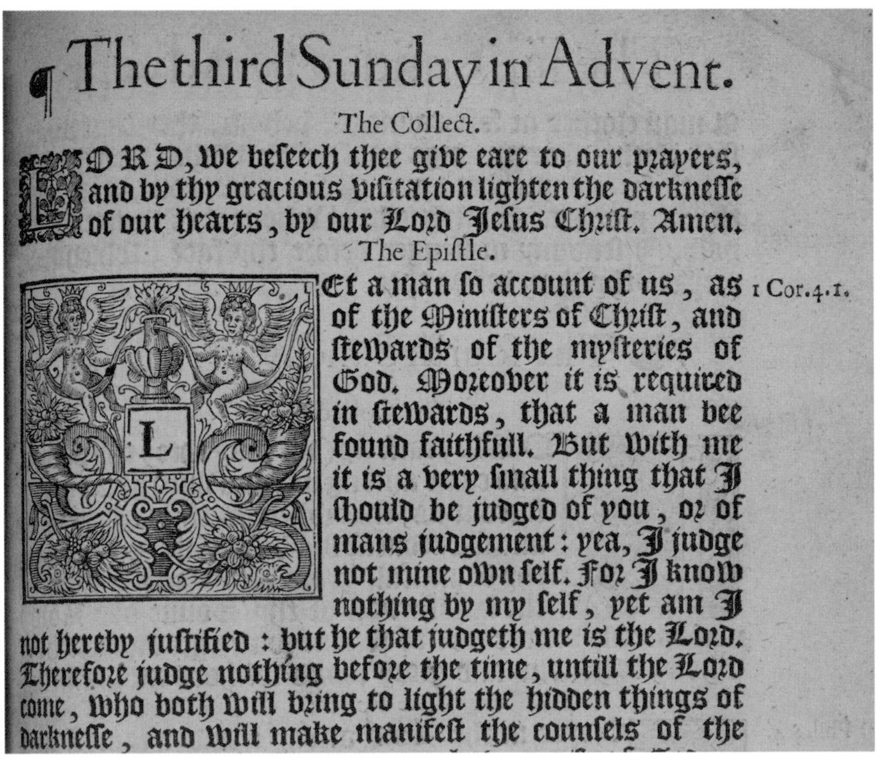

¶ The third Sunday in Advent.

The Collect.

LORD, we beſeech thee give eare to our prayers, and by thy gracious viſitation lighten the darkneſſe of our hearts, by our Lord Jeſus Chriſt. Amen.

The Epiſtle.

Let a man ſo account of us, as of the Miniſters of Chriſt, and ſtewards of the myſteries of God. Moreover it is required in ſtewards, that a man bee found faithfull. But with me it is a very ſmall thing that I ſhould be judged of you, or of mans judgement: yea, I judge not mine own ſelf. For I know nothing by my ſelf, yet am I not hereby juſtified: but he that judgeth me is the Lord. Therefore judge nothing before the time, untill the Lord come, who both will bring to light the hidden things of darkneſſe, and will make manifeſt the counſels of the 1 Cor. 4. 1.

different booksellers involved. Sometimes, books whose sheets had sat around unsold for some years were reissued with a new title leaf, with a new date and possibly different wording of the title, to try to convince customers that something new was on offer, although the entire book (apart from the first leaf) was actually made up of the sheets printed some years before.

Popular books which were reprinted several times within a short space of time – the Bible is an obvious example – can present all kinds of complexities to those who try to understand their publishing history, as copies of sheets from different distinct printings, months or possibly years apart, could be mixed up together to make up complete books, and it is quite common to find multiple copies of books like this with identical title leaves followed by text made up from a different mix of sheets from different printings. Even books printed apparently only once can present considerable variety. The Scottish prayer book of 1637, an attempt to impose the Book of Common Prayer on the Scots, which resulted in civil uprising, has a bibliographical history which mirrors the controversy it generated. It was in production for a year and half, during which time parts of the book were typeset more than once, with numerous corrections and changes made during the printing process. Some quires were printed in different typesettings (the same words and page layout, but different original pages of type), and within particular settings there are variants where text was changed or suppressed. The result is that no two copies are likely to be quite identical, although they may look so at first glance. If you put two surviving copies side by side you are likely to find that they have different readings, different layouts or different ornaments at various points in the text.

For all these reasons, the printing process may introduce variety into print runs, so that the multiple uniformity which we might expect to see in an edition of a book is not what we actually find. They are on the whole accidental reasons, from the book buyer's point of view, in the sense that they are things that happen in the printing house or bindery without the buyer's knowledge. This point is worth making in order to distinguish these kinds of differences from other kinds which also result from the printing process, but which were deliberately presented to the buyer as choices.

OPPOSITE
The fact that these two pages from two copies of the Scottish Prayer Book of 1637 are different settings is most obviously apparent from the fact that the big decorative borders (called factotums) around the capital 'L' are different. The wording and layout is the same in each case, but there are other subtle differences which become apparent from close scrutiny. Each page originated from a different block of locked-up type

OVERLEAF
This seventeenth-century Bible is made up from a mixture of printed sheets from two separate editions—the page on the right hand side of the opening is in Roman type, that on the left is in black letter. Such mixing may take place at various points in a book's history – not only at the time of issue, but also later, if owners or booksellers chose to 'perfect' individual volumes by making up missing or defective pages from another copy

19 A [e] seruant will not bee chastised with wordes: though hee vnderstand, yet hee will not || answere.

e He that is of a seruile and rebellious nature.
|| Or, regard.

20 Seest thou a man hastie in his matters? there is more hope of a foole, then of him.

21 He that delicately bringeth vp his seruant from youth, at length he wil be euen as his sonne.

22 * An angry man stirreth vp strife, and a furious man aboundeth in transgression.

Chap. 15.18.

23 * The pride of a man shall bring him low: but the humble in spirit shall enioy glory.

Iob 22.29.

24 Hee that is partner with a theefe, hateth his owne soule: he heareth cursing and declareth it not.

25 The feare of man bringeth a [f] snare: but he that trusteth in the LORD shall bee exalted.

f He that feareth man more then God, falleth into a snare, and is destroyed.

26 Many doe seeke the face of the ruler: but euery mans [g] iudgement commeth from the LORD.

g Hee needeth not to flatter the ruler: for what God hath appointed, that shall come to him.

27 A wicked man is abomination to the iust, and he that is vpright in his waye, is abomination to the wicked.

CHAP. XXX.

2 To humble our selues in consideration of Gods workes 5 The word of God is perfit. 11 Of the wicked and hypocrites. 15 Of things that are neuer saciate. 18 Of others that wonderfull.

¶ The words of [a] AGVR the sonne of IAKEH.

The prophecie which the man spake vnto Ithiel, euen to [b] Ithiel and Ucal.

a Who was an excellent man in vertue & knowledge in the time of Salomon.
b Which were Agurs schollers or friends.

2 Surely I am more [c] foolish then any man, and haue not the vnderstanding of a man in me.

c Herein hee declareth his great humilitie, who would not attribute any wisedome to himselfe, but all vnto God.

3 For I haue not learned wisedome, nor attained to the knowledge of holy things.

4 Who hath ascended vp to [d] heauen, and descended? Who hath gathered the winde in his fist? Who hath bound the waters in a garment? Who hath established all the ends of the world? What is his name, and what is his sonnes name, if thou canst tell?

d Meaning, to know the secrets of God, as though he would say, None.

5 * Euery word of God is pure: he is a shield to those that trust in him.

Psal. 19.8.

6 * Put nothing vnto his words, lest hee reprooue thee, and thou be found a liar.

Deut. 4.2. and 12.32.

7 Two [e] things haue I required of thee: denie me them not before I die.

8 Remooue farre from mee vanitie and lies: giue me not pouertie, nor riches: feede me with food conuenient for me,

e He maketh this request to God.

9 Lest I bee full and denie thee, and say, [f] Who is the LORD? or lest I bee poore, and steale and take the Name of my God in vaine.

f Meaning, that they that put their trust in their riches, forget God, & that by too much wealth men haue an occasion to the same.

10 Accuse not a seruant vnto his master, lest hee curse thee [g] when thou hast offended.

g In accusing him without

11 There is a generation that curseth their father, and doeth not blesse their mother.

12 There is a generation that are pure in their owne conceit, and yet are not washed from their filthinesse.

13 There is a generation, whose eyes are haughty, and their eye lids are lifted vp.

14 ... vp the afflicted out of the earth, & the poore from among men.

15 The horseleach hath two [h] daughters, which cry, Giue, giue. There be three things that will not be satisfied: yea, foure that say not, It is enough.

16 The graue, and the barren wombe: the earth that cannot bee satisfied with water, and the fire that saith not it is enough.

17 The eye that mocketh his father, and despiseth the instruction of his mother, let the rauens [i] of the valley picke it out, and the yong eagles eate it.

18 There bee three things hid from mee, yea, foure that I know not.

19 The way of an eagle in the ayre, the way of a serpent vpon a stone, the way of a ship in the mids of the sea, and the way of a man with a maide.

20 Such is the way also of an adulterous woman: she eateth, and [k] wipeth her mouth, and saith, I haue not committed iniquitie.

21 For three things the earth is mooued: yea, for foure it cannot susteine it selfe:

22 For a [l] seruant when he reigneth, and a foole when he is filled with meate,

23 For the hatefull woman when she is married, and for a handmaid that is [m] heire to her mistresse.

24 These bee foure small things in the earth, yet they are [n] wise, and full of wisedome:

25 The pismires a people not strong, yet prepare they their meate in summer:

26 The conies a people not mightie, yet make they their houses in the rocke,

27 The grashopper hath no king, yet goe they forth all by bands.

28 The spider taketh holde [o] with her hands, and is in kings palaces.

29 There be three things that order well their going: yea, foure are comely in going.

30 A lion which is strong among beasts, and turneth not at the sight of any:

31 A lusty grayhound, and a goate, and a king against whom there is no rising vp.

32 If thou hast beene foolish in lifting thy selfe vp, and if thou hast thought wickedly, lay thine hand [p] vpon thy mouth.

33 When one churneth milke, he bringeth foorth butter: and he that wringeth his nose, causeth blood to come out: so he that forceth wrath bring foorth strife.

CHAP. XXXI.

2 He exhorteth to chastitie and iustice, 10 And sheweth the conditions of a wise and worthy woman.

¶ 1 THE WORDS OF KING [a] LEMVEL: The [b] prophesie which his mother taught him.

What my sonne! and what the sonne of [c] my wombe! and what O sonne of my desires!

3 Giue not thy strength vnto women, [d] nor

b The doctrine which his mother Bath-sheba taught this often repetition of one thing, she declareth

him.
21 He that delicately bringeth up his servant
from a childe, shall have him become *his* son at the
length.
22 * An angry man stirreth up strife, and a
furious man aboundeth in transgression.
23 * A mans pride shall bring him low: but
honour shall uphold the humble in spirit.
24 Whoso is partner with a thief, hateth
his own soul: he heareth cursing, and bewrayeth
it not.
25 The fear of man bringeth f a snare: but
whoso putteth his trust in the LORD, † shall
be safe.
26 * Many seek † the rulers favour, but every
mans g judgement *cometh* from the LORD.
27 An unjust man *is* an abomination to the
just: and he that *is* upright in the way, *is* abomination to the wicked.

CHAP. XXX.

Agurs confession of his faith. 7 The two points of his prayer. 10 The meanest are not to be wronged. 11 Four wicked generations. 15 Four things insatiable. 17 Parents are not to be despised. 18 Four things hard to be known. 21 Four things untolerable. 24 Four things exceeding wise. 29 Four things stately. 32 Wrath is to be prevented.

THe words of a Agur the son of Iakeh, *even*
the prophecie: the man spake unto Ithiel,
even unto b Ithiel and Ucal.
2 Surely I *am* more c brutish then *any* man,
and have not the understanding of a man.
3 I neither learned wisdom, nor † have the
knowledge of the holy.
4 * Who hath ascended up into d heaven, or
descended? * who hath gathered the winde in
his fists? who hath bound the waters in a garment? who hath established all the ends of the
earth? what *is* his name, and what *is* his sons
name, if thou canst tell?
5 * Every word of God *is* † pure: he *is* a
shield unto them that put their trust in him.
6 * Adde thou not unto his words, lest he
reprove thee, and thou be found a liar.
7 e Two things have I required of thee, † denie me *them* not before I die.
8 Remove farre from me vanitie and lies; give
me neither poverty, nor riches, * feed me with
food † convenient for me:
9 * Lest I be full, and † deny *thee*, and say,
Who *is* the LORD? or lest I be poor, and steal,
and take the name of my God *in vain*.
10 † Accuse not a servant unto his master, lest
he curse thee, and thou be found g guilty.
11 *There is* a generation *that* curseth their father, and doth not blesse their mother.
12 *There is* a generation *that are* pure in
their own eyes, and yet is not washed from their
filthinesse.
13 *There is* a generation, O how * lofty are
their eyes! and their eye-lids are lifted up.
14 * *There is* a generation, whose teeth *are as*
swords, and their jaw-teeth *as* knives, to devour
the poor from off the earth, and the needy from
among men.
15 The horsleach hath h two daughters,
crying, Give, give. There are three things *that*
enough:
16 The grave, and the barren womb, the earth
that is not filled with water, and the fire *that*
saith not, *It is* enough.
17 The eye *that* mocketh at *his* father, and
despiseth to obey his mother, the ravens of || the
i valley shall pick it out, and the young eagles
shall eat it.
18 There be three things *which* are too wonderfull for me; yea, four which I know not:
19 The way of an eagle in the air, the way of
a serpent upon a rock, the way of a ship in the
† midst of the sea, and the way of a man with a
maid.
20 Such *is* the way of an adulterous woman;
she eateth, and k wipeth her mouth and saith, I
have done no wickednesse.
21 For three things the earth is disquieted, and
for four *which* it cannot bear:
22 * For l a servant when he reigneth, and a
fool when he is filled with meat,
23 For an odious *woman* when she is married,
and an handmaid that is m heir to her mistresse.
24 There be four things which are little upon
the earth, but they *are* † n exceeding wise:
25 * The ants *are* a people not strong, yet they
prepare their meat in the summer;
26 The conies *are but* a feeble folk, yet make
they their houses in the rocks;
27 The locusts have no king, yet go they forth
all of them † by bands;
28 The spider taketh hold with her o hands,
and is in kings palaces.
29 There be three things which go well, yea
four are comely in going:
30 A lion *which is* strongest among beasts, and
turneth not away for any,
31 A || † grey-hound, an he-goat also, and a
king against whom *there is* no rising up.
32 If thou hast done foolishly in lifting up thy
self, or if thou hast thought evil, * p *lay* thine hand
upon thy mouth.
33 Surely the churning of milk bringeth forth
butter, and the wringing of the nose bringeth
forth blood: so the forcing of wrath bringeth
forth strife.

CHAP. XXXI.

1 Lemuels lesson of chastity and temperance. 6 The afflicted are to be comforted and defended. 10 The praise and properties of a good wife.

THe words of king a Lemuel, the prophecie that
his b mother taught him.
2 What, my son? and what, the c son of my
womb? and what, the son of my vows?
3 Give not thy strength unto women, nor thy
wayes to that which d destroyeth kings.
4 *It is* not for kings, O Lemuel, *it is* not for
kings to drink wine, nor for princes, e strong
drink:
5 Lest they drink, and forget the law, and † per-
vert the judgement † of any of the afflicted.
6 * Give strong drink unto him that is ready
to perish, and wine to those that be † of heavy
hearts.
7 Let him drink and forget his poverty, and
remember his misery f no more.
8 Open thy mouth for the g dumb in the
cause of all † such as are appointed to destruction.

|| Or, *the brook*.
i Which haunt in the valley for carrions.
† Heb. *heart*.
k She hath her desires, and after counterfeiteth as though she were an honest woman.
* Chap. 19. 10.
l These commonly abuse the state whereunto they are called.
m Which is married to her master after the death of her mistresse.
† Heb. *wise, made wise*.
n They contain great doctrine and wisdom.
* Chap. 6. 6, &c.
† Heb. *gathered together*.
o If man be not able to compasse these common things by his wisdom, we cannot attribute wisdom to man but folly.
|| Or, *horse*.
† Heb. *girt in the loins*.
* Job 21. 5. and 40. 4.
p Make a stay, and continue not in doing evil.
a That is, of Solomon, who was called Lemuel, that is, of God, because God had ordained him to be king over Israel.
b The doctrine which his mother Barth-sheba taught him.
c By this often repetition of one thing she declareth her motherly affection.
d Meaning, that women are the destruction of kings, if they haunt them.
e That is, the king must not give himself to wantonnesse, and neglect

e same.
* Chap. 6.
†Heb. *hurt not with thy tongue*. g In accusing him

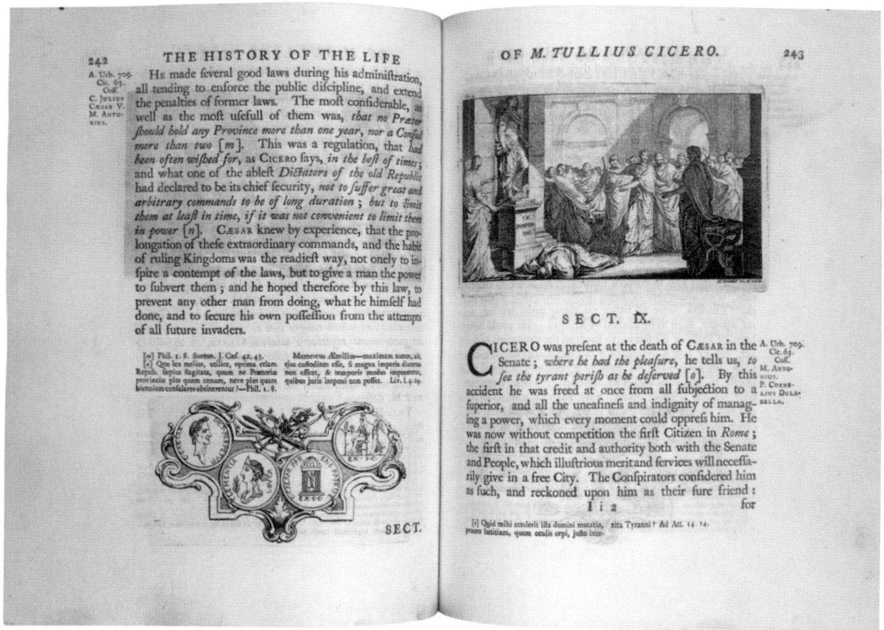
242 THE HISTORY OF THE LIFE

A. Urb. 709. Cic. 63. Coſſ. C. Julius Cæsar V. M. Antonius.

He made ſeveral good laws during his adminiſtration, all tending to enforce the public diſcipline, and extend the penalties of former laws. The moſt conſiderable, as well as the moſt uſefull of them was, *that no Prætor ſhould hold any Province more than one year, nor a Conſul more than two* [*m*]. This was a regulation, that *had been often wiſhed for*, as Cicero ſays, *in the beſt of times*; and what one of the ableſt *Dictators of the old Republic* had declared to be its chief ſecurity, *not to ſuffer great and arbitrary commands to be of long duration; but to limit them at leaſt in time, if it was not convenient to limit them in power* [*n*]. Cæsar knew by experience, that the prolongation of theſe extraordinary commands, and the habit of ruling Kingdoms was the readieſt way, not onely to inſpire a contempt of the laws, but to give a man the power to ſubvert them; and he hoped therefore by this law, to prevent any other man from doing, what he himſelf had done, and to ſecure his own poſſeſſion from the attempts of all future invaders.

[*m*] Phil. 1. 8. Sueton. J. Cæſ. 42, 43.
[*n*] Quæ lex melior, utilior, optima etiam Repub. ſæpius flagitata, quam ne Prætoriæ provinciæ plus quam annum, neve plus quam biennium conſulares obtinerentur!—Phil. 1. 8. Mamercus Æmilius—maximam autem, ait, ejus cuſtodiam eſſe, ſi magna imperia diuturna non eſſent, & temporis modus imponeretur, quibus juris imponi non poſſet. Liv. l. 4. 24.

SECT.

OF M. TULLIUS CICERO. 243

SECT. IX.

A. Urb. 709. Cic. 63. Coſſ. M. Antonius. P. Cornelius Dolabella.

CICERO was preſent at the death of Cæsar in the Senate; *where he had the pleaſure*, he tells us, *to ſee the tyrant periſh as he deſerved* [*o*]. By this accident he was freed at once from all ſubjection to a ſuperior, and all the uneaſineſs and indignity of managing a power, which every moment could oppreſs him. He was now without competition the firſt Citizen in *Rome*; the firſt in that credit and authority both with the Senate and People, which illuſtrious merit and ſervices will neceſſarily give in a free City. The Conſpirators conſidered him as ſuch, and reckoned upon him as their ſure friend: for

I i 2

[*o*] Quid mihi attulerit iſta domini mutatio, ... ptatem lætitiam, quam oculis cepi, juſto interitu Tyranni? Ad Att. 14. 14.

When printing was invented in the fifteenth century paper was well established as a medium for handwritten books and documents and it was the natural choice for mass production, but vellum (specially dried calfskin) was the preferred option for high quality, permanent texts. The earliest printers therefore often ran off a number of copies of their books printed on vellum as well as paper, to offer purchasers a choice and a luxury option; the typesetting would be exactly the same and the paper copies would normally constitute the bulk of the edition. This tradition goes back to the very beginning of printing (the first printed book, the Gutenberg Bible, was issued on vellum as well as on paper), and continued throughout the handpress era. The use of vellum as the material for luxury copies became less common after the early sixteenth century, though it never quite died out and there are examples of eighteenth- and nineteenth-century books with a vellum issue. What became much more common was the idea of offering a choice based on paper, with sheets of an edition run off on different qualities of paper of varying thickness or whiteness. The great multivolume

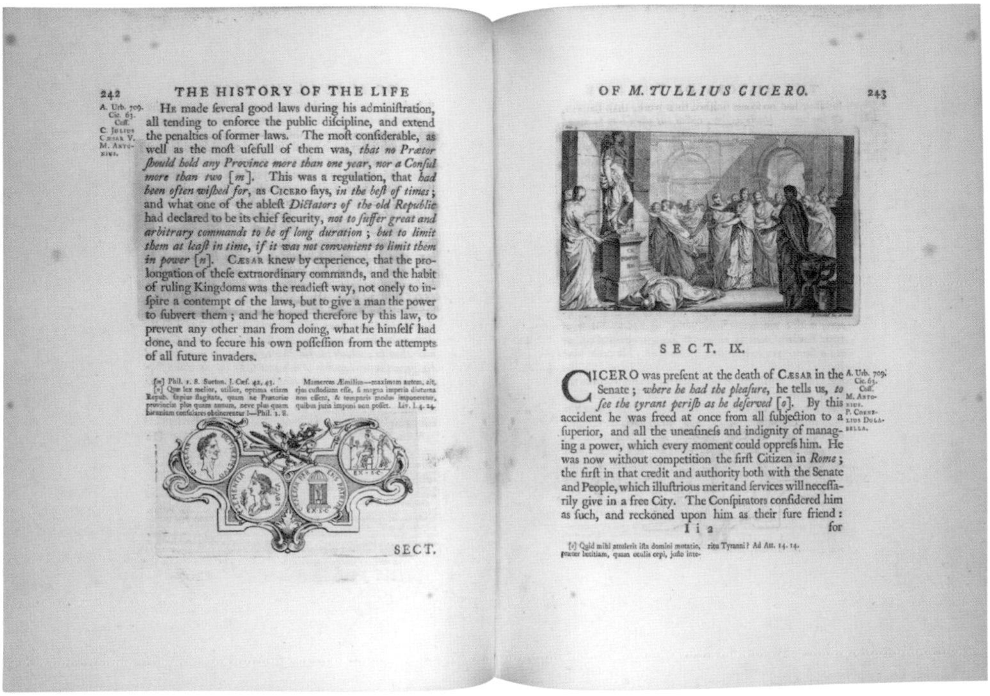

242 THE HISTORY OF THE LIFE

HE made feveral good laws during his adminiftration, all tending to enforce the public difcipline, and extend the penalties of former laws. The moft confiderable, as well as the moft ufefull of them was, *that no Prætor fhould hold any Province more than one year, nor a Conful more than two* [m]. This was a regulation, that *had been often wifhed for*, as CICERO fays, *in the beft of times*; and what one of the ableft *Dictators of the old Republic* had declared to be its chief fecurity, *not to fuffer great and arbitrary commands to be of long duration; but to limit them at leaft in time, if it was not convenient to limit them in power* [n]. CÆSAR knew by experience, that the prolongation of thefe extraordinary commands, and the habit of ruling Kingdoms was the readieft way, not onely to infpire a contempt of the laws, but to give a man the power to fubvert them; and he hoped therefore by this law, to prevent any other man from doing, what he himfelf had done, and to fecure his own poffeffion from the attempts of all future invaders.

SECT.

OF *M. TULLIUS CICERO.* 243

SECT. IX.

CICERO was prefent at the death of CÆSAR in the Senate; *where he had the pleafure*, he tells us, *to fee the tyrant perifh as he deferved* [o]. By this accident he was freed at once from all fubjection to a fuperior, and all the uneafinefs and indignity of managing a power, which every moment could opprefs him. He was now without competition the firft Citizen in *Rome*; the firft in that credit and authority both with the Senate and People, which illuftrious merit and fervices will neceffarily give in a free City. The Confpirators confidered him as fuch, and reckoned upon him as their fure friend:

I i 2 for

polyglot Bible printed by Christopher Plantin at Antwerp between 1569 and 1572 was offered for sale on four different types of paper, or on vellum, variously priced according to quality. As well as using multiple types of plain white paper, printers would also sometimes mark out subsets of their editions by printing them on coloured paper, to create something of a novelty.

The other trick that could be incorporated into the printing process, to create *de luxe* options for particular books, was the production of large paper copies. Here, the locked-up pages of type would be spaced further apart, before running the press again using larger sheets of paper. The result was the same book, textually and typographically, but more generously spaced out with wider margins. This appealed to discerning and affluent book buyers and was a common habit particularly towards the end of the hand-press period, in the eighteenth century. Large paper copies can be distinguished from the ordinary paper versions by comparing the widths of the inner margins, which cannot be trimmed during the bookbinding process as the outer ones were.

Variety, and a luxury option for discerning customers, could be introduced by printing large paper copies of books. The typesetting remains the same but the locked-up pages of type were moved further apart and printed on larger sheets of paper, to give more generous margins. Here are ordinary, and large-paper copies of Conyers Middleton's Life of Cicero *(1741)*

IV. THE SACRIFICE.

OH all ye, who paſs by, whoſe eyes and m
To worldly things are ſharp, but to me
To me, who took eyes that I might you find:
Was ever grief like mine.

The Princes of my people make a head
Againſt their Maker: they do wiſh me dead,
Who cannot wiſh, except I give them bread:
Was ever grief like mine

Without me each one, who doth now me bra
Had to this day been an Egyptian ſlave.
They uſe that power againſt me, which I gave
Was ever grief like mine

Mine own Apoſtle, who the bag did bear,
Though he had all I had, did not forbear
To ſell me alſo, and to put me there:
Was ever grief like mine?

For thirty pence he did my death deviſe,
Who at three hundred did the ointment prize,
Not half ſo ſweet as my ſweet ſacrifice:
Was ever grief like mine

Therefore my ſoul melts, and my heart's dear tr
Drops blood (the only beads) my words to mea
O let this cup paſs, if it be thy pleaſure:
Was ever grief like mine?

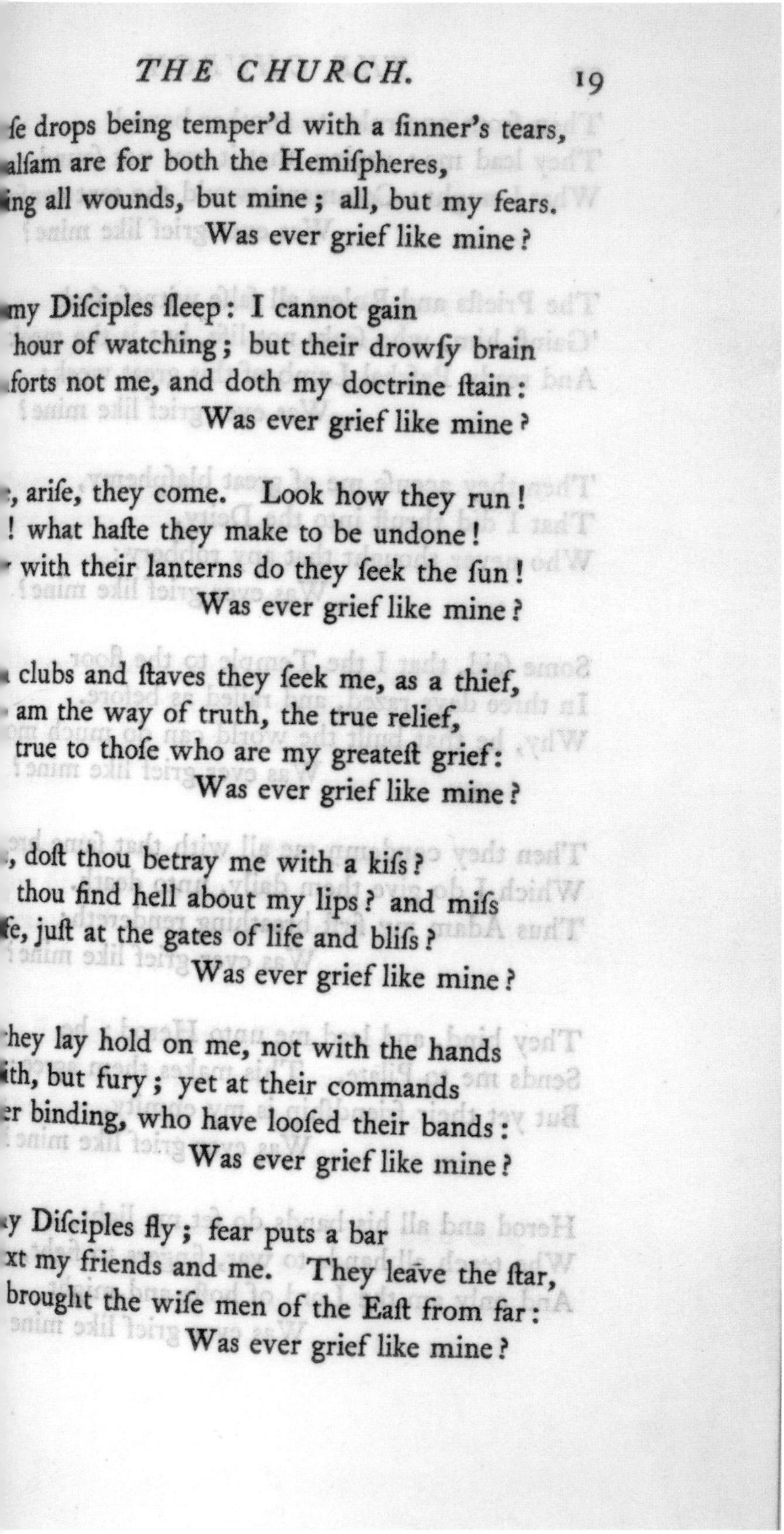

THE CHURCH. 19

ſe drops being temper'd with a ſinner's tears,
alſam are for both the Hemiſpheres,
ing all wounds, but mine; all, but my fears.
Was ever grief like mine?

my Diſciples ſleep: I cannot gain
hour of watching; but their drowſy brain
forts not me, and doth my doctrine ſtain:
Was ever grief like mine?

, ariſe, they come. Look how they run!
! what haſte they make to be undone!
with their lanterns do they ſeek the ſun!
Was ever grief like mine?

clubs and ſtaves they ſeek me, as a thief,
am the way of truth, the true relief,
true to thoſe who are my greateſt grief:
Was ever grief like mine?

, doſt thou betray me with a kiſs?
thou find hell about my lips? and miſs
fe, juſt at the gates of life and bliſs?
Was ever grief like mine?

hey lay hold on me, not with the hands
ith, but fury; yet at their commands
er binding, who have looſed their bands:
Was ever grief like mine?

y Diſciples fly; fear puts a bar
xt my friends and me. They leave the ſtar,
brought the wiſe men of the Eaſt from far:
Was ever grief like mine?

William Pickering's 1844 edition of George Herbert's The Temple *was issued with some copies printed on vellum (as this one), to offer a luxury option to purchasers*

Exhortation to auoid hast, and to work by good aduisement.

Epistle of vartuous busines, eschewing idlenesse.

A Ballad to the Sheriffes and Aldermen of London on a May morning.

A disguising before the Mayor of London by the Mercers.

A disguising before the Mayor by the Goldesmithes.

A mumming before the king at Eltham.

A disguising before the king in the castle of Hartford.

A disguising before the great estates of the land.

A mumming before the king at Windsore.

A balad giuen to Hen. the 6. and his mother, on Newyeres day at Hartford.

All thinges are right, so as the Crab goeth forward.

Chusing loues of S. Valentines day.

Of an Esquire that serued in Loues court.

Of a gentlewoman that loued a man of great estate.

Of the ladie of Holland, and Duke of Glocest before their marriage.

Of Iacke Wat that could pluck the lining out a blacke boll.

Gallaunts, England may waile that euer th came here.

Æsops Fables moralised in mitre.

The churle and the bird.

The horse, sheepe, and goose.

Gwy Earle of Warwick, & Colbrond the Da

Prouerbs of Lidgate.

Complaint for departing of T. Chaucer in France embassadour.

Of two mōstrous beasts, Bicorn, & Chichefac

The serpent of diuision.

The temple of Glasse.

The life and martyrdome of S. Edmond King the East Angles.

The roiall receiuing of Hen. the 6. into his n ble citie of London, after his returne out France, Iohn Wells being Maior.

Lidgates Testament.

Heywoods prouerbs, with his, & Sir Thomas Mores Epigrams, may serue for sufficient supplies of manie of theis deuises. And now translated Petrarch, Ariosto, Tasso, & Bartas himself deserue curious comparison with Chaucer, Lidgate, & owre best English, auncient & moderne. Amongst which, the Countesse of Pembrokes Arcadia, & the Faerie Queene ar now freshest in request: & Astrophil, & Amyntas ar none of the idlest pastimes of sum fine humanists. The Earle of Essex much commendes Albions England: and not unworthily, for diverse notable pageants, before, & in the Chronicle. Sum English, & other Histories nowhere more sensibly described, or more inwardly discouered. The Lord Mountioy ma the like account of Daniels peece of the Chronicle, touching th usurpation of Henrie of Bullingbrooke. which in deede is a f sententious, & politique peece of Poetrie: as proffitable, as pleasura The younger sort takes much delight in Shakespeares Venus, & Adonis: but his Lucrece, & his tragedie of Hamlet, Prince of Denmarke, haue in them, to please the wiser sort. Or such poets: or better: or none.

Vilia miretur vulgus: mihi flavus Apollo Pocula Castaliae plena ministret aquae: quoth Sir Edward Dier, betw iest, & earnest. Whose written deuises farr excell most of the sonets, an cantos in print. His Amaryllis, & Sir Walter Raleighs Cynthia, how fine & sweet inventions? Excellent matter of emulation for Spencer Constable, France, Watson, Daniel, Warner, Chapman, Siluester, Shakespeare, & the rest of owr florishing metricians. I looke for much aswell in verse, as in prose, from mie two Oxford frends, Doctor Gager, & M. Hac both rarely furnished for the purpose: & I haue a phansie to Owens new Epig as pithie as elegant, as plesant as sharp, & sumtime as weightie as breife: & amo so manie gentle, noble, & royall spirits meethinkes I see sum heroical thing in clowdes: mie soueraine hope. Axiophilus shall forgett himself, or will remer to make do use of so manie rhapsodies, Can

CHAPTER FOUR

VARIETY THROUGH OWNERSHIP

Although the printing process may introduce various kinds of individuality into apparently identical books, it is really once they leave the printer that the opportunities multiply. Let us imagine a printer running off, say, 1000 copies of a new book, that we can visualise as 1000 sets of unbound sheets sitting in a pile waiting to be delivered to binders and booksellers. In fact, those 1000 sets may not all be quite identical, through deliberate or accidental quirks of printing, but we can think of them as 1000 items sitting at pretty much the same point on a starting line from which they set off on truly individual paths.

Each one of those copies then has its own subsequent and unique history, developing over time. The 1000 sets may be parcelled out to the retail trade in such a way that groups of them begin by being put into very similar bindings, but once each one passes to a first purchaser it begins a journey from owner to owner, which can extend over many generations, that can only be unique. Some of them may be transferred through a string of individual owners, some of them may end up in institutional libraries (with or without an initial period of individual ownership). Some of them may end up being destroyed, maybe within a few years of production, maybe several hundred years later; we must not forget that countless numbers of printed books have perished over the centuries, through accidental or deliberate means. If we gather up the survivors of a particular print run and put them side by side today, we will see that no two are the same; the Folger Shakespeare Library in Washington is famous for having 82 copies of Shakespeare's First Folio and every one of those copies has its own unique characteristics as regards binding, markings, ownership history and make-up of printed sheets.

How much does this matter? A lot depends on what traces of individual history each copy retains. Books have influenced people, and shaped as well as reflected their interests. The mere fact of recorded ownership in a particular book at a particular time can tell us something about both owner and text; it can allow us to make deductions about the tastes, intellectual abilities or financial means of the owner, and it can show the reception of the text at different periods of history. If the book is annotated, we can see further into that world of private relationship between reader and text, and the impact of books in their contemporary contexts. The history of reading, using surviving evidence to gain a better understanding of the ways in which individual or whole generations of readers interacted with their books, has become a thriving academic discipline, with numerous books, articles and online databases produced during the last decade or so.

There are numerous types of evidence which can be found in books to shed light on their individual histories, but not all books are equally endowed in this respect. While many owners over the centuries have marked their books in various ways, many have not; it is not uncommon to find a seventeenth-century book with no inscriptions, bookplates or other signs to show what hands it has passed through over the years. Books have been repaired and rebound, sometimes more than once, and while those staging points are themselves part of the historical record, with messages we can interpret, they have also all too often been times when evidence is lost by discarding and replacing earlier bindings and endleaves. Fashion in book collecting in generations gone by tended to prefer books to be clean and unsullied by the scribbles of previous owners, and markings were sometimes deliberately removed by washing out inscriptions and taking out bookplates. Libraries have typically assumed that the interest in their books lies solely with their texts, and they have focused their activities accordingly. Library catalogues have traditionally concentrated on authors and titles, with scant attention given (until recently) to copy-specific information on owners and bindings. Repair work has been directed first and foremost on the need to have a sturdy vehicle for the reading of texts. These kinds of values are turned on their head by the new ease with which texts can be circulated in digital or other facsimile. A sixteenth-century edition of Chaucer in a twentieth-century binding, with no annotations and all traces of

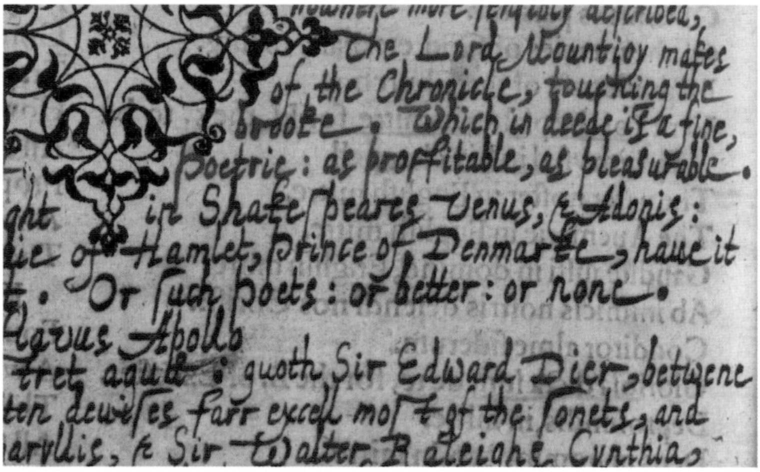

Gabriel Harvey's extensively annotated copy of the 1598 edition of Chaucer's Works *is particularly noteworthy for containing the first known reference to Shakespeare's* Hamlet *(p. 92, detail left)*

previous ownership removed through rebinding processes, is still a historic object, but what it has to offer to readers and scholars is often equally well provided by the multitude of electronic and paper-based surrogates which are now available. It also has little that distinguishes it from another copy which has had similar treatment. Gabriel Harvey's copy of the 1598 Chaucer, on the other hand, with his inscription and copious notes on contemporary poets, including the earliest known reference to *Hamlet*, is clearly a unique and irreplaceable object.

OWNERS' MARKINGS

There are numerous ways in which people have left traces of their ownership in books; they have written their names on the titlepage, they have pasted in printed bookplates, they have put their names or arms on the binding, they have used codes and mottoes. They have not always identified themselves like this, but they may still have reacted to the text by writing notes in the margins to highlight particular passages, disagree with particular authorial views, or add supplementary information.

Owners' annotations in books may be anything from occasional side notes to copious outpourings which cover every available piece of white space. Just a few examples from the countless thousands

WAYS OF MARKING OWNERSHIP: I

Individuals, and institutions, have used a variety of means to indicate their ownership of books, some of which are straightforward to interpret, others less so.

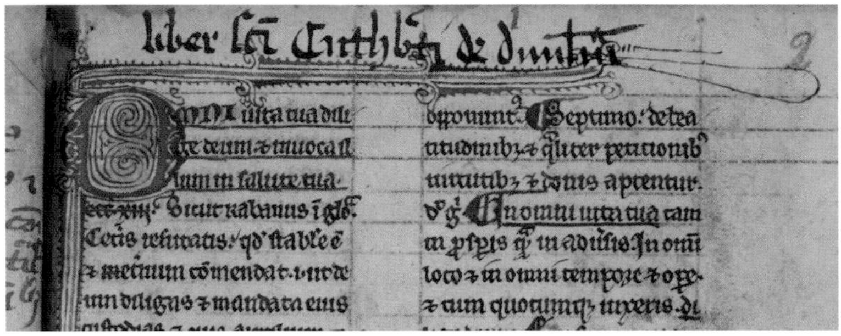

Inscriptions in books have a long history; here is a 14th-century ownership marking of Durham Priory; a 17th-century titlepage inscription by the Restoration period book collector Arthur Annesley, Earl of Anglesey (1614-86); and a 19th-century inscription by someone named E H Bentall, a crewman or passenger on a ship, the Samson

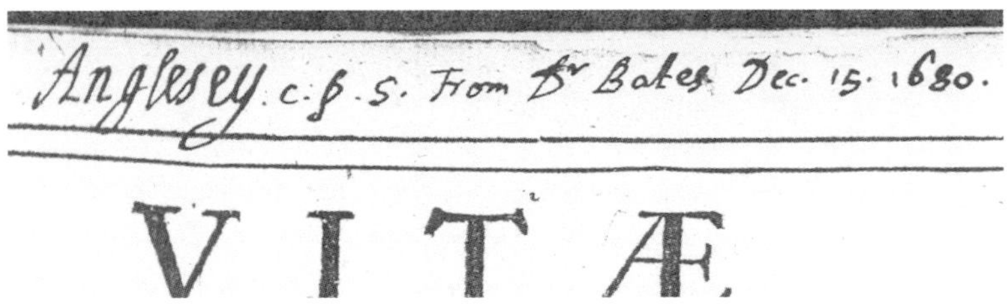

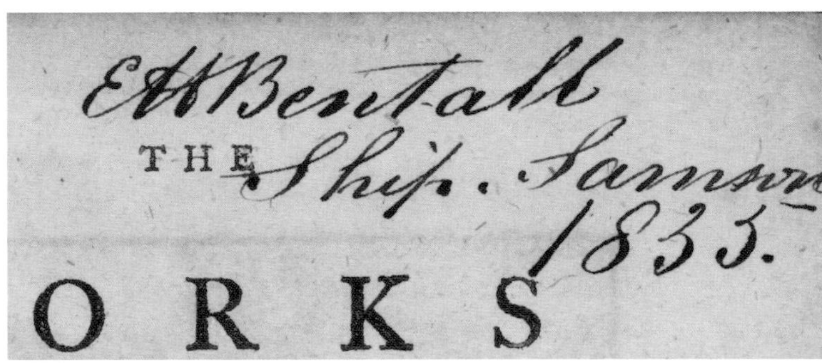

Owners have sometimes preferred more cryptic forms of inscription; here the collector C. M. Cracherode has written his monogram rather than his name. The books of Sir Hans Sloane, whose collection helped to found the British Museum, can often be recognised from the distinctive code which he used to indicate the prices he paid

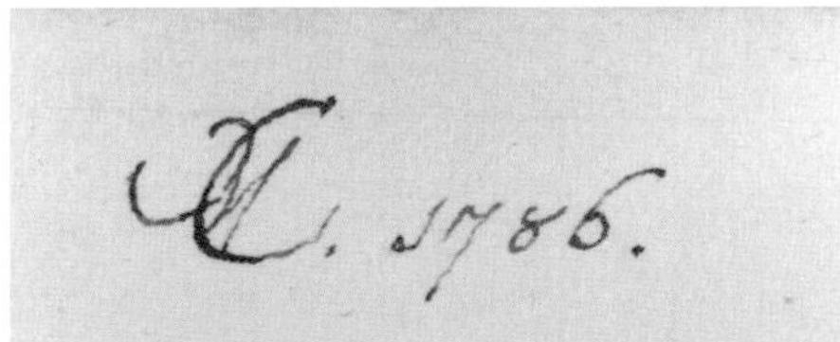

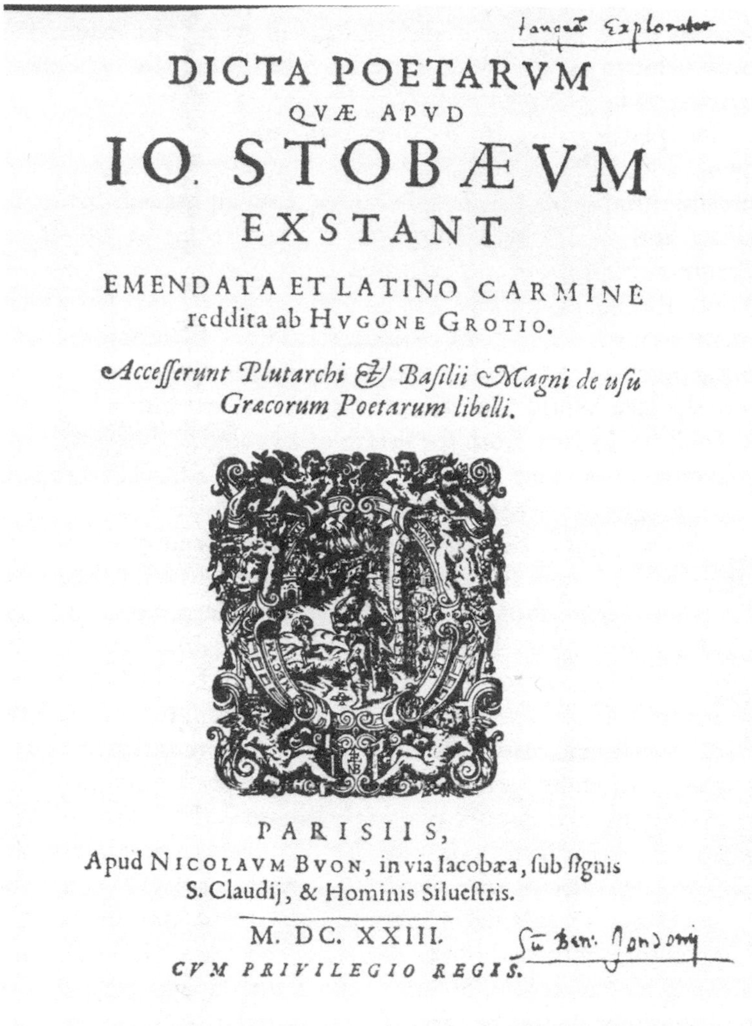

tanquã Explorator
DICTA POETARVM
QVÆ APVD
IO. STOBÆVM
EXSTANT
EMENDATA ET LATINO CARMINE
reddita ab HVGONE GROTIO.
Accesserunt Plutarchi & Basilii Magni de usu
Græcorum Poetarum libelli.
PARISIIS,
Apud NICOLAVM BVON, in via Iacobæa, sub signis
S. Claudij, & Hominis Siluestris.
M. DC. XXIII.
CVM PRIVILEGIO REGIS.
Sũ Ben: Jonsonij

Early owners sometimes added a favourite motto alongside their name, like the early 17th-century dramatist Ben Jonson, who typically wrote 'tanquam exploratur' ('as an explorer') in his books as well as his name

Ink stamps, like that of the 18th-century doctor Thomas Frewen or Sion College Library, have been used by individuals and libraries, particularly since the late 18th century; stencils, like that of Thomas Clark (left), are sometimes found in 18th- and 19th-century books

WAYS OF MARKING OWNERSHIP: II

Bookplates have a long history, going back to the 15th century, and many thousands of owners have used them. Book labels (like that of Erasmus Head) have also been extensively used—like bookplates, these are printed on separate pieces of paper and pasted into the books, but are made using letterpress rather than by engraving.

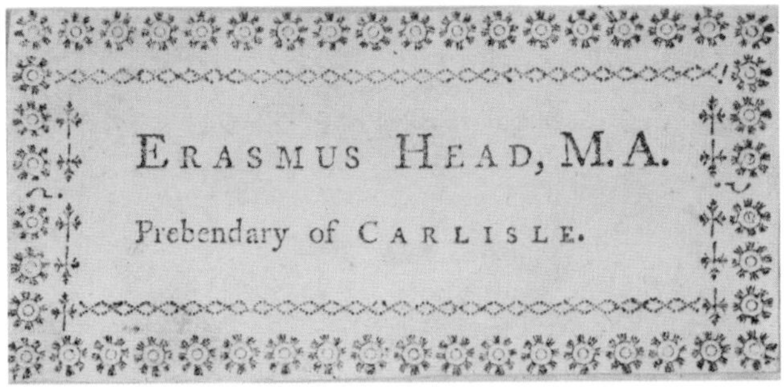

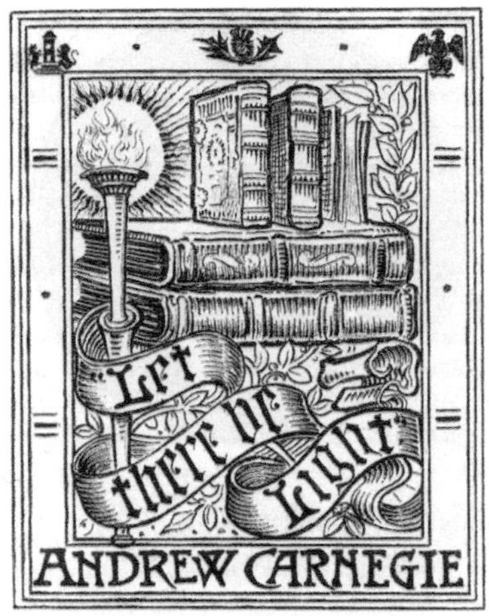

OPPOSITE
The outsides of books have also offered extensive opportunities for indicating ownership, either by impressing a name or initials, or by using an armorial or other heraldic stamp. These techniques have been common in England since the middle of the 16th century.

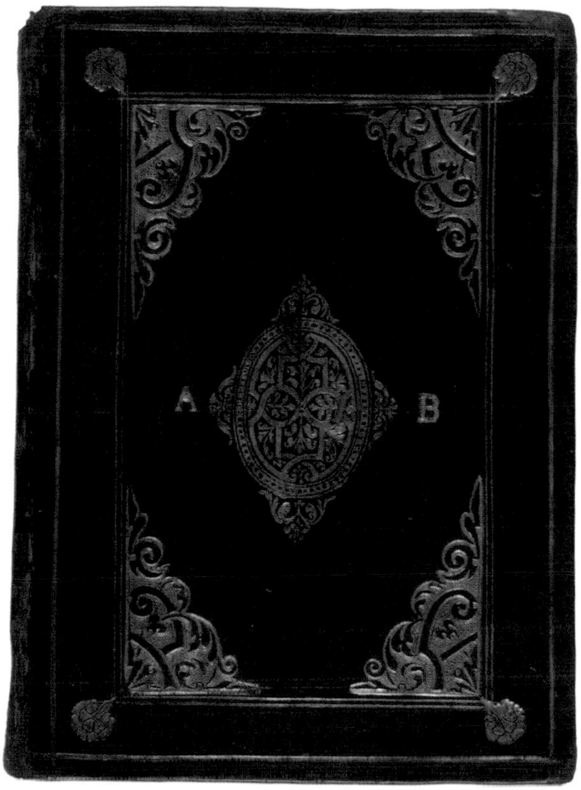
A
B

WILLIAM
MADAN
1769

" plain the meaning of its contents in words adapted to the
" ideas of my thought: then he replied, " The contents are
" these: FROM THIS TIME ENTER YE INTO THE MYS-
" TERIES OF THE WORD, WHICH BEFORE WAS CLOSED
" UP; FOR ALL ITS TRUTHS ARE SO MANY MIRRORS
" OF THE LORD."

The doctrine of man's Will in its relations to the divine grace, prevenient and co-operating, is expressed with sufficient accuracy as to the *fact*, tho' imperfectly grounded & evolved as to the *posse*, by the spiritual Philagathocalethists who represent the Author's own sentiments. But the worst fault, I can find in the (declared) evil and heretical spirits, amounts to little more, than an inconvenient phraseology.— & the horrid punishments attached the latter solely on account of a supposed error, which is not declared to have influenced their lives or to preclude the love of God or of their neighbor, breathe a spirit of theological Hate akin to persecution.— Swedenborg says— From God the Lord Man received a ~~power~~ of Will, and thro' God's effective presence he receives the power to exert this Will. The other party, meaning the same thing, says— It is God that is within us both to will and to do as far as we will and do righteously.— Without the operations of the Spirit Man would be as *spiritually* dead as a Stock or Stone.— Then (retorts Sw.) he would be no longer a Man.— Be it so." (reply the Others, tho' this depends on the choice of the definition— what sound objection can be made to the position, that deserted by God Man would become a Dog, a Brute, or a Devil— according to the *kind* of Support withdrawn— from him & from which he had withdrawn?

that have come down to us are illustrated here. Francis Hargrave (1741-1821), a regular annotator whose books are now in the British Library, was particularly exercised by a pamphlet on the Temple Church, whose margins he covered with historical and legal notes ranging around the subject of the text. The poet and lawyer Gabriel Harvey (1545?-1630), adversary of Thomas Nashe, has already been mentioned as an annotator; he was a furious scribbler in books and his Chaucer is only one of many surviving books from his personal library which are covered in notes and comments. Coleridge, the Romantic poet, is another celebrated annotator whose notes in his books have been studied by literary critics.

The dedicated commentator may go a stage further and have books bound up with blank pages interleaved between the printed ones, to ensure ample room for writing. John Warner – probably a late seventeenth-century nonconformist minister of that name – had a small-format Bible bound up this way with larger blank pages so that he could cover them with notes, expositions and references to earlier commentators. Interleaved lecture notes, such as those of the early nineteenth-century Cambridge student Walter Trevelyan, show us how chemistry was being taught and absorbed at that time. Peter van Veen, an early seventeenth-century Dutch lawyer who admired the writings of Montaigne, took a copy of the *Essais* and turned it into a gift for his son not by interleaving it, but by writing a personal memoir on the endleaves, highlighting and commenting on important passages, and enlivening the margins with pen and ink drawings.

If a previous owner is someone famous, we may succumb to a buzz of association of the kind explored more fully below (see p.132); here we hold in our hand something that was once held by Milton, or Byron, or any personal hero or villain who once owned books. There is often value beyond the merely associational, though, for reasons already stated: books offer a window onto intellectual influences and developing thought processes. We know what William Blake thought about Sir Joshua Reynolds from the inscription he added to the titlepage of a copy of Reynolds's *Works*: 'This man was hired to depress art'. Henry VIII's books, a number of which survive in the British Library, are interesting not only because they were once handled by the man himself, but

OPPOSITE
The liberal annotations which the poet Samuel Taylor Coleridge often added to his books have long been valued by literary scholars, for their window into Coleridge's ideas

OVERLEAF
Francis Hargrave's habit of copious annotation is well illustrated in this example from his collection, where he fills the margins of a pamphlet on the history of the Temple Church in London

and faithful reporter of the decisions of our Courts of Justice,) on the north side of the Church, was repaired and beautified. Dugdale also makes mention of the Effigy, in grey marble, of a Bishop, near the Communion-table, and truly observes that it is most excellently cut: but he adds, that of this Bishop we have no memorial.

Stow speaks of the five Effigies above-mentioned, that are inclosed within the iron-work in the Round Tower, and agrees with the other writers as to some of them, and particularly with Camden, who observes, that the reverence for the holiness of the Knights Templars who were buried there, and for that of the place itself, was such, that King Henry the Third, and many Noblemen of that time, of the highest rank and eminence in the kingdom, were desirous of being buried in this Church.

Accordingly it has been supposed that the following six persons of high rank have been buried in it; namely:—

First.—*Geoffrey de Mandeville*, or, as he is sometimes called, *de Magnaville*, or, in Latin, *de Magnâ villâ*, Earl of Essex; the shield being charged with his arms. *[The patent of Empress Maud creating him Earl of Essex to him & his heirs is in Seld. Tit. of Honor. but he had been previously made by King S…]*

[see 1. Dugd. Bar. 204]

[Sir George Jerningham heir of the body of the Geoffrey de Mandeville]

It is expressly stated in an antient manuscript account of the foundation of Walden Abbey, in Essex, by this Geoffrey de Mandeville, that he was buried in the Temple Church. See *Dugdale's Monasticon, Vol. 1*, page 448. *[My conjecture is, that he was buried in the church of St. Dunstan in the West next Temple Bar London. J. H.]*

[Temple Bar is mentioned with reference to a church there. The Temple church not literally mentioned.]

But there seems to be some doubt upon the subject, on account of the time of this Nobleman's death, which is thought to have taken place before the year 1185, (a) in which the Temple Church was consecrated.

[This Geoffrey Earl of Essex is expressly mentioned by Dugdale in Baronage to have dyed upon the 16 … & so it is in the manuscript account which … is in 1. Dugd. Monastic. AA]

Secondly.—*William, Earl of Pembroke*, Earl-Marshal of England; who was Guardian of the Realm in the minority of King Henry the Third. He was, says Camden, "a powerful man in his time." He died in the year 1219, which was thirty-four years after the building of the Temple Church.

[The story of this Earl William is largely given in 1. Dugd. Bar. 600. to 602. At the end of it he is mentioned to have dyed 3. Hen. 3. at Caversham & to have been thence carried to Reading, & after to Westm.r Abbey & from thence to the New Church in the Temple & there to have been solemnly interred. Dugdale refers to Mathew Paris 304: for all this; & in Walt. &c.[?]: the account is confirmed. J. H.]

"On

"On the tomb of this William," says Camden, "I read, *Comes Pembrochiæ*, and this verse:—

Miles eram Martis; Mars multos viceràt armis.

His arms are on his shield.

Thirdly.—*William, Earl of Pembroke,* Earl-Marshall, son of the former William. He died in the year 1231.

Fourthly.—*Gilbert, Earl of Pembroke,* another son of the first William. He died in the year 1241, being slain in a Tournament at Hertford.

Touching the manner of Gilbert's death, *Weever*, in his *Antient Funeral Monuments*, page 443, observes as follows:—

"*Matthew Paris* recounts, that in the year 1241, Gilbert pro-
" claimed a Tournament in Hertford in scorn of the King's authority,
" by which such sports had been forbidden. It happened that
" himself running was, by the flinging of his horse, cast out of the
" saddle, and the horse gave him such a stroke on the breast that he
" died the same day. His bowels were interred in the Abbey of
" Hertford with the bowels of one *Sir Robert de Say*, a gallant gen-
" tleman slain in the same exercise.

Fifthly.—Here also, say both Stow and Maitland, lies *Robert Rosse*, called Fursan. The arms of Rossé are on his shield.

And Weever, in page 443, speaks more particularly of this person, whom he calls *Sir Robert Rosse, Knight,* and mentions the following Epitaph on him, as having formerly been seen in the Temple Church.

HIC REQUIESCIT

R........ EQ......... QUONDAM VISITATOR GENERALIS

ORDINIS MILITIÆ TEMPLI IN ANGLIA, FRANCIA, ET IN ITALIA.

"This

A contemporary owner took this 1671 Bible and had it interleaved to turn it into his personal compendium of Bible studies, in which he could intersperse notes and observations with interpretations of other writers

Cap. 3. 15. it shall bruise thy head, & thou shalt bruise his heel.

Sept. Cap. 3. 16. thy desire shall be to thy husband.

Cap. 4. 7. If thou doest well shalt thou not be accepted? & if thou doest not well sin lieth at the door. and upto thee shall be his desire, & thou shalt rule over him.

and ye shall be as gods, know-
and evil.
when the woman saw that the
good for food, and that it *was*
o the eyes, and a tree to be de-
nake *one* wise ; she took of the
of, and did eat, and gave also
usband with her, and he did eat.
e eyes of them both were open-
y knew that they *were* naked :
sewed fig-leaves together, and
nselves aprons.
ey heard the voice of the LORD
ing in the garden in the cool of
d Adam and his wife hid them-
m the presence of the LORD
gst the trees of the garden.
he LORD God called unto A-
aid unto him, Where *art* thou ?
he said, I heard thy voice in the
and I was afraid, because I *was*
d I hid my self.
he said, Who told thee that
naked ? Hast thou eaten of the
reof I commanded thee, that
dest not eat ?
the man said, The woman
u gavest *to be* with me, she gave
ree, and I did eat.
the LORD God said unto the
What *is* this *that* thou hast done?
voman said, The serpent beguil-
I did eat.
the LORD God said unto the
ecause thou hast done this, thou
above all cattel, and above
st of the field : upon thy belly
go, and dust shalt thou eat all
f thy life.
I will put enmity between thee
woman, and between thy seed
ed : it shall bruise thy head,
halt bruise his heel.
to the woman he said, I will
ltiply thy sorrow and thy con-
in sorrow thou shalt bring forth
and thy desire *shall be* to thy
and he shall rule over thee.
unto Adam he said, Because
earkened unto the voice of thy
hast eaten of the tree of which
ded thee, saying, Thou shalt
it : cursed *is* the ground for
in sorrow shalt thou eat *of* it
s of thy life.
rns also and thistles shall it
h to thee : and thou shalt eat
f the field.
e sweat of thy face shalt thou eat
thou return unto the ground ;
it wast thou taken : for dust
and unto dust thou shalt return.
Adam called his wives name
use she was the mother of all

o Adam also and to his wife did
God make coats of skins, and
em.

22 ¶ And the LORD God said, Behold,
the man is become as one of us, to know
good and evil. And now lest he put forth
his hand, and take also of the tree of life,
and eat, and live for ever :
23 Therefore the LORD God sent him
forth from the garden of Eden, to till the
ground, from whence he was taken.
24 So he drove out the man : and he
placed at the east of the garden of Eden,
cherubims, and a flaming sword, which
turned every way, to keep the way of the
tree of life.

CHAP. IV.

1 The birth of Cain and Abel. 8 The murder of Abel. 11 The curse of Cain. 19 Lamech and his two wives.

AND Adam knew Eve his wife: and she
conceived, and bare Cain, and said,
I have gotten a man from the LORD.
2 And she again bare his brother Abel.
And Abel was a keeper of sheep, but Cain
was a tiller of the ground.
3 And in process of time it came to
pass, that Cain brought of the fruit of the
ground an offering unto the LORD.
4 And Abel, he also brought of the
firstlings of his flock, and of the fat
thereof. And the LORD had respect unto *
Abel, and to his offering :
5 But unto Cain and to his offering he
had not respect. And Cain was very
wroth, and his countenance fell.
6 And the LORD said unto Cain, Why
art thou wroth ? and why is thy countenance fallen ?
7 If thou doest well, shalt thou not be accepted ? and if thou doest not well, sin lieth at the door. And unto thee *shall be* his
desire, and thou shalt rule over him.
8 And Cain talked with Abel his brother : and it came to pass when they were
in the field, that Cain rose up against
Abel his brother, and slew him.
9 And the LORD said unto Cain,
Where *is* Abel thy brother ? and he said,
I know not : *Am* I my brothers keeper ?
10 And he said, What hast thou done ?
the voice of thy brothers bloud crieth unto me from the ground.
11 And now *art* thou cursed from the
earth, which hath opened her mouth to
receive thy brothers bloud from thy
hand.
12 When thou tillest the ground, it
shall not henceforth yield unto thee her
strength. A fugitive and a vagabond shalt
thou be in the earth.
13 And Cain said unto the LORD, My
punishment *is* greater then I can bear.
14 Behold, thou hast driven me out
this day from the face of the earth : and
from thy face shall I be hid, and I shall
be a fugitive and a vagabond in the earth
and it shall come to pass, that every one
that findeth me shall slay me.
15 And the LORD said unto him, There-

fore

[illegible]odotion vertit ἐνεπύρισεν inflamavit. i.e. igne de
[illegible] sumpsit & sic grata esse probavit. vid Crit: in loco.

[illegible] Cain [illegible] est, nec [illegible] puniretur tam gravi a caede [illegible] quoniam ad poenam, & omnium exemplum vult superesse [illegible] quam diu torqueri. Lyran. Abulens. Carthusian. [illegible] & distinguunt. Omnis qui occiderit Cain, subaudi [illegible] ut Symmachus vertit, septimus punietur, Cain scilicet quia [illegible] vitae dedit [illegible] ad poenam & exemplum. [illegible] septimum, ut vertit Symmachus, sed septuplum significat. [illegible] (i.e. septima generatione) [illegible] Dei ergo [illegible] τὸ μὴ ἀνελεῖν αὐτὸν πάντα τὸν εὑρίσκοντα αὐτόν [illegible] semper [illegible] ad monstrandam viam qua [illegible] in ex nominis sui positum in frontem. Alii temporarium signum [illegible] durabile & perpetuum fuisse putat. Sunt [illegible] omnia [illegible] mallem his adstipulari qui sortiunt signum [illegible] hominum. Quod conjiciunt ex eo quod dicitur, Vagus & [illegible] Septuagint reddiderunt στένων καὶ τρέμων ἔσῃ ἐπὶ τῆς [illegible] super terram. Fagius. Corn: a Lap: dicit

Cap. 4. 26. οὗτος ἤλπισεν ἐπικαλεῖσθαι τὸ ὄνομα κυρίου τοῦ θεοῦ. Sept.

אָז הוּחַל לִקְרֹא בְּשֵׁם. Then [began me]n to call upon the name of the Lord.

[Cap. 5.] 3. Ἔζησε δὲ Ἀδὰμ τριάκοντα καὶ [διακόσ]ια ἔτη. Sept. Cap. 4. 4. ἐγένοντο δὲ [αἱ ἡμέρ]αι Ἀδὰμ, ἃς ἔζησε μετὰ τὸ γεννῆ[σαι αὐτ]ὸν τὸν Σὴθ, ἔτη ἑπτακόσια. Sept. [6.] Ἔζησε δὲ Σὴθ πέντε καὶ δια[κόσια ἔ]τη. Cap. 5. 7. καὶ ἔζησε Σὴθ μετὰ [τὸ γεννῆσ]αι αὐτὸν τὸν Ἐνὼς, ἑπτὰ ἔ[τη καὶ ἑ]πτακόσια. Sept.

[illegible] morti addictus videtur ergo Seth pius [illegible] filium [illegible], [illegible] peccatum addicti sumus. [illegible] homo, Enos dici a radice [illegible] oblivioni tradendus, ad hoc Etymon alludit Psalm. 8. Quid [illegible] ἐπικαλεῖσθαι τὸ ὄνομα τοῦ θεοῦ [illegible] [illegible] sed et sperare significat a radice iachal, & spes est [illegible] nominis Domini, quasi tempore Enos coeperat Idololatria, a chol sed a chalal [illegible] quod in hiphil habet [illegible] est. Corn: a Lap: [illegible] ἤλπισεν [illegible] Drusius [illegible] puto ustendum, tunc [illegible] est invocari nomen Domini [illegible] [illegible]

consolabitur nos ab operibus [illegible]
[illegible] laborisae agriculturae molestias, jungendo
[illegible] Animalia. (Clar.)

[illegible] probat. ut velut Dei ad hominis [illegible] propterea Dei [illegible] ut Angeli solent. [illegible] 6. 2. & 4. Filios Dei [illegible] interpretatur Enochi posteros. Aquila videtur hoc voluisse [illegible] transtulit, τότε ἤρχθη τοῦ καλεῖσθαι ἐν ὀνόματι κυρίου. [illegible] huic sensui Irenaeus 4. 30. Grotius

Adam

it) Individuam mariti et uxoris societatem [co]mmendat. Hoc enim dicendi genus signi[f]icat post ordinatum conjugium fuisse utrumque [tan]quam instar unius hominis. (Clarius ait) vocavit [n]omen eorum Adam, ut ipsa appellatione disc[er]ent se insolescere [illegible] se a terra [illegible] vasa [illegible] constare recordarentur. Significat enim Adam [illegible], etiam et rubrum significat.

A printed summary of lecture topics in chemistry has been interleaved by a Cambridge student around the turn of the 19th century to create a notebook which was presumably filled out when, or shortly after, the lectures were delivered

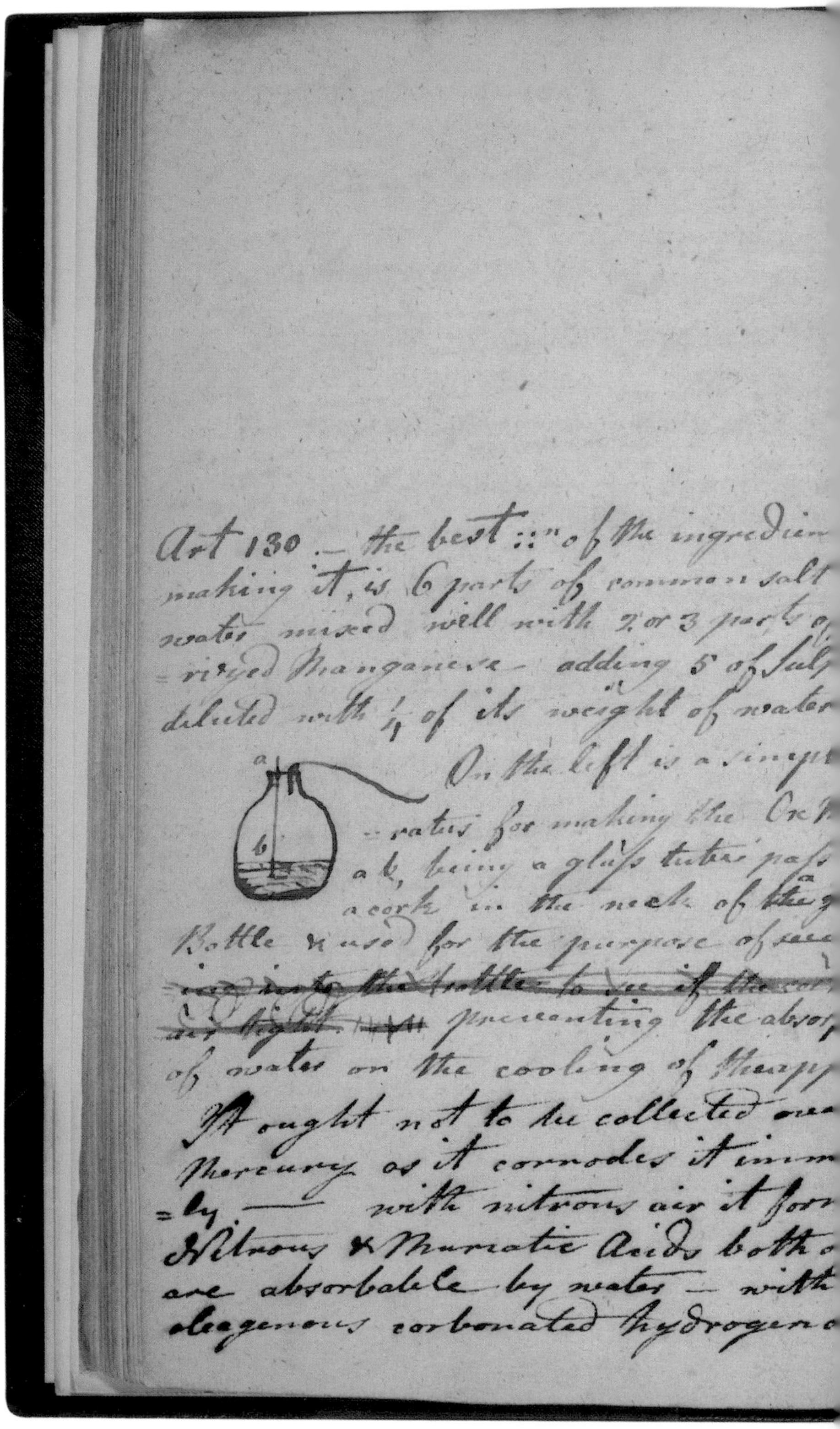

Art 130 – the best :: of the ingredien
making it, is 6 parts of common salt
water mixed well with 2 or 3 parts of
=rized Manganese – adding 5 of Sul
diluted with 1/4 of its weight of water
a
On the left is a singu
b
=ratus for making the Ox
a b, being a glass tube pas
a cork in the neck of the
Bottle & used for the purpose of
preventing the absor
of water on the cooling of the app
It ought not to be collected over
Mercury as it corrodes it imm
=ly — with nitrous air it for
Nitrous & Muriatic Acids both
are absorbable by water – with
oleagenous carbonated hydrogen

127. Properties of ſal ammoniac.

Its volatility, ſolubility in water, and ſpirits of wine.

Cold produced.

128. Sal ammoniac decompoſed by various methods.

129. The effects of muriatic acid on water and oils.

130. Oxygenation of the muriatic acid—ol. dephlogiſticated marine acid.

Properties of oxygenated muriatic acid.

Its uſes.

131. Oxygenated muriatic acid combined with alkali.

132 Oxygenated muriatic acid mixed with oils, with ſpirit of wine.

Muriatic æther.

MIXTURES of ACIDS.

133. Nitro-muriatic acid—ol. aqua regia.

Its properties and uſes.

134. Sulphuric acid impregnated with nitrous vapour.

135. Nitro-ſulphuric acid—aqua reginalis.

Its properties and uſe.

BORACIC

Peter van Veen, an early 17th-century Dutch lawyer, personalised this copy of Montaigne's *Essais* by adding extensive notes in the margins and endleaves, marking significant passages, and providing a lively series of pen and ink drawings throughout the book; it was intended to become an heirloom for his son

116 ESSAIS DE MICHEL DE MONTAIG
tous accidens humains regardent. Escoutons y seule
nous nous disons, tout ce, dequoy nous auons princ
ment besoin. Qui se souuient de s'estre tant & tant d
mesconté de son propre iugement, est-il pas vn sot, d
entrer pour iamais en deffiance? Quand ie me trouue
uaincu par la raison d'autruy, d'vne opinion faulse, ie
prens pas tant, ce qu'il m'a dit de nouueau, & cette ig
ce particuliere, ce seroit peu d'acquest, comme en ge
i'apprens ma debilité, & la trahison de mon entender
d'où ie tire la reformation de toute la masse. En toute
autres erreurs, ie fais de mesme: & sens de cette regle
de vtilité à la vie. Ie ne regarde pas l'espece & l'indi
comme vne pierre où i'aye bronché. I'apprens à crai
mon alleure par tout: & m'attens à la regler. D'appre
qu'on a dit ou fait vne sottise, ce n'est rien que cela. I
apprendre, qu'on n'est qu'vn sot. Instruction bien plu
ple, & importante. Les faux pas, que ma memoire m'a
souuent, lors mesme qu'elle s'asseure le plus de soy, ne
pas inutilement perdus. Elle a beau me iurer à cette h
& m'asseurer: ie secoue les oreilles: la premiere oppos
qu'on fait à son tesmoignage, me met en suspens. Et n'
rois me fier d'elle, en chose de poids: ny la garantir s
faict d'autruy. Et n'estoit, que ce que ie fay par faute de
moire, les autres le font encore plus souuët, par faute de
ie prendrois tousiours en chose de faict, la verité de la b
che d'vn autre, plustost que de la mienne. Si chacun es
de prés les effects & circonstances des passions qui le r
tent, comme i'ay faict de celle à qui i'estois tombé en p
ge, il les verroit venir: & rallentiroit vn peu leur impetu
té & leur course. Elles ne nous sautent pas tousiours au
let d'vn prinsault, il y a de la menasse & des degrez.

Fluctus vti primò cœpit cùm albescere ponto,
Paulatim sese tollit mare, & altiùs vndas
Erigit, inde imo consurgit ad æthera fundo.

Le iugement tient chez moy vn siege magistral, au moi
s'en efforce soigneusement. Il laisse mes appetits aller

&la haine & l'amitié, voire & celle que ie me porte à
-mesme, sans s'en alterer & corrompre. S'il ne peut re-
er les autres parties selō soy, au moins ne se laisse-il pas
:mer à elles : il fait son jeu à part. L'aduertissement à
ın de se cognoistre, doit estre d'vn important effect:
ue ce Dieu de science & de lumiere le fit plāter au frōt
n temple : comme comprenant tout ce qu'il auoit
us conseiller. Platon dit aussi, que prudence n'est
chose, que l'execution de cette ordonnāce : & Socra-
: verifie par le menu en Xenophon. Les difficultez &
:urité, ne s'apperçoiuent en chacune science, que par
qui y ont entree. Car encore fault-il quelque degré
elligence, à pouuoir remarquer qu'on ignore : & faut
:er à vne porte, pour sçauoir qu'elle nous est close. D'où
cette Platonique subtilité, que ny ceux qui sçauent,
à s'enquerir, dautant qu'ils sçauēt: ny ceux qui ne sça-
, dautant que pour s'enquerir, il fault sçauoir, dequoy
:nquiert. Ainsi, en cette cy de se cognoistre soy-mes-
: que chacun se void si resolu & satisfait, ce que chacū
se estre suffisamment entendu, signifie que chacun n'y
ıd rien du tout, comme Socrates apprend à Euthyde-
loy, qui ne fais autre profession, y trouue vne profon-
& varieté si infinie, que mon apprentissage n'a autre
, que de me faire sentir, combien il me reste à appren-
ma foiblesse si souuēt recogneuë, ie dois l'inclination
ıy à la modestie: à l'obeïssance des creāces qui me sōt
:ites : à vne constante froideur & moderation d'opi-
: & la haine de cette arrogance importune & querel-
se croyant & fiant tout à soy, ennemie capitale de dis-
e & de verité. Oyez les regenter. Les premieres sotti-
ıils mettent en auant, c'est au style qu'on establit les
ons & les loix. *Nihil est turpius quam cognitioni & perce-
assertionem approbationémque præcurrere.* Aristarchus disoit,
ciennement, à peine se trouua-il sept sages au monde,
: de son temps à peine se trouua-il sept ignorans. Au-
nous pas plus de raison que luy, de le dire en nostre
s? L'affirmation & l'opiniastreté, sont signes exprez de

William Blake's views on Sir Joshua Reynolds are pithily encapsulated in the comment he wrote on the titlepage of a copy of Reynolds's Works: *'This man was hired to depress art'. Blake's notes elsewhere in the book expand on his negative assessment*

also because he marked passages which caught his eye for political or moral purposes. Students of Reformation history also value the books from the personal library of Henry's Archbishop of Canterbury, Thomas Cranmer, partly because collectively they provide an insight into what he read, but also because his marginal notes capture his thoughts and responses on particular ideas.

Scholars have long valued the marginalia of earlier experts. When the books of Anthony Askew, a celebrated eighteenth-century collector, were auctioned in 1774, the catalogue made

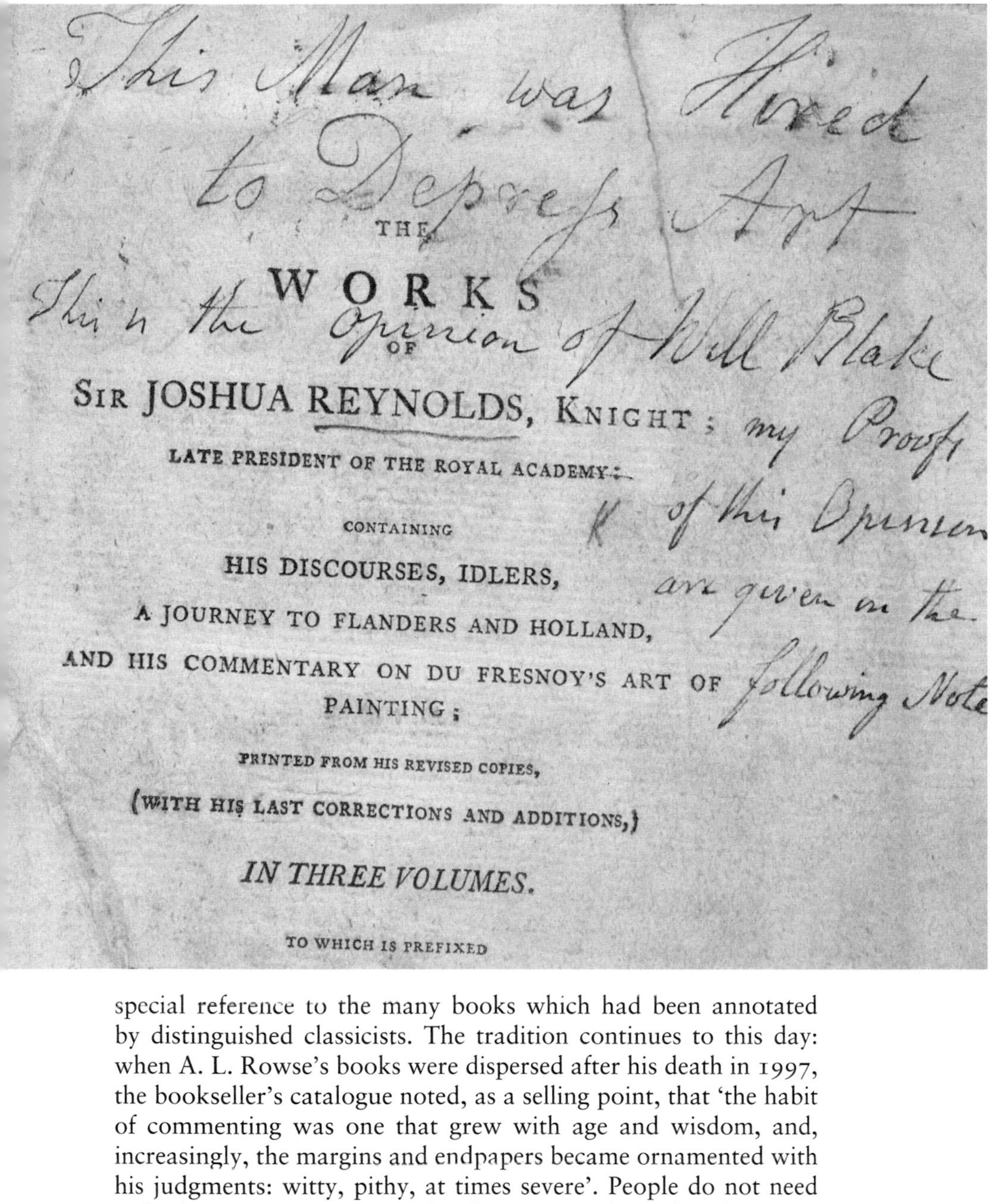

This Man was Hired to Depress Art

THE WORKS OF SIR JOSHUA REYNOLDS, KNIGHT; LATE PRESIDENT OF THE ROYAL ACADEMY:

CONTAINING HIS DISCOURSES, IDLERS, A JOURNEY TO FLANDERS AND HOLLAND, AND HIS COMMENTARY ON DU FRESNOY'S ART OF PAINTING;

PRINTED FROM HIS REVISED COPIES, (WITH HIS LAST CORRECTIONS AND ADDITIONS,)

IN THREE VOLUMES.

TO WHICH IS PREFIXED

This is the Opinion of Will Blake my Proofs of this Opinion are given in the following Note

special reference to the many books which had been annotated by distinguished classicists. The tradition continues to this day: when A. L. Rowse's books were dispersed after his death in 1997, the bookseller's catalogue noted, as a selling point, that 'the habit of commenting was one that grew with age and wisdom, and, increasingly, the margins and endpapers became ornamented with his judgments: witty, pithy, at times severe'. People do not need to be famous, or important, for their marginalia to be of interest; the notes of obscure or anonymous former readers can provide

RIGHT

Many of the books which survive from Henry VIII's personal collection are annotated by him, against passages that interested him. Here he marks a section from a work by Erasmus, noting the shortcomings of priests

OPPOSITE

Students of Reformation history will recognise the importance of a book with the distinctive 'Thomas Cantuarien.' inscription on the titlepage, showing that it came from the library of Thomas Cranmer, Henry VIII's Archbishop of Canterbury; they will value it yet more if it has annotations or other evidence of his direct interaction with the text

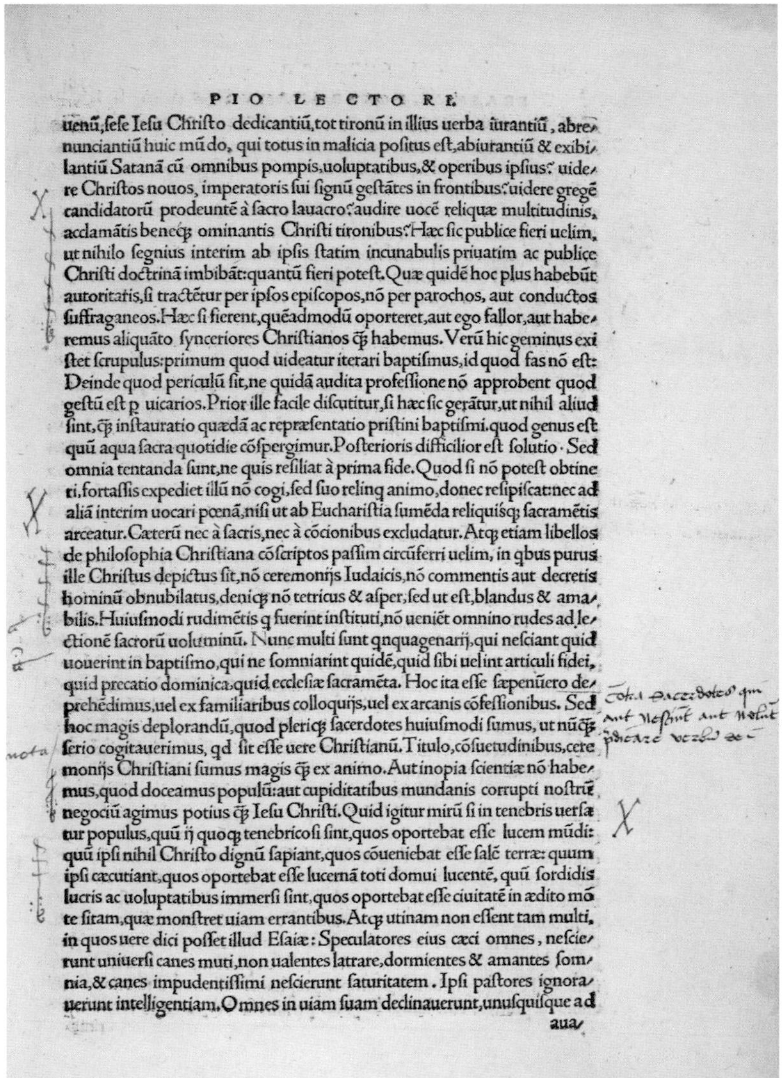

PIO LECTORI.

uenũ, ſeſe Ieſu Chriſto dedicantiũ, tot tironũ in illius uerba iurantiũ, abre-
nunciantiũ huic mũdo, qui totus in malicia poſitus eſt, abiurantiũ & exibi-
lantiũ Satanã cũ omnibus pompis, uoluptatibus, & operibus ipſius: uidere Chriſtos nouos, imperatoris ſui ſignũ geſtãtes in frontibus: uidere gregẽ
candidatorũ prodeuntẽ à ſacro lauacro: audire uocẽ reliquæ multitudinis,
acclamãtis beneq; ominantis Chriſti tironibus: Hæc ſic publice fieri uelim,
ut nihilo ſegnius interim ab ipſis ſtatim incunabulis priuatim ac publice
Chriſti doctrinã imbibãt: quantũ fieri poteſt. Quæ quidẽ hoc plus habebũt
autoritatis, ſi tractẽtur per ipſos epiſcopos, nõ per parochos, aut conductos
ſuffraganeos. Hæc ſi fierent, quẽadmodũ oporteret, aut ego fallor, aut habe-
remus aliquãto ſynceriores Chriſtianos q̃ habemus. Verũ hic geminus exi
ſtet ſcrupulus: primum quod uideatur iterari baptiſmus, id quod fas nõ eſt:
Deinde quod periculũ ſit, ne quidã audita profeſſione nõ approbent quod
geſtũ eſt p uicarios. Prior ille facile diſcutitur, ſi hæc ſic gerãtur, ut nihil aliud
ſint, q̃ inſtauratio quædã ac repræſentatio priſtini baptiſmi. quod genus eſt
quũ aqua ſacra quotidie cõſpergimur. Poſterioris difficilior eſt ſolutio. Sed
omnia tentanda ſunt, ne quis reſiliat à prima fide. Quod ſi nõ poteſt obtine
ri, fortaſſis expediet illũ nõ cogi, ſed ſuo relinq animo, donec reſipiſcat: nec ad
aliã interim uocari pœnã, niſi ut ab Euchariſtia ſumẽda reliquiſq; ſacramẽtis
arceatur. Cæterũ nec à ſacris, nec à cõcionibus excludatur. Atq; etiam libellos
de philoſophia Chriſtiana cõſcriptos paſſim circũferri uelim, in qbus purus
ille Chriſtus depictus ſit, nõ ceremonijs Iudaicis, nõ commentis aut decretis
hominũ obnubilatus, deniq; nõ tetricus & aſper, ſed ut eſt, blandus & ama-
bilis. Huiuſmodi rudimẽtis q fuerint inſtituti, nõ uenient omnino rudes ad le-
ctionẽ ſacrorũ uoluminũ. Nunc multi ſunt qnquagenarij, qui neſciant quid
uouerint in baptiſmo, qui ne ſomniarint quidẽ, quid ſibi uelint articuli fidei,
quid precatio dominica, quid eccleſiæ ſacramẽta. Hoc ita eſſe ſæpenũero de-
prehẽdimus, uel ex familiaribus colloquijs, uel ex arcanis cõfeſſionibus. Sed
hoc magis deplorandũ, quod pleriq; ſacerdotes huiuſmodi ſumus, ut nũq̃
ſerio cogitauerimus, qd ſit eſſe uere Chriſtianũ. Titulo, cõſuetudinibus, cere
monijs Chriſtiani ſumus magis q̃ ex animo. Aut inopia ſcientiæ nõ habemus, quod doceamus populũ: aut cupiditatibus mundanis corrupti noſtrũ
negociũ agimus potius q̃ Ieſu Chriſti. Quid igitur mirũ ſi in tenebris uerſa
tur populus, quũ ij quoq; tenebricoſi ſint, quos oportebat eſſe lucem mũdi:
quũ ipſi nihil Chriſto dignũ ſapiant, quos cõueniebat eſſe ſalẽ terræ: quum
ipſi cæcutiant, quos oportebat eſſe lucernã toti domui lucentẽ, quũ ſordidis
lucris ac uoluptatibus immerſi ſint, quos oportebat eſſe ciuitatẽ in ædito mõ
te ſitam, quæ monſtret uiam errantibus. Atq; utinam non eſſent tam multi,
in quos uere dici poſſet illud Eſaiæ: Speculatores eius cæci omnes, neſcierunt uniuerſi canes muti, non ualentes latrare, dormientes & amantes ſom-
nia, & canes impudentiſſimi neſcierunt ſaturitatem. Ipſi paſtores ignora-
uerunt intelligentiam. Omnes in uiam ſuam declinauerunt, unuſquiſque ad

aua-

sit extendi, semper uerò à domino indiget adiuuari. C

Et ubi est, quod regulari definitione præmissum est, Non solùm actuum, uerùm etiam cogitationum bonarum ex Deo esse principium: qui & incipit, quæ bona sunt, & exequitur, & consummat in nobis? Ecce hic etiam si bonis cœptis necessarium Dei fateris auxilium: ipsos tamen laudabiles motus, appetitusq; uirtutum, remota gratia Dei, nudæ libertati adscribis arbitrij: ut boni salubresq; conatus nequeant quidem proficere, nisi Deus adiuuet: possunt tamen, etiam si non à Deo inspirentur, incipere. Deinde ut euidentius definias, quid hoc ex libero arbitrio habeat, quid sumat ex gratia Dei, addis, & dicis:

Nec enim cùm uoluerit quis, sanitate perfruitur: aut de ægritudinis morbo pro arbitrij sui desiderio liberatur.

Doces ergo, non posse quidem hominem per semetipsum apprehendere sanitatem, sed habere eum à semetipso desiderium sanitatis. Et sua tantum sponte uenire ad medicum: non etiam hoc ipsum medici esse, quòd ueniat. Quasi uerò anima ipsa non langueat, & corpori suo remedium sana prospiciat. Atqui totus homo ex ipsa & cum ipsa in profundum miseriæ suæ decidit, ubi eam prius, quàm à medico notitiam suæ calamitatis accipiat, iacère delectat, amantem errores suos, & amplectentem falsa pro ueris. Cuius salus prima est, ut sibi incipiat displicere, & uetustatem suæ debilitatis odisse. Sequens uerò est, ut & sanari desideret, D & à quo sananda sit, nouerit. Quæ curationem ipsius sic præcedunt, ut ei ab illo, qui eam curaturus sit, inserantur. Ne, cùm ei ullo modo hæc inesse possint, merito uideatur saluata, non gratia. Deinde adijcis:

Vt autem euidentius clareat, etiam per naturæ bonum (quod beneficio creatoris non dubium est) nonnunquam bonarum uoluntatum prodire principia: quæ tamen, nisi à Deo dirigantur, ad consummationem uirtutum uenire non possunt,

Rom. 7. *Apostolus testatur, dicens: Velle enim adiacet mihi: perficere autem bonum non inuenio.*

Falsò ergo secundum hanc definitionem antè dixisti, Non solùm actuum, uerùm etiam cogitationum bonarum ex Deo esse principium: qui & incipit, quæ bona sunt, & exequitur, & consummat in nobis. Sed hoc nullo modo ex aliqua parte potest esse falsum. Cui nequaquam inferri contraria debuerunt: ut, quod rectè professus es ex gratia incipere, id postea confirmares per naturæ bonum, & per liberum arbitrium nos habere. Dixit quidem beatus Apostolus: Velle enim adiacet mihi, per-

2. Cor. 3. ficere autem bonum non inuenio. Sed idem dixit: Non quòd idonei simus, cogitare aliquid ex nobis ipsis: sed sufficientia nostra ex Deo est. Et

Phil. 2. idem dixit: Deus est enim, qui operatur in nobis & uelle, & perficere, pro bona uoluntate. Non ergo Apostolus sibi contrarius est. Sed cùm donatum nobis fuerit bonum uelle, non statim inuenimus & facere, nisi quæren

A quærentibus, petentibus, atque pulsantibus, qui dedit desiderium, præstet effectum. Vox nanque ista dicentis: Velle enim adiacet mihi, perficere autem bonum, non inuenio: uocati est, sub gratia constituti: qui condelectatur quidem legi Dei secundum interiorem hominem: sed uidet aliam legem in membris suis, repugnantem legi mentis suæ, & captiuantem se in lege peccati. Et quamuis acceperit scientiam rectè uolendi, uirtutem tamen in se non inuenit, eorum quæ optat, operandi: donec pro bona uoluntate, quam sumpsit, mereatur inuenire quî faciat. Post hæc ponis plurima testimonia, quibus nunc ualidum, nunc infirmum liberum arbitrium demonstretur. Quasi quidam sint, qui proprijs uiribus impleant, quod alij facere Deo non adiuuante non possunt: aut ob aliud homo accipiat præceptum, nisi ut diuinum quærat auxilium. Concludis ergo, & dicis: Rom. 7.

Et ita sunt quodammodo indiscretè permista, atque confusa, ut quid ex quo pendeat, inter multos magna quæstione uoluatur. Id est: Vtrum, quia initium bonæ uolũtatis præbuerimus, misereatur nostri Deus: an quia Deus misereatur, consequamur bonæ uoluntatis initium. Multi enim singula hæc credentes, ac iusto amplius asserentes, uarijs, sibiq; contrarijs sunt erroribus inuoluti.

Ecce, ut tibi uidetur, quæ confusa erant, discreta sunt: & quæ explicari

B non poterant, absoluta. Duos enim contrarios sibi definis errores, quibus, inter liberum arbitrium & gratiam contentiosè disputantes, quid tenendum sit, implicentur. Et in uno cõstituis eos, qui dicunt, gratiam dari secundum merita nostra: in alio autem illos ponis, qui dicunt, ex misericordia à Deo bonarum uoluntatum prodire principia: eos intelligi uolens, qui inimicos gratiæ debellarunt. Si ergo error est, initia bonæ uoluntatis non adiuto diuinitus homini adscribere: & error, confiteri quoniam præparatur uoluntas à domino, quò dirigendi sumus: ut utrunque uitemus. Si utrunque, inquis, sequamur, nos nulli errori acquiescimus. Tu nos subdis duobus, & geminas, sicut intelligis, prauitates: diuidendo damnas, miscendo iustificas. Hac lege ac regula poteris prædicare, quòd tam errent, qui dicunt, Semper esse fallendum: quàm qui definiunt, Nunquam esse fallendum. Sed ut in neutro peccetur, utrũque sectandum: quia nec semper declinanda sit seueritas. Fallit te prorsus opinio tua: De duobus malis, unum fieri bonum non potest: Vnam uirtutem duo uitia non gignunt: Vnum uerum, duo falsa non faciunt. Quæ enim paria sunt, meritò non minuuntur coëundo, sed crescunt. Non itaque oportuit eos bonarum uoluntatum initia, quæ ex Dei asserunt aspiratione generari, ea sententia reprehendi, qua arguuntur qui adhuc liberum arbitrium putant sibi sine opere gratiæ posse sufficere. Harum enim definitionum, una ab ecclesia expugnata est, alia defensa.

The early 17th-century London surgeon Jospeh Fenton used the flyleaves of one of his books to make a list of the surgical books he had on his shelves

equally valuable testimony of the ways in which books were being absorbed or reacted to in the past.

People have used books not only to write notes relating directly to the text, but to realise the potential of the space provided on flyleaves and other blank pages to record other things that mattered to them. The surgeon Joseph Fenton (d.1634), a contemporary of William Harvey at St Bartholomew's Hospital in London in the early seventeenth century, used the flyleaf of one of his medical texts for 'a note of all the bookes of chyrurgerye that I have in my studye'. John Robartes, 2nd Lord Robartes (1606-85), a major figure in building up the remarkable library at Lanhydrock House in Cornwall, used flyleaves in a number of his books to make notes about deer in the park, and bucks shot in particular years, without any apparent connection with the subjects of the books. Endleaves in school books often bear witness to the wandering attention spans of earlier generations of students; the bawdy rhyme on the flyleaf of a collection of tracts originally owned by a monk of Rochester testifies to the worldly knowledge of the cloister. Abstract markings may also be less directly connected with textual interpretation than might initially be thought; the books which Samuel Johnson used in compiling his *Dictionary* are full of sigla written in to capture word usages which were useful for citations.

There is a whole world of various kinds of markings which people have left in books, some of which are easier to interpret than others. Words in margins may seem fairly straightforward, although they may (or may not) relate to the printed text in different ways; they may be commenting on it, indexing it, summarising it or translating it. It is also common to find underlinings or lines drawn against margins, and a variety of symbols like stars, ticks or drawn-in pointing hands. Students of the history of reading are increasingly looking at this range of interactions between books and their users to categorise and distinguish them. Marginalia may sometimes look like a game of ping-pong between author and reader, bouncing ideas between them; sometimes they suggest something more like synthesis, when a reader's markings create an individual work of reference which has become more useful, in that personal arena, than it was before.

Copies of plays which have been used for dramatic performances

A note of all the bookes of Chyrurgerye that I have in my studye.

Hipocrates
Pauly Ægineta
...ius
...do w^t the
...er onlie Chy
...gions bounde.
...ultius
...eus.
...oppius
...relius Celsus
...reus a Cruce
...omius
...yrurgia Chyrurgice
...moteus.
...raeus.
...reas Alchazar.
...britius ab Aqua=
...pendente.
...anthus
...racelsus.
...ridanus Sanctus.
...raeus.
...orcitanus.
...uralis
...rus de Argillata.
...naldus de
...lla noua
...dus Vidius
...iacotius
...rmelinus
...lielmus Fabritius
...atheus Roßius

Ioßennius
Andreas Vesalius
Andreas Laurentius
de strumis

This copy of a mid 18th-century book by Isaac Watts was marked up by Samuel Johnson when he was quarrying words for his Dictionary

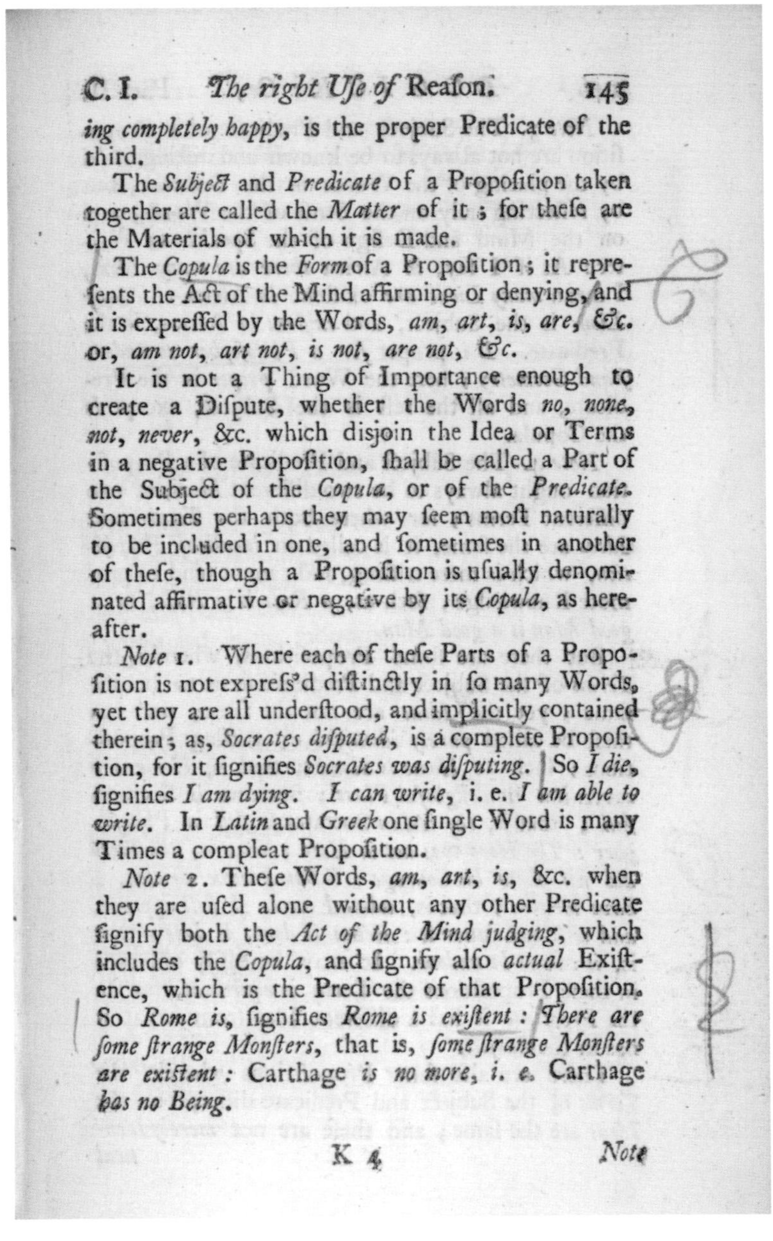

C. I. *The right Uſe of* Reaſon. 145

ing completely happy, is the proper Predicate of the third.

The *Subject* and *Predicate* of a Propoſition taken together are called the *Matter* of it; for theſe are the Materials of which it is made.

The *Copula* is the *Form* of a Propoſition; it repreſents the Act of the Mind affirming or denying, and it is expreſſed by the Words, *am*, *art*, *is*, *are*, *&c.* or, *am not*, *art not*, *is not*, *are not*, *&c.*

It is not a Thing of Importance enough to create a Diſpute, whether the Words *no*, *none*, *not*, *never*, &c. which disjoin the Idea or Terms in a negative Propoſition, ſhall be called a Part of the Subject of the *Copula*, or of the *Predicate*. Sometimes perhaps they may ſeem moſt naturally to be included in one, and ſometimes in another of theſe, though a Propoſition is uſually denominated affirmative or negative by its *Copula*, as hereafter.

Note 1. Where each of theſe Parts of a Propoſition is not expreſs'd diſtinctly in ſo many Words, yet they are all underſtood, and implicitly contained therein; as, *Socrates diſputed*, is a complete Propoſition, for it ſignifies *Socrates was diſputing*. So *I die*, ſignifies *I am dying*. *I can write*, i. e. *I am able to write*. In *Latin* and *Greek* one ſingle Word is many Times a compleat Propoſition.

Note 2. Theſe Words, *am*, *art*, *is*, &c. when they are uſed alone without any other Predicate ſignify both the *Act of the Mind judging*, which includes the *Copula*, and ſignify alſo *actual* Exiſtence, which is the Predicate of that Propoſition. So *Rome is*, ſignifies *Rome is exiſtent*: *There are ſome ſtrange Monſters*, that is, *ſome ſtrange Monſters are exiſtent*: Carthage *is no more*, *i. e.* Carthage *has no Being*.

K 4 *Note*

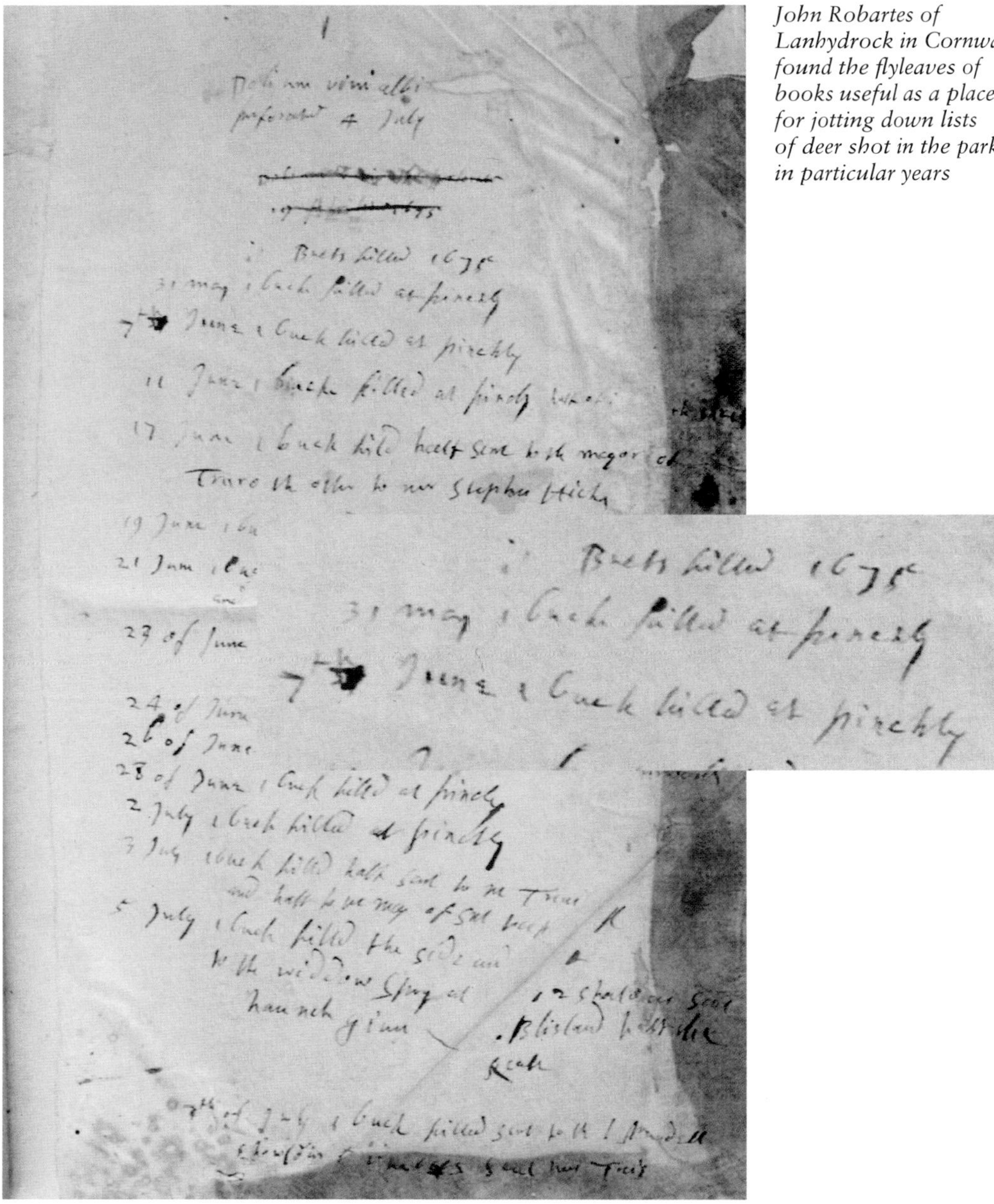

John Robartes of Lanhydrock in Cornwall found the flyleaves of books useful as a place for jotting down lists of deer shot in the park in particular years

M. T. CICERONIS Oration[illegible] XII. Selectarum Liber. Editio cum OLIVET, aliisque notæ melioris Exemplaribus collata, et in usum studiosæ Juventutis edita, 1785. 2s. 6d.

M. T. CICERONIS OPUSCULA; hoc est, Cato Major, seu, de Senectute; Lælius, seu, de Amicitia; Paradoxa; Somnium Scipionis. Præfigitur ejusdem M. T. Ciceronis Vita Literaria nunc primùm in lucem data. Editio nova. 2s.

DE FIDE et Officiis Christianorum, ex cl. Burneti et Grotii libellis, in usum Juventutis Christianæ. Editio altera. 1s. 6d.

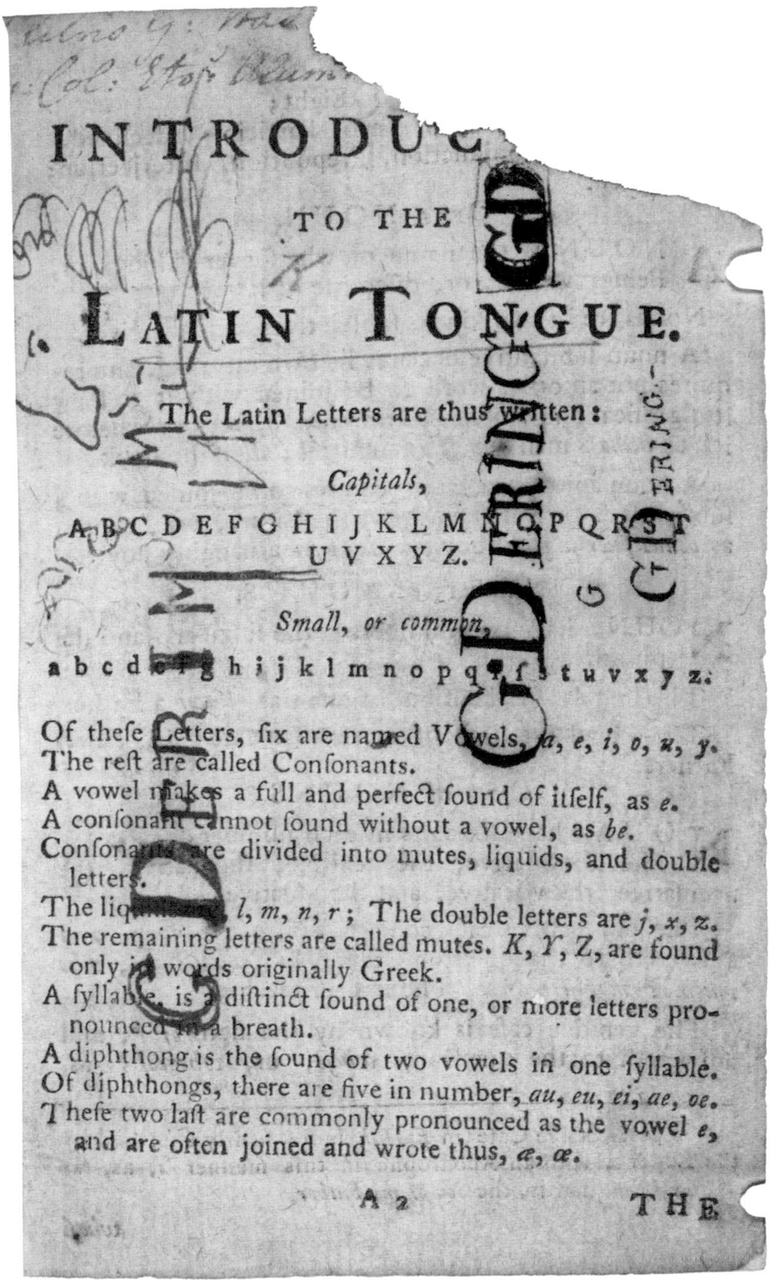

INTRODUC[TION]

TO THE

LATIN TONGUE.

The Latin Letters are thus written:

Capitals,

A B C D E F G H I J K L M N O P Q R S T
U V X Y Z.

Small, or common,

a b c d e f g h i j k l m n o p q r ſ s t u v x y z.

Of theſe Letters, ſix are named Vowels, *a, e, i, o, u, y.*
The reſt are called Conſonants.
A vowel makes a full and perfect ſound of itſelf, as *e.*
A conſonant cannot ſound without a vowel, as *be.*
Conſonants are divided into mutes, liquids, and double letters.
The liquids are, *l, m, n, r*; The double letters are *j, x, z.*
The remaining letters are called mutes. *K, Y, Z,* are found only in words originally Greek.
A ſyllable, is a diſtinct ſound of one, or more letters pronounced in a breath.
A diphthong is the ſound of two vowels in one ſyllable.
Of diphthongs, there are five in number, *au, eu, ei, ae, oe.*
Theſe two laſt are commonly pronounced as the vowel *e,* and are often joined and wrote thus, *æ, œ.*

A 2 THE

The scribbles and drawings in this copy of a Latin grammar were written by the Duke of Wellington and his friend George Hammond while they were schoolboys at Eton

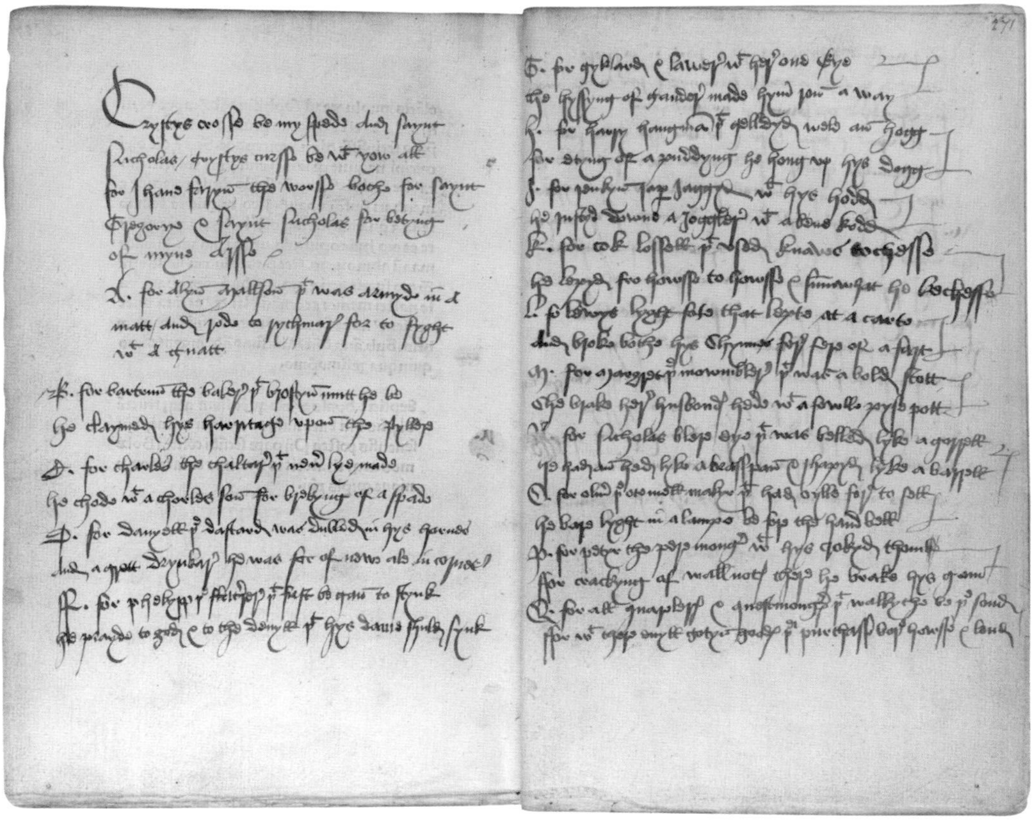

or as prompt copies are sometimes marked up with changes or cuts, or stage directions, to show how they were acted. Bibles have often been used for a particular kind of annotation, to record significant events in the lives of a family, a reflection of the special significance of the Word of the Lord, and of its physical manifestation in printed Bibles as an appropriate place to list those details. The record of births and deaths in the Brundrit family in the early nineteenth century, recorded in their Bible at the opening of the New Testament (p.124-5), is typical of countless others which survive in family Bibles of ordinary households of years gone by.

Annotations in books may be important not only because of what they can tell us about the annotator and his views on the world, but also because they may contain significant information about the text and its publication, which may not be available elsewhere. George Thomason (1600?-66), a bookseller in London

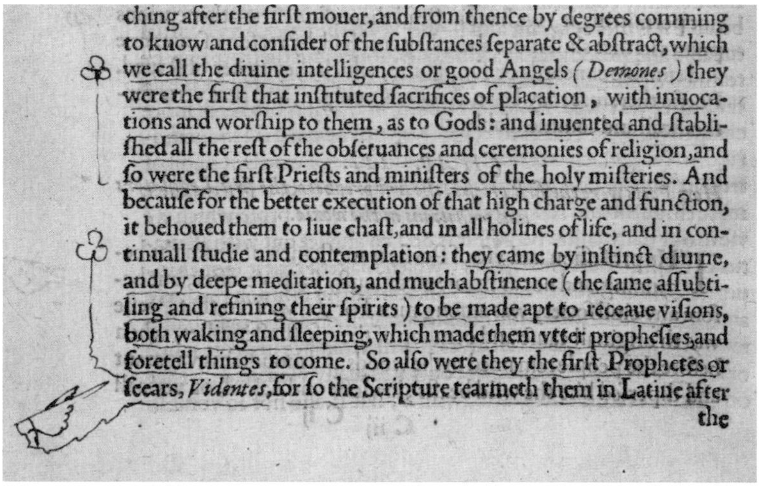
ching after the firſt mouer, and from thence by degrees comming
to know and conſider of the ſubſtances ſeparate & abſtract, which
we call the diuine intelligences or good Angels (*Demones*) they
were the firſt that inſtituted ſacrifices of placation, with inuoca-
tions and worſhip to them, as to Gods: and inuented and ſtabli-
ſhed all the reſt of the obſeruances and ceremonies of religion, and
ſo were the firſt Prieſts and miniſters of the holy miſteries. And
becauſe for the better execution of that high charge and function,
it behoued them to liue chaſt, and in all holines of life, and in con-
tinuall ſtudie and contemplation: they came by inſtinct diuine,
and by deepe meditation, and much abſtinence (the ſame aſſubti-
ling and refining their ſpirits) to be made apt to receaue viſions,
both waking and ſleeping, which made them vtter propheſies, and
foretell things to come. So alſo were they the firſt Prophetes or
ſeears, *Videntes*, for ſo the Scripture tearmeth them in Latine after
the

during the Civil War, assembled a unique collection of about 23,000 of the pamphlets, tracts, handbills and news-sheets which poured from the press during that period of political upheaval. Their value as texts for historians is enhanced by Thomason's habit of noting the actual day of publication on each item, so the exact sequence of squib and counter-squib can be established. Many books have been published anonymously or pseudonymously over the centuries, where the authors of contentious texts have wished to hide their identity, although some readers of the time may have known the truth, or at least had strong suspicions. It is not uncommon to find such books with contemporary notes on the titlepages allegedly naming the author, and the standard multivolume reference work on anonymous books – Halkett and Laing's *Dictionary of anonymous and pseudonymous publications in the English language* – relies extensively on annotated copies like this for its identifications. Sometimes these notes are right, sometimes they aren't, but either way they expand our knowledge of contemporary perceptions.

Author's own copies of the books they publish can be particularly interesting if they use them to record their later thoughts on the texts which become frozen and unchangeable once the printing press has done its work (unlike texts we write today and hold in

OPPOSITE
This collection of late 15th-century printed tracts owned by John Noble, a monk of Rochester Priory, and subsequently added to Henry VIII's library, has on its flyleaf a manuscript rhyme of contemporary bawdy verse. 'As an example of the sort of humour which appealed to the average reader of that day, this poem has an importance quite out of proportion to its literary value', as its 20th-century editor observed:
... L for Lewys light-fote that lepte at a carte
And broke bothe hys shynnes for fere of a fart
M for Margret the mowmbler that was a bold stott
She brake her husbondes hede with a fowlle pyse-pott
N for Nicholas blere-eye was bellyed lyke a gorrell
He had an hed lyke a brasspan and shapyd lyke a barrel ...

ABOVE LEFT
People have marked their books with all kinds of symbols and lines

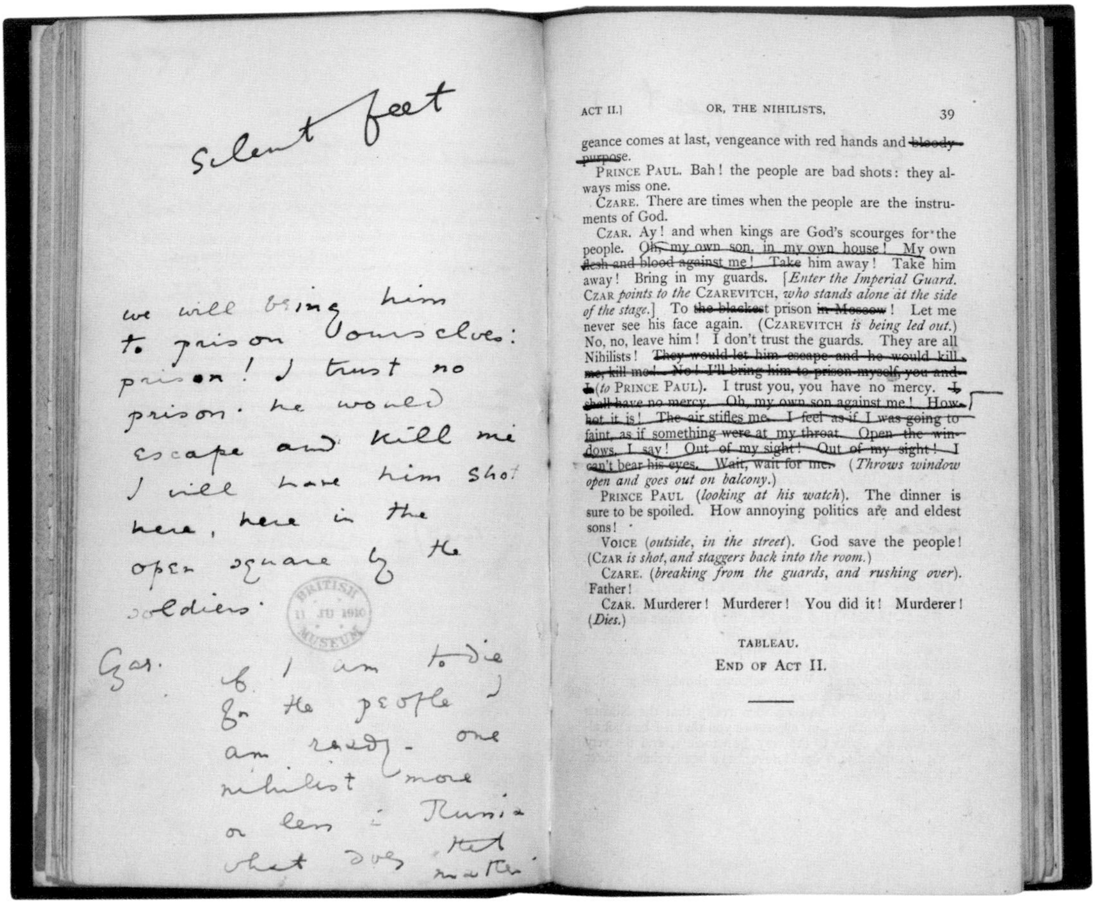

This copy of Oscar Wilde's first play, Vera, *was used as a prompt copy when it was performed in New York in 1882, showing the alterations from the original text made in performance*

electronic form). They may note corrections, additions, or changes of their ideas, or they may mark them up to become the copy text for later editions which may or may not have come to publication.

The additions which people may make to books are not limited to words, they may also include images. They may draw in their books as well as write in them (like Peter van Veen shown earlier), or they may have illustrative material bound in with the text leaves, additional to any pages of plates originally issued as part of the publication. This was easy to organise before books were always

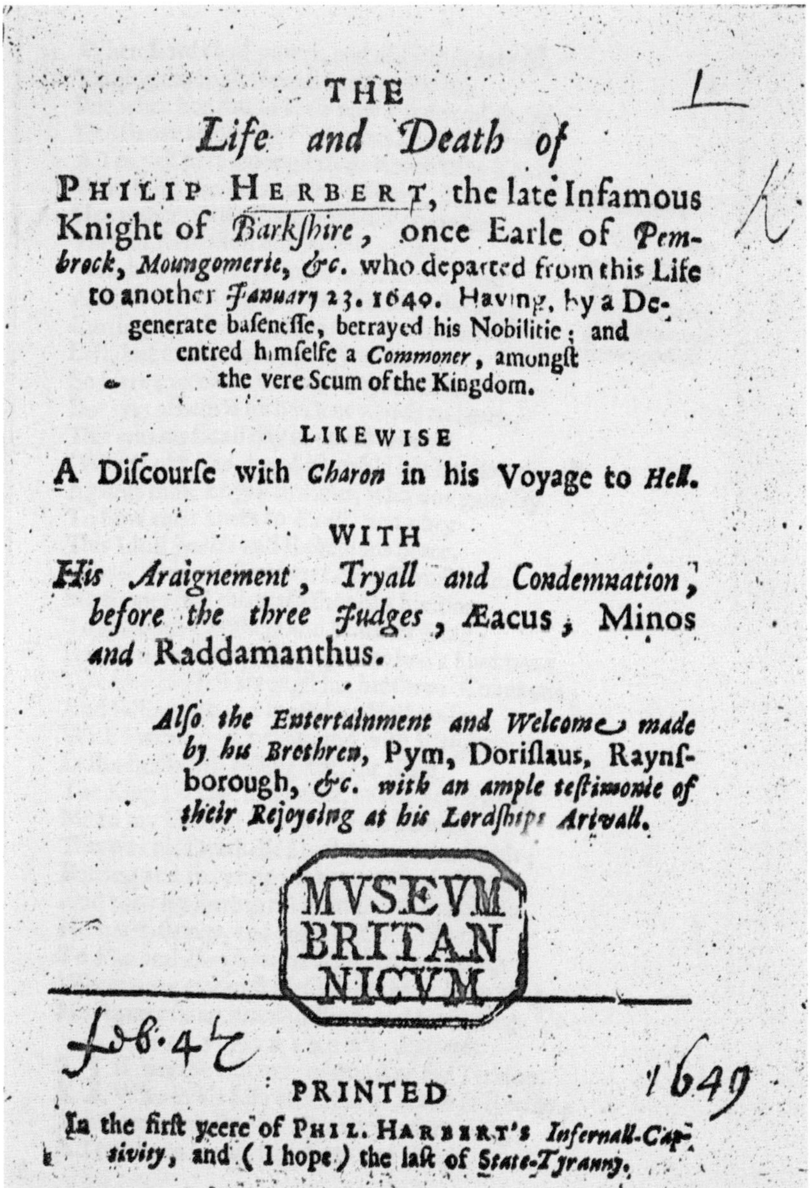

THE
Life and Death of
PHILIP HERBERT, the late Infamous Knight of *Barkshire*, once Earle of *Pembrock*, *Moungomerie*, *&c.* who departed from this Life to another *January* 23. 1649. Having, by a Degenerate basenesse, betrayed his Nobilitie; and entred himselfe a *Commoner*, amongst the vere Scum of the Kingdom.

LIKEWISE
A Discourse with *Charon* in his Voyage to *Hell*.

WITH
His Araignement, Tryall and Condemnation, *before the three Judges*, Æacus, Minos *and* Raddamanthus.

Also the Entertainment and Welcome made by his Brethren, Pym, Dorislaus, Raynsborough, *&c. with an ample testimonie of their Rejoycing at his Lordships Arrivall.*

MVSEVM BRITANNICVM

1649

PRINTED
In the first yeere of PHIL. HARBERT's *Infernall-Captivity*, and (I hope) the last of *State-Tyranny*.

LEFT
The Civil War bookseller George Thomason did posterity a service not only by amassing a unique collection of newsbooks and pamphlets from the 1640s and 50s, but also by annotating them in his own hand to give details of the exact time of publication

OVERLEAF
The record of births, marriages and deaths written in the Bible by members of the Brundrit family in the early 19th century is typical of similar lists kept in family Bibles and devotional books in many households

Ann Owen Brundrit
Born 22nd August 1820
at 5 Oclock in the after[noon]
Died Oct 19th 1826 at half past three in the

Elizabeth Brundrit
Born 7th of February 1823
at half past 9 Oclock at m[orning]

Ellen Brundrit Born Jany 28
1826 at 1/2 past two in the Mor[ning]
Died July 4th 1826 at 1/2 past three in the

William Wright Brundrit
born 13th September 1827 at half
past three in the Morning

Robt Wright Brundrit born Apr[il]
18th 1830 at eleven Oclock in the fore[noon]

John Brundrit Born Jany 4th 183[.]
at 1/4 before 1 Oclock in the Morning

oseph Brundrit born 16th May 1835.
Died December 19 1835.

THE GOSPEL according to St. MATTHEW.

CHAP. I.

The genealogy of Christ: 18 His conception and birth: 21, 23 His names.

HE book of the generation of Jesus
Christ, the son of David, the son of
braham.
2 ¶ Abraham begat Isaac; and Isaac
egat Jacob; and Jacob begat Judas
nd his brethren;
3 And Judas begat Phares and Zara of
hamar; and Phares begat Esrom; and
srom begat Aram;
4 And Aram begat Aminadab; and
minadab begat Naasson; and Naasson
egat Salmon;
5 And Salmon begat Booz of Rachab;
d Booz begat Obed of Ruth; and Obed
egat Jesse;
6 And Jesse begat David the king;
d David the king begat Solomon of
er *that had been the wife* of Urias;
7 And Solomon begat Roboam; and Ro-
oam begat Abia; and Abia begat Asa;
8 And Asa begat Josaphat; and Josa-
hat begat Joram; and Joram begat
zias;
9 And Ozias begat Joatham; and
oatham begat Achaz; and Achaz begat
zekias;
10 And Ezekias begat Manasses; and
Ianasses begat Amon; and Amon begat
osias;
11 And Josias begat Jechonias and his
rethren, about the time they were
arried away to Babylon;
12 And after they were brought to
abylon, Jechonias begat Salathiel; and
alathiel begat Zorobabel;
13 And Zorobabel begat Abiud; and
biud begat Eliakim; and Eliakim
egat Azor;
14 And Azor begat Sadoc; and Sadoc
egat Achim; and Achim begat Eliud;
15 And Eliud begat Eleazar; and
leazar begat Matthan; and Matthan
egat Jacob.
16 And Jacob begat Joseph the husband
f Mary, of whom was born Jesus, who
s called Christ.
17 So all the generations from Abraham
o David *are* fourteen generations; and
rom David until the carrying away into
Babylon *are* fourteen generations; and
rom the carrying away into Babylon
nto Christ *are* fourteen generations.
18 ¶ Now the birth of Jesus Christ was
n this wise: When as his mother Mary
vas espoused to Joseph, before they
ame together, she was found with child
f the Holy Ghost.
19 Then Joseph her husband, being
a just *man*, and not willing to make her
a public example, was minded to put
her away privily.
20 But while he thought on these things,
behold, the angel of the LORD appeared
unto him in a dream, saying, Joseph,
thou son of David, fear not to take unto
thee Mary thy wife; for that which is
conceived in her is of the Holy Ghost.
21 And she shall bring forth a son,
and thou shalt call his name JESUS: for
he shall save his people from their sins.
22 Now all this was done, that it
might be fulfilled which was spoken of
the Lord by the prophet, saying,
23 Behold, a virgin shall be with child,
and shall bring forth a son, and they shall
call his name Emmanuel; which being
interpreted, is, God with us.
24 Then Joseph, being raised from
sleep, did as the angel of the Lord had
bidden him, and took unto him his wife:
25 And knew her not till she had
brought forth her first-born son: and he
called his name JESUS.

CHAP. II.

1 The wise men coming to Christ, 11 worship him. 14 Joseph fleeth into Egypt.

NOW when Jesus was born in Bethlehem of Judea, in the days of
Herod the king, behold, there came wise
men from the east to Jerusalem,
2 Saying, Where is he that is born King
of the Jews? for we have seen his star
in the east, and are come to worship him.
3 When Herod the king had heard
these things, he was troubled, and all
Jerusalem with him.
4 And when he had gathered all the
chief priests and scribes of the people
together, he demanded of them where
Christ should be born.
5 And they said unto him, In Bethlehem of Judea: for thus it is written by
the prophet,
6 And thou Bethlehem, *in* the land of
Juda, art not the least among the princes
of Juda: for out of thee shall come
a Governor, that shall rule my people
Israel.
7 Then Herod, when he had privily
called the wise men, inquired of them
diligently what time the star appeared.
8 And he sent them to Bethlehem;
and said, Go and search diligently for
the young child; and when ye have found
him, bring me word again, that I may
come and worship him also.
9 When they had heard the king, they
departed: and, lo, the star, which they
saw in the east, went before them, till it

Mary Jane Brundrit, born 10 March 1837.
at half past nine in the morning

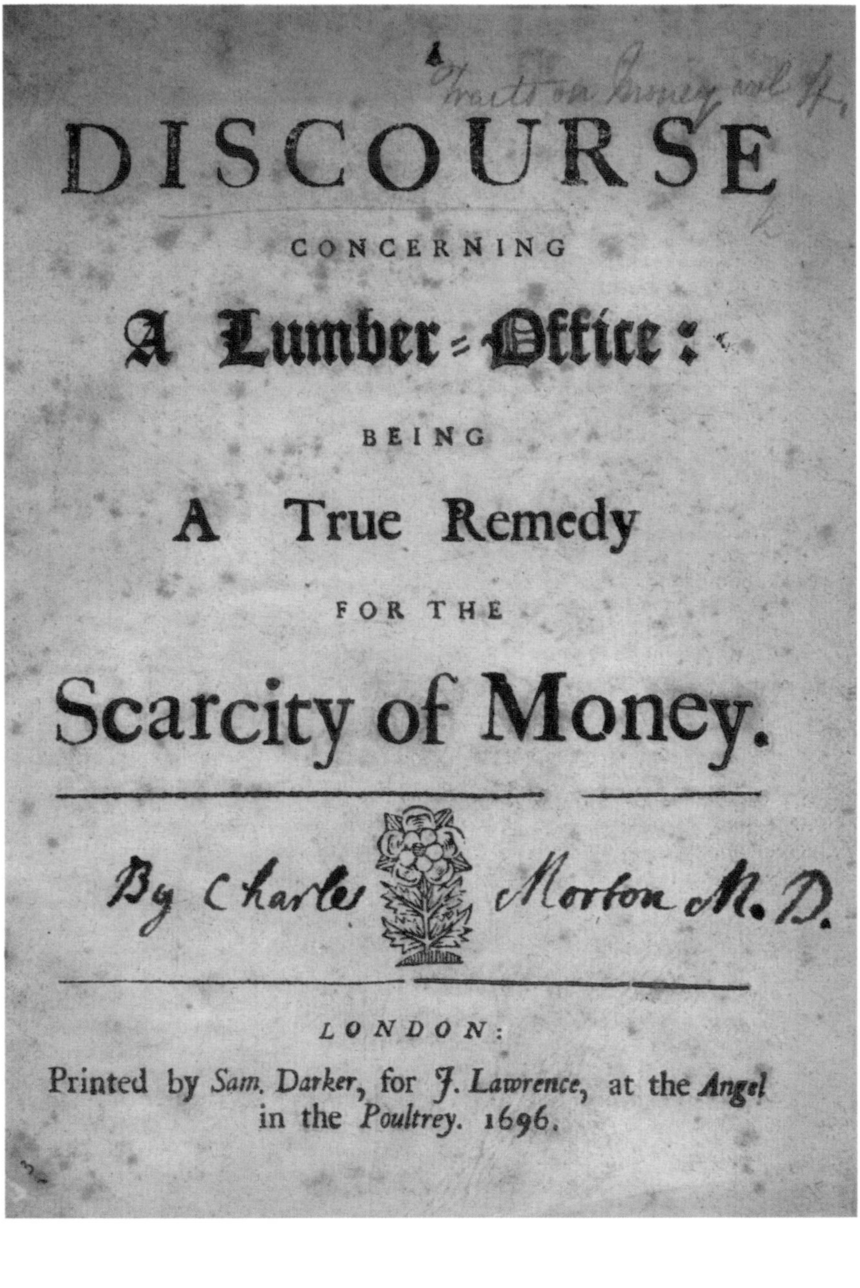

A

DISCOURSE

CONCERNING

A Lumber-Office:

BEING

A True Remedy

FOR THE

Scarcity of Money.

By Charles Morton M.D.

LONDON:

Printed by *Sam. Darker*, for *J. Lawrence*, at the *Angel* in the *Poultrey*. 1696.

Books published anonymously or pseudonymously, because authors wished to keep their identities hidden, sometimes have notes added by contemporary people to reveal their names (or guess at them), which can be very useful to later generations

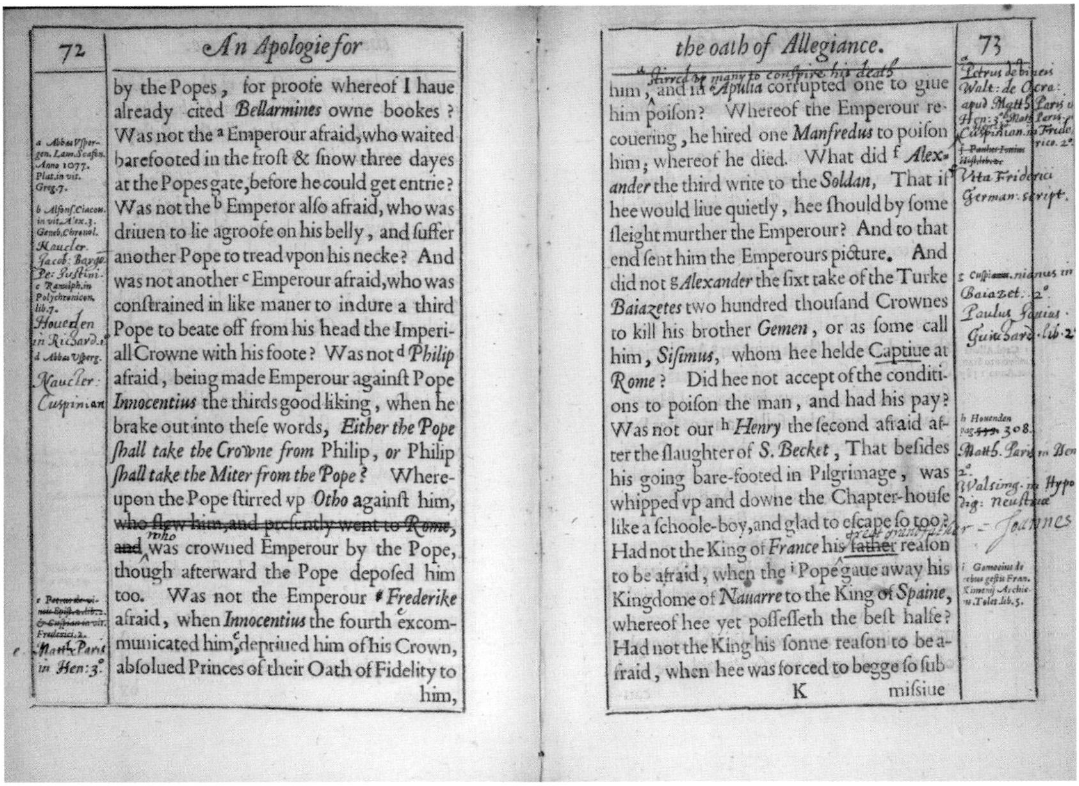

72 An Apologie for

by the Popes, for proofe whereof I haue already cited *Bellarmines* owne bookes? Was not the [a] Emperour afraid, who waited barefooted in the frost & snow three dayes at the Popes gate, before he could get entrie? Was not the [b] Emperor also afraid, who was driuen to lie agroofe on his belly, and suffer another Pope to tread vpon his necke? And was not another [c] Emperour afraid, who was constrained in like maner to indure a third Pope to beate off from his head the Imperiall Crowne with his foote? Was not [d] *Philip* afraid, being made Emperour against Pope *Innocentius* the thirds good liking, when he brake out into these words, *Either the Pope shall take the Crowne from* Philip, *or* Philip *shall take the Miter from the Pope?* Whereupon the Pope stirred vp *Otho* against him, who slew him, and presently went to *Rome*, and was crowned Emperour by the Pope, though afterward the Pope deposed him too. Was not the Emperour [e] *Frederike* afraid, when *Innocentius* the fourth excommunicated him, depriued him of his Crown, absolued Princes of their Oath of Fidelity to him,

the oath of Allegiance. 73

him, and in *Apulia* corrupted one to giue him poison? Whereof the Emperour recouering, he hired one *Manfredus* to poison him, whereof he died. What did [f] *Alexander* the third write to the *Soldan*, That if hee would liue quietly, hee should by some sleight murther the Emperour? And to that end sent him the Emperours picture. And did not [g] *Alexander* the sixt take of the Turke *Baiazetes* two hundred thousand Crownes to kill his brother *Gemen*, or as some call him, *Sisimus*, whom hee helde Captiue at *Rome*? Did hee not accept of the conditions to poison the man, and had his pay? Was not our [h] *Henry* the second afraid after the slaughter of *S. Becket*, That besides his going bare-footed in Pilgrimage, was whipped vp and downe the Chapter-house like a schoole-boy, and glad to escape so too? Had not the King of *France* his father reason to be afraid, when the [i] Pope gaue away his Kingdome of *Nauarre* to the King of *Spaine*, whereof hee yet possesseth the best halfe? Had not the King his sonne reason to be afraid, when hee was forced to begge so sub-

K missiue

This copy of James I's tract Triplici nodo, triplex cuneus—*a contribution to the fierce pamphlet warfare of the time between the protestant and catholic causes—was annotated by the King, personally, to mark up changes for a subsequent edition*

put on sale ready bound to the publisher's specifications, as sheets could be interspersed with the text leaves before being bound up. The process was partly facilitated by a flourishing trade in prints, i.e. engraved or etched pictures printed and sold in multiple copies, which could be kept as pictures, in a portfolio or on a wall, or bound up in a book. Sets of prints illustrating Biblical events were sold throughout the seventeenth and eighteenth centuries with this purpose in mind, and Bibles are not uncommonly found containing such pictures, added according to the purchaser's wishes. Books with pictures bound in to an owner's specification are sometimes referred to as extra-illustrated, sometimes as Grangerised, in memory of the author and print collector James Granger (1723-76), whose *Biographical history of England* (1769) was noted for

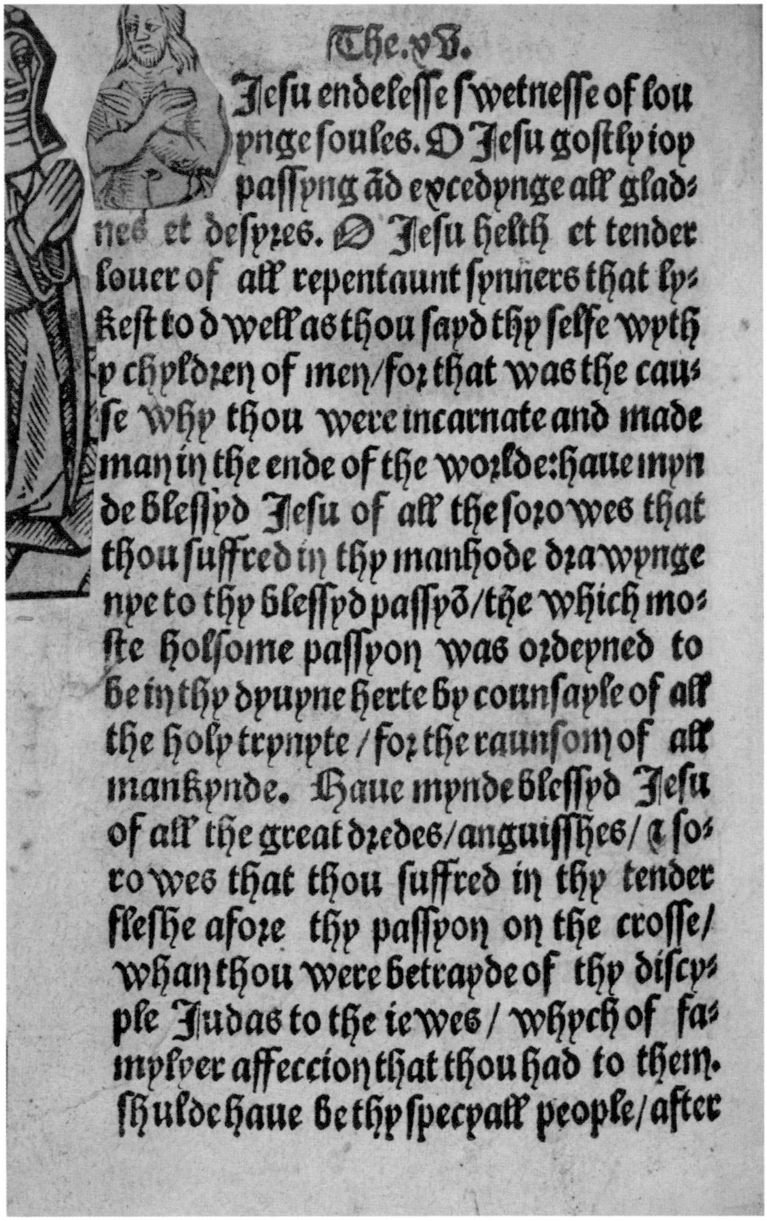
The.xv.
Jesu endelesse swetnesse of lou
ynge soules. O Jesu gostly ioy
passyng ād excedynge all glad-
nes et desyres. O Jesu helth et tender
louer of all repentaunt synners that ly-
kest to dwell as thou sayd thy selfe wyth
ÿ chyldren of men/for that was the cause why thou were incarnate and made
man in the ende of the worlde: haue myn
de blessyd Jesu of all the sorowes that
thou suffred in thy manhode drawynge
nye to thy blessyd passyō/the which mo-
ste holsome passyon was ordeyned to
be in thy dyuyne herte by counsayle of all
the holy trynyte/for the raunsom of all
mankynde. Haue mynde blessyd Jesu
of all the great dredes/anguisshes/& sorowes that thou suffred in thy tender
fleshe afore thy passyon on the crosse/
whan thou were betrayde of thy discy-
ple Judas to the iewes/whych of fa-
myler affeccion that thou had to them.
shulde haue be thy specyall people/after

A page from an English primer of 1532 which has been embellished with pasted-in woodcuts of Jesus with a kneeling nun; the book belonged at that time to a member of Syon Abbey, a Bridgettine house for monks and nuns

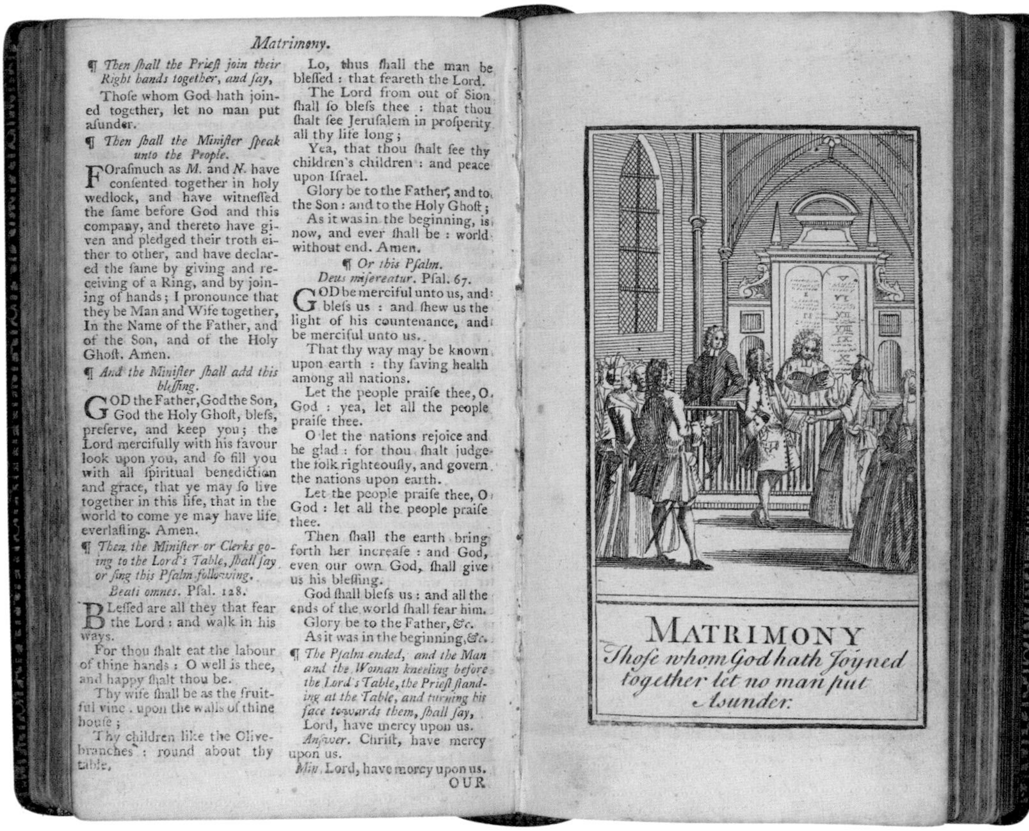

Matrimony.

¶ *Then ſhall the Prieſt join their Right hands together, and ſay,*

Thoſe whom God hath joined together, let no man put aſunder.

¶ *Then ſhall the Miniſter ſpeak unto the People.*

FOraſmuch as *M.* and *N.* have conſented together in holy wedlock, and have witneſſed the ſame before God and this company, and thereto have given and pledged their troth either to other, and have declared the ſame by giving and receiving of a Ring, and by joining of hands; I pronounce that they be Man and Wife together, In the Name of the Father, and of the Son, and of the Holy Ghoſt. Amen.

¶ *And the Miniſter ſhall add this bleſſing.*

GOD the Father, God the Son, God the Holy Ghoſt, bleſs, preſerve, and keep you; the Lord mercifully with his favour look upon you, and ſo fill you with all ſpiritual benediction and grace, that ye may ſo live together in this life, that in the world to come ye may have life everlaſting. Amen.

¶ *Then the Miniſter or Clerks going to the Lord's Table, ſhall ſay or ſing this Pſalm following.*

Beati omnes. Pſal. 128.

BLeſſed are all they that fear the Lord : and walk in his ways.

For thou ſhalt eat the labour of thine hands : O well is thee, and happy ſhalt thou be.

Thy wife ſhall be as the fruitful vine : upon the walls of thine houſe;

Thy children like the Olive-branches : round about thy table.

Lo, thus ſhall the man be bleſſed : that feareth the Lord.

The Lord from out of Sion ſhall ſo bleſs thee : that thou ſhalt ſee Jeruſalem in proſperity all thy life long;

Yea, that thou ſhalt ſee thy children's children : and peace upon Iſrael.

Glory be to the Father, and to the Son : and to the Holy Ghoſt;

As it was in the beginning, is now, and ever ſhall be : world without end. Amen.

¶ *Or this Pſalm.*

Deus miſereatur. Pſal. 67.

GOD be merciful unto us, and bleſs us : and ſhew us the light of his countenance, and be merciful unto us.

That thy way may be known upon earth : thy ſaving health among all nations.

Let the people praiſe thee, O God : yea, let all the people praiſe thee.

O let the nations rejoice and be glad : for thou ſhalt judge the folk righteouſly, and govern the nations upon earth.

Let the people praiſe thee, O God : let all the people praiſe thee.

Then ſhall the earth bring forth her increaſe : and God, even our own God, ſhall give us his bleſſing.

God ſhall bleſs us : and all the ends of the world ſhall fear him.

Glory be to the Father, &c.

As it was in the beginning, &c.

¶ *The Pſalm ended, and the Man and the Woman kneeling before the Lord's Table, the Prieſt ſtanding at the Table, and turning his face towards them, ſhall ſay,*

Lord, have mercy upon us.

Anſwer. Chriſt, have mercy upon us.

Min. Lord, have mercy upon us.

OUR

An 18th-century prayer book which has been individualised by adding in a set of illustrations—the book was not published like this, the pictures were bought separately and bound in, but suites of plates were marketed for such purposes

the popular habit of binding copies up with portraits added. The practice is however much older than this, as there are numerous instances of manuscripts or printed books from the fifteenth and sixteenth centuries with pasted-in pictures added by early owners. As well as pictures, owners have sometimes inserted autographs and manuscript material relating to a book's text.

People have added to books by writing things in them; they have also taken things away, by deleting things they find offensive or unsuitable. Mutilation is another way of giving a book an individual history, albeit a rather negative one. Sixteenth-century English church service books, which survived the upheavals of the Reformation, will often be found to have been systematically subjected to the edict of Henry VIII, issued in 1542, that all references to the Pope, and to Saint Thomas à Becket, should be expunged. The offending words will have been crossed out, or cut out, so

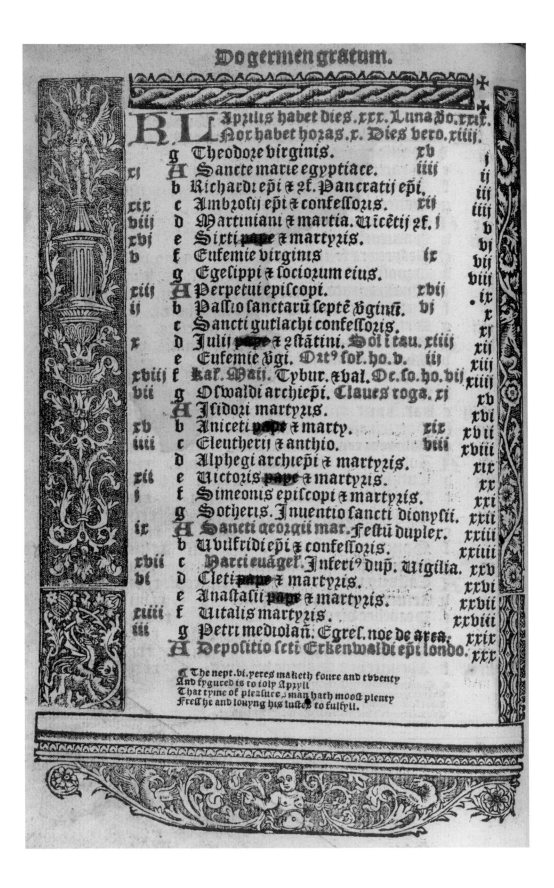

KL Aprilis habet dies. xxx. Luna vo. xxix.
Nox habet horas. x. Dies vero. xiiij.

	g	Theodore virginis.	xv	j
xj	A	Sancte marie egyptiace.	iiij	ij
	b	Richardi epi & cf. Pancratij epi.		iij
xix	c	Ambrosij epi & confessoris.	xij	iiij
viij	d	Martiniani & martia. Vicētij cf.	j	v
xvj	e	Sixti [redacted] & martyris.		vj
v	f	Eufemie virginis	ix	vij
	g	Egesippi & sociorum eius.		viij
xiij	A	Perpetui episcopi.	xvij	ix
ij	b	Passio sanctarū septē vginū.	vj	x
	c	Sancti gutlachi confessoris.		xj
x	d	Julij [redacted] & cstātini. Sol i tau.	xiiij	xij
	e	Eufemie vgi. Ort⁹ sol. ho. v.	iij	xiij
xviij	f	Kal. Maij. Tybur. & val. Oc. so. ho. vij		xiiij
vij	g	Oswaldi archiepi. Claues roga.	xj	xv
	A	Isidori martyris.		xvi
xv	b	Aniceti [redacted] & marty.	xix	xvii
iiii	c	Eleutherij & anthio.	viii	xviii
	d	Alphegi archiepi & martyris.		xix
xii	e	Victoris [redacted] & martyris.		xx
j	f	Simeonis episcopi & martyris.		xxi
	g	Sotheris. Inuentio sancti dionysii.		xxii
ix	A	Sancti georgii mar. Festū duplex.		xxiii
	b	Vuilfridi epi & confessoris.		xxiiii
xvii	c	Marci euāgel. Inferi⁹ dup. Vigilia.		xxv
vi	d	Cleti [redacted] & martyris.		xxvi
	e	Anastasii [redacted] & martyris.		xxvii
xiiii	f	Vitalis martyris.		xxviii
iii	g	Petri mediolan. Egres. noe de arca.		xxix
	A	Depositio scti Erkenwaldi epi londo.		xxx

¶ The next. vi. yeres maketh foure and twenty
And fygured is to ioly Apryll
That tyme of pleasure, man hath moost plenty
Fresshe and louyng his lustes to fulfyll.

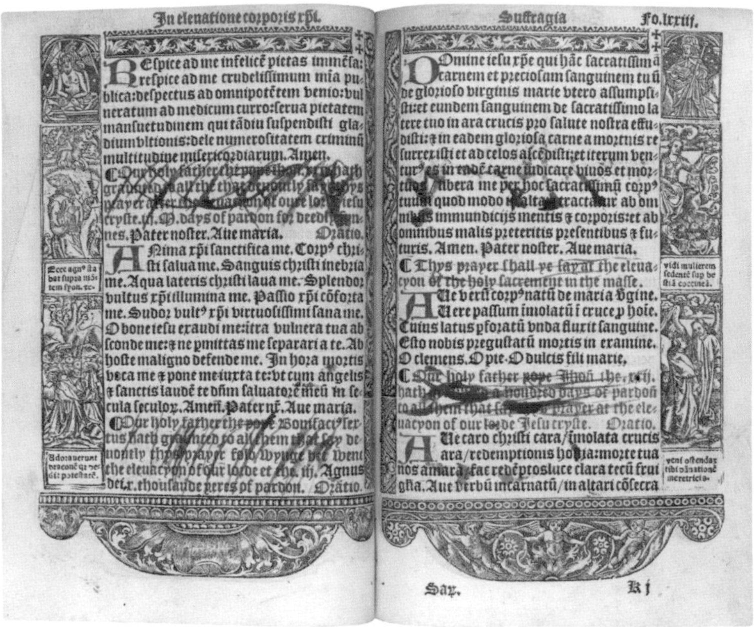

In elenatione corporis xpi.

Respice ad me infelicẽ pietas immẽsa: respice ad me crudelissimum mia publica: despectus ad omnipotẽtem venio: vulneratum ad medicum curro: serua pietatem mansuetudinem qui tãdiu suspendisti gladium vltionis: dele numerositatem criminũ multitudine misericordiarum. Amen.
¶ Our holy father the pope [illegible] hath graunted to all them that deuoutly say thys prayer after the eleuacyon of oure lorde iesu cryste. iij. M. days of pardon for dedly synnes. Pater noster. Aue maria. Oratio.
Anima xpi sanctifica me. Corp9 christi salua me. Sanguis christi inebria me. Aqua lateris christi laua me. Splendor vultus xpi illumina me. Passio xpi cõforta me. Sudor vult9 xpi virtuosissimi sana me. O bone iesu exaudi me: itra vulnera tua absconde me: & ne pmittas me separari a te. Ab hoste maligno defende me. In hora mortis voca me & pone me iuxta te: vt cum angelis & sanctis laudẽ te dñm saluatorẽ meũ in secula seculor. Amen. Pater nr. Aue maria.
¶ Our holy father the pope Bonifaci9 sextus hath graunted to all them that say deuoutly thys prayer [illegible] wene the eleuacyon of our lorde et [illegible] iij. Agnus dei. x. thousande yeres of pardon. Oratio.

Ecce agn9 stabat supra mõtem syon. &c.

Adorauerunt draconẽ qz dedit potestatẽ.

Suffragia Fo. lxxiij.

Domine iesu xpe qui hãc sacratissimã carnem et preciosam sanguinem tuũ de glorioso virginis marie vtero assumpsisti: et eundem sanguinem de sacratissimo latere tuo in ara crucis pro salute nostra effudisti: & in eadem gloriosa carne a mortuis resurrexisti et ad celos ascẽdisti: et iterum ventur9 es in eadẽ carne iudicare viuos et mortuos/ libera me per hoc sacratissimũ corp9 tuum quod modo in altari tractatur ab omnibus immundicijs mentis & corporis: et ab omnibus malis preteritis presentibus & futuris. Amen. Pater noster. Aue maria.
¶ Thys prayer shall ye say at the eleuacyon of the holy sacrement in the masse.
Aue verũ corp9 natũ de maria virgine. Uere passum imolatũ i cruce p hoie. Cuius latus pforatũ vnda fluxit sanguine. Esto nobis pregustatũ mortis in examine. O clemens. O pie. O dulcis fili marie.
¶ Our holy father pope Iohñ the. xxij. hath [illegible] a hondred days of pardon to all them that say [illegible] prayer at the eleuacyon of our lorde Iesu cryste. Oratio.
Aue caro christi cara/ imolata crucis ara/ redemptionis hostia: morte tua nos amara/ fac redẽptos luce clara tecũ frui gloria. Aue verbũ incarnatũ/ in altari cõsecra

vidi mulierem sedentẽ sup bestiã coccineã.

veni ostendam tibi dãnationẽ meretricis.

Sar. K j

OPPOSITE AND LEFT
In this copy of a Book of Hours printed for the English market in 1527, a contemporary owner has obeyed Henry VIII's edict and scratched out all references to the Pope or the Holy Father

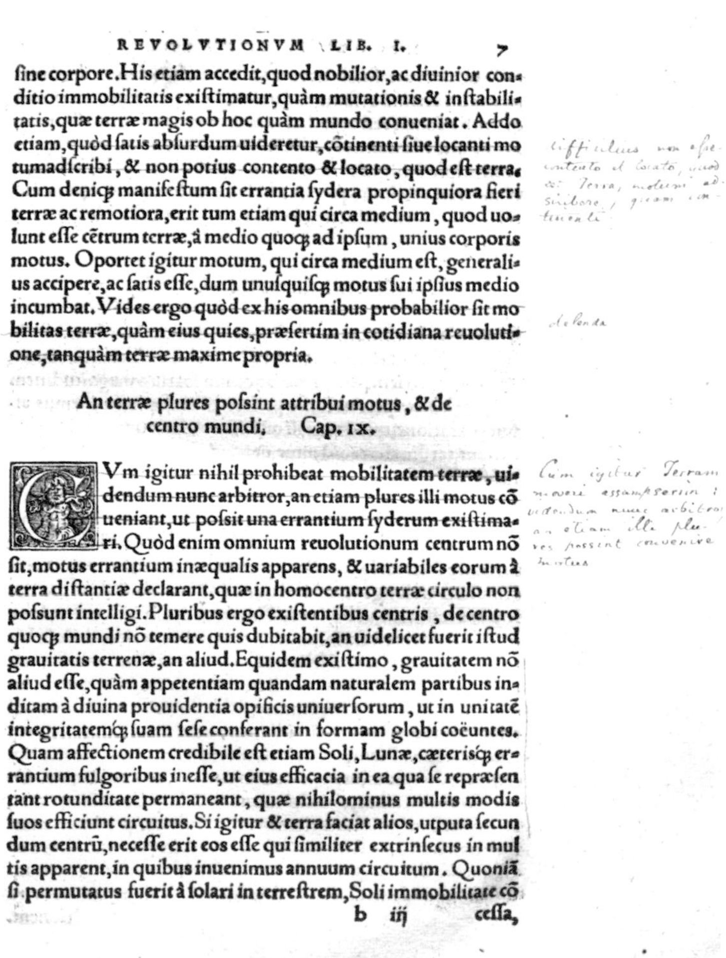

REVOLVTIONVM LIB. I. 7

fine corpore. His etiam accedit, quod nobilior, ac diuinior conditio immobilitatis existimatur, quàm mutationis & instabilitatis, quæ terræ magis ob hoc quàm mundo conueniat. Addo etiam, quòd satis absurdum uideretur, cõtinenti siue locanti motum adscribi, & non potius contento & locato, quod est terra. Cum denique manifestum sit errantia sydera propinquiora fieri terræ ac remotiora, erit tum etiam qui circa medium, quod uolunt esse cẽtrum terræ, à medio quoque ad ipsum, unius corporis motus. Oportet igitur motum, qui circa medium est, generalius accipere, ac satis esse, dum unusquisque motus sui ipsius medio incumbat. Vides ergo quòd ex his omnibus probabilior sit mobilitas terræ, quàm eius quies, præsertim in cotidiana reuolutione, tanquàm terræ maxime propria.

difficilius non esse contento et locato, quod est Terra, motum adscribere, quam continenti

delenda

An terræ plures possint attribui motus, & de centro mundi, Cap. IX.

CVm igitur nihil prohibeat mobilitatem terræ, uidendum nunc arbitror, an etiam plures illi motus cõueniant, ut possit una errantium syderum existimari. Quòd enim omnium reuolutionum centrum nõ sit, motus errantium inæqualis apparens, & uariabiles eorum à terra distantiæ declarant, quæ in homocentro terræ circulo non possunt intelligi. Pluribus ergo existentibus centris, de centro quoque mundi nõ temere quis dubitabit, an uidelicet fuerit istud grauitatis terrenæ, an aliud. Equidem existimo, grauitatem nõ aliud esse, quàm appetentiam quandam naturalem partibus inditam à diuina prouidentia opificis uniuersorum, ut in unitatẽ integritatemque suam sese conferant in formam globi coëuntes. Quam affectionem credibile est etiam Soli, Lunæ, cæterisque errantium fulgoribus inesse, ut eius efficacia in ea qua se repræsentant rotunditate permaneant, quæ nihilominus multis modis suos efficiunt circuitus. Si igitur & terra faciat alios, utputa secundum centrũ, necesse erit eos esse qui similiter extrinsecus in multis apparent, in quibus inuenimus annuum circuitum. Quoniã si permutatus fuerit à solari in terrestrem, Soli immobilitate cõ

b iij cessa,

Cum igitur Terram moveri assumpserim, videndum nunc arbitror an etiam illi plures possint convenire motus

Copernicus's famous book setting out his theory of the revolution of the earth round the sun was subject to the attentions of the Roman Catholic Church's censors in 1620, when it was decreed that a number of passages should be excised. Here, an owner has been through a copy of the original 1543 edition deleting and amending passages from the text, in accordance with these instructions

ABOVE & OPPOSITE
The manuscript reputedly used by St Boniface to ward off the blows of his murderers, complete with slash marks, has long been a venerated relic of the Cathedral at Fulda (opposite). The Saint has often been depicted with the book, skewered on the point of a sword (above)

that the books could continue to be used. Various other kinds of censorship, for political or theological reasons, can be found exercised on books down the ages.

VENERATION THROUGH ASSOCIATION

Books with an association with a famous individual or historical event have long been regarded as special or collectable; this is the oldest kind of interest in book provenance. The Cathedral of Fulda preserves an early theological manuscript whose wooden covers are reputedly scored with the marks of sword blows received when St Boniface, a German evangelist in the eighth century, used the book as a shield to ward off a pagan attack. The book was none too effective in this respect, and Boniface was killed, but the book has been held as a treasured relic ever since.

The sixth-century Gospels of St Augustine now at Corpus Christi College, Cambridge would be a much treasured book in any circumstances, as the oldest illuminated gospel manuscript now extant, but it is the fact that this book was brought to England by St Augustine in 597 AD, when he came to Christianise the country, that makes it particularly special. We know that books like this have long been venerated for their holiness by association; a fifteenth-century drawing of the high altar in the church of St Augustine's Abbey, Canterbury, shows this book, and others believed to have belonged to St Augustine, standing displayed behind the altar along with other precious relics. Contemporary tradition had it that a local peasant who had sworn a false oath on one of these books was struck blind.

Books do not need to be associated with saints to become special. Any book which has been owned or used by a noteworthy historical figure, whether hero or villain, is likely to acquire this kind of aura, or be regarded as a particularly desirable thing to possess. Second-hand and antiquarian books will increase in price if they are association copies, in proportion with the level of interest or notoriety of the previous owner. A book which would normally change hands for a small amount in a second-hand bookshop will sell for significantly more if it has the signature on the flyleaf of Winston Churchill, or John Lennon. This phenomenon can be viv-

idly seen in the prices which signed offprints of important scientific papers can command: an offprint of the famous 1953 *Nature* article unravelling the structure of DNA, and autographed by Crick and Watson, will change hands for five-figure sums, although the three pages of text are readily available as photocopies or printouts from a website.

'Association' books can be especially fascinating if they can be linked with a particular historical event. The manuscript prayer manual which belonged to Lady Jane Grey, which she is believed to have carried onto the scaffold in 1554, and which contains her handwritten additions, is a touching object. Association is also valued when it comes about through presentation, when we have a copy of a book which has been given by the author to a friend or colleague.

The 6th-century Gospel Book brought to Britain by St Augustine in 597 A.D. is a venerated object because of its history and association; it is still used as the book on which incoming Archbishops of Canterbury swear their oath (opposite). A late medieval drawing of the High Altar at St Augustine's Abbey, Canterbury shows this book, with others believed to have belonged to the Saint, propped up among the community's most holy 'relics' (right)

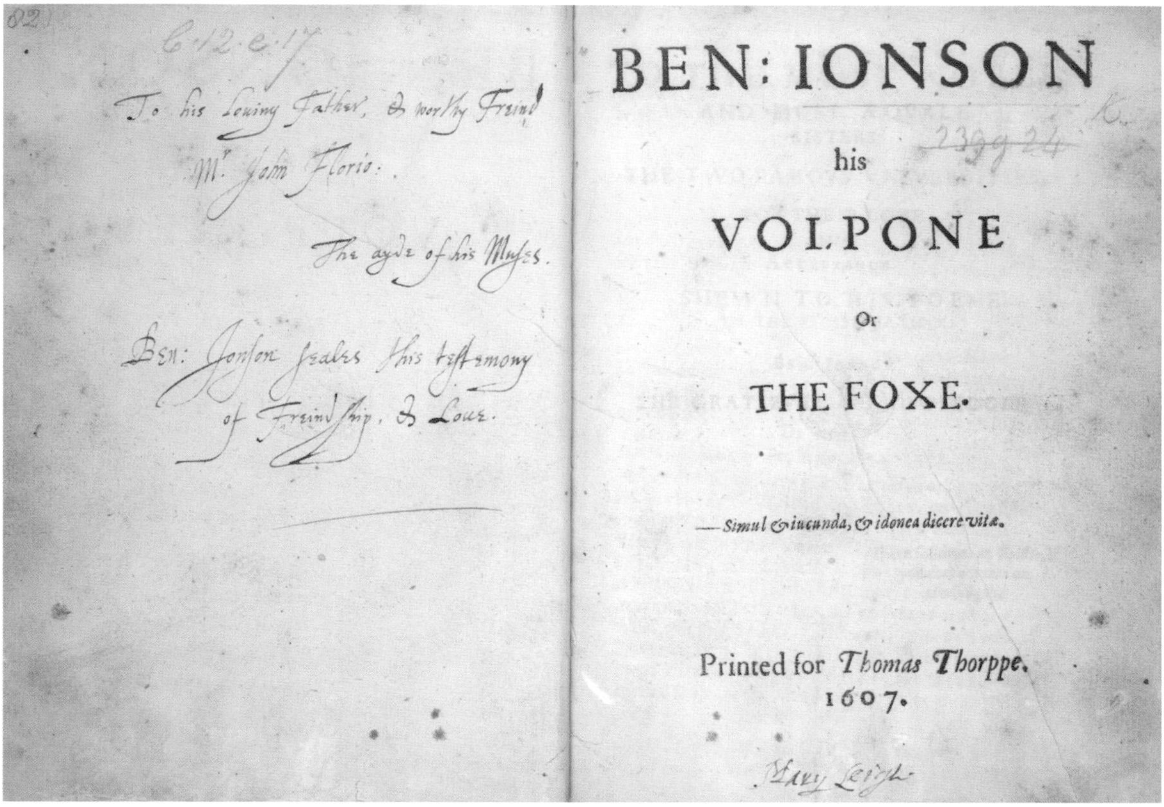

ABOVE
A copy of the first printing of Ben Jonson's play Volpone, inscribed by him to the contemporary author and dictionary-compiler John Florio

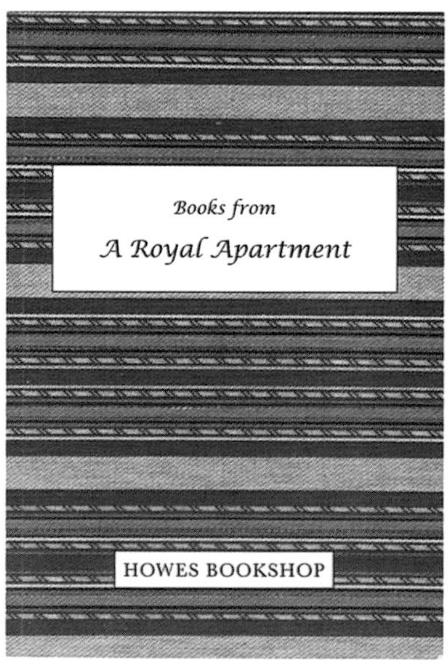

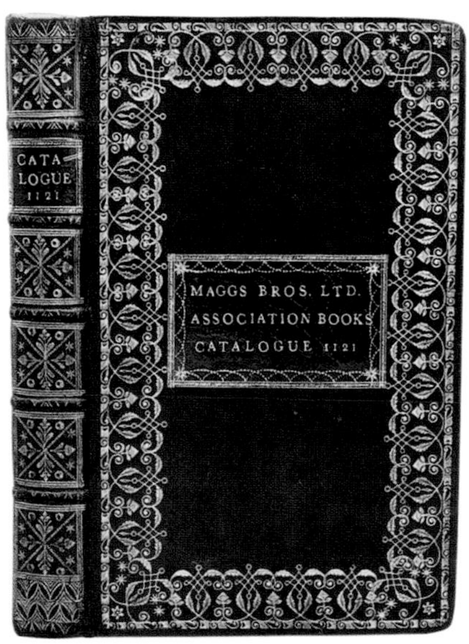

RIGHT
Books which can be associated with celebrated people have always been regarded as desirable and collectible, as these booksellers' catalogues show

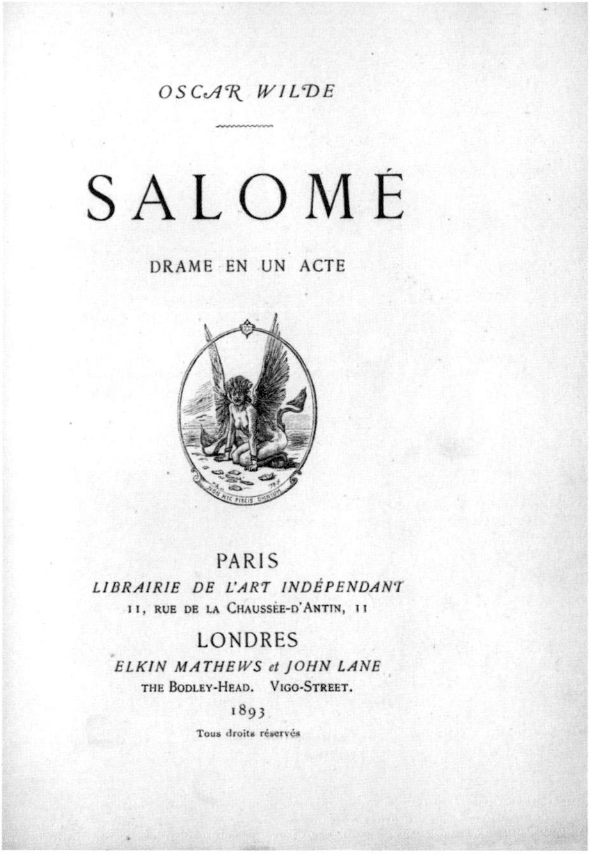

OSCAR WILDE

SALOMÉ

DRAME EN UN ACTE

PARIS
LIBRAIRIE DE L'ART INDÉPENDANT
11, RUE DE LA CHAUSSÉE-D'ANTIN, 11
LONDRES
ELKIN MATHEWS et JOHN LANE
THE BODLEY-HEAD. VIGO-STREET.
1893
Tous droits réservés

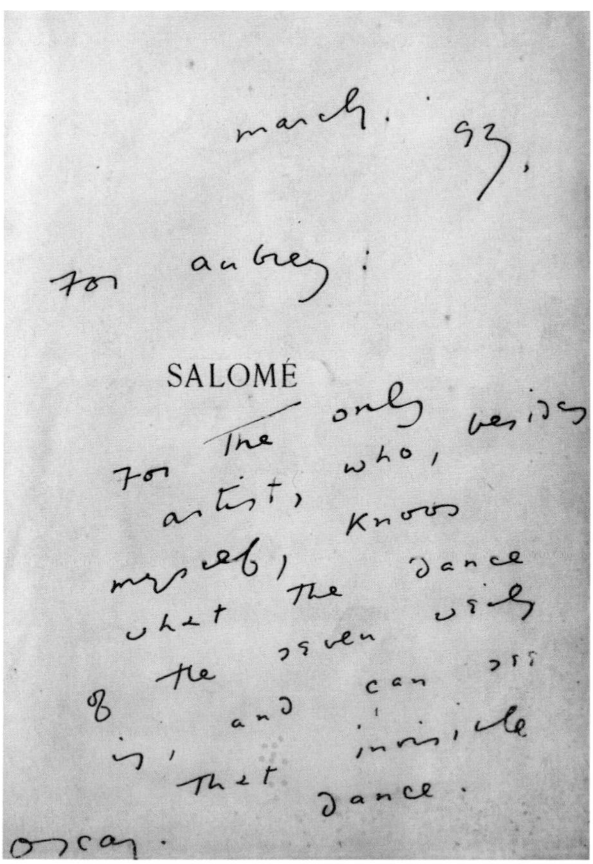

march. 93.

For aubrey:

SALOMÉ

For the only artist, who, besides myself, knows what the dance of the seven veils is, and can see that invisible dance.

Oscar.

LEFT
The special interest of this copy of Oscar Wilde's Salomé *comes from the presentation inscription on the half-title, from the author to Aubrey Beardsley: 'For Aubrey: for the only artist, who, besides myself, knows what the dance of the seven veils is, and can see that invisible dance. Oscar'*

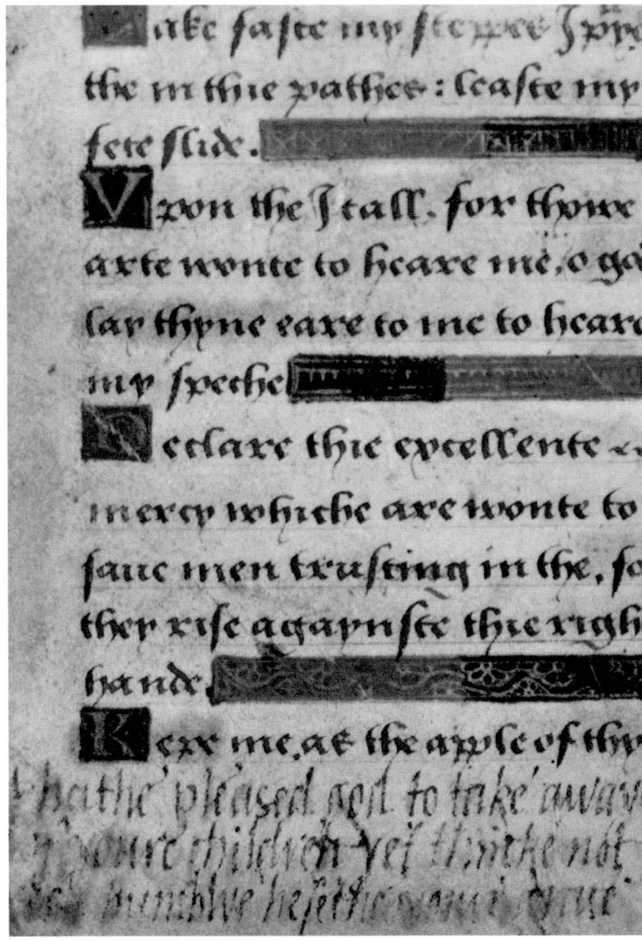

ake faste my steppes lorde
the in thine pathes : leaste my
fete slide.
Vpon the I call. for thou
arte wonte to heare me, o god
lay thyne eare to me to heare
my speche
eclare thie excellente
mercy whiche are wonte to
saue men trusting in the, for
they rise agaynste thie right
hande
Kepe me, as the apple of thyn
hathe pleased god to take awaye
youre children yet thinke not
humblye

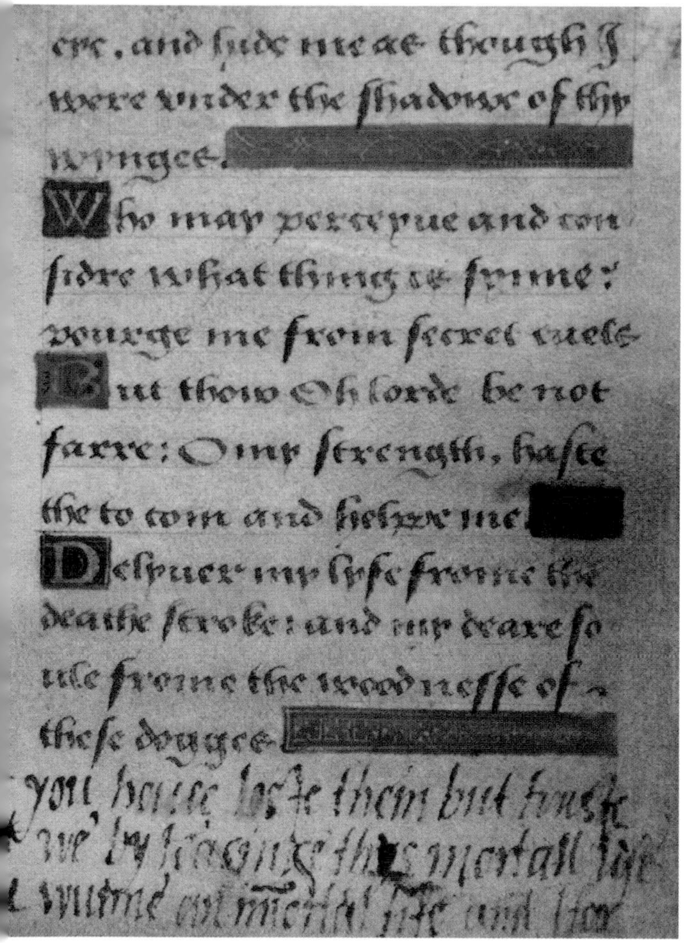
eye, and hyde me as though I
were under the shadowe of thy
wynges.
Who may perceyve and con
sidre what thing is synne:
pourge me from secret euels.
But thow Oh lorde be not
farre: O my strength, haste
the to com and helpe me.
Delyuer my lyfe frome the
deathe stroke: and my deare so
ule frome the woodnesse of
these dogges.

The prayer book of Lady Jane Grey, executed at the Tower of London in 1554, contains handwritten notes by her addressed to her father, and to the Lieutenant of the Tower, reflecting on mortality

'He filled their listening ears with wondrous things'

CHAPTER FIVE

VARIETY THROUGH BINDING

OPPOSITE
The introduction of cloth edition binding techniques in the mid 19th-century allowed Victorian designers to create imaginative and colourful covers

The outer covers of books, their bindings, comprise another important arena for displaying their individual and unique histories. Like printing, binding was for many centuries a handcrafted process, until increasing demand, coupled with technological opportunity, brought about major changes to the industry in the nineteenth century. Books today are issued in uniform bindings, mass produced according to publishers' specifications, with little or no choice available to the purchaser at point of sale apart perhaps from the option to have a paperback rather than a hardback, if these are simultaneously on offer. The roots of this way of doing things lie in the 1830s, when a breakthrough was made in creating a cloth-covered binding which could be mechanically decorated and lettered. This new technique hastened the move away from leather, which had been the standard outer covering of books since the Middle Ages, to the cheaper alternatives of cloth and paper, while also making it possible to issue whole editions of books in genuinely identical bindings. It also brought about the development of the pictorial outer covers and dust jackets which we take for granted today; book covers could be both colourful and decorated in the handpress period, but the ornamentation was essentially abstract and bore no relation to the contents of the book. The change took place during the Victorian era, when designers began to exploit the opportunities provided by the new cloth covers, and evolved into the decorative conventions which continue today.

Before the nineteenth century bookbinding, like printing, was carried out by trained artisans working either individually or in small workshops with only a handful of people. The binders took the printed sheets which came from the printers and turned them into books ready for use by folding and sewing the leaves and putting them into protective covers, which would typically be covered with leather. It follows from this that every book of

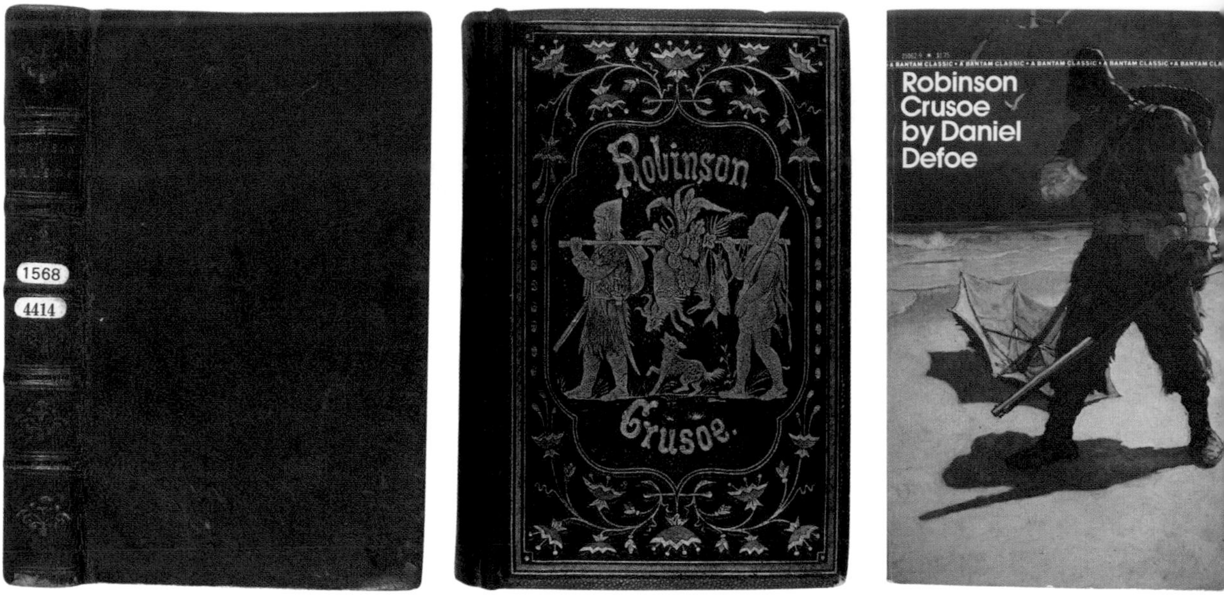

The creation of pictorial outer covers, reflecting and advertising the contents of the books, was a 19th-century development: here are 18th, 19th and 20th-century editions of Robinson Crusoe, *in contemporary bindings*

this period is a unique handmade object, in the same way that a handwritten manuscript will always be unique, and that bindings are more individually distinct objects than the printed sheets they contain. Even if a binder sets out to make two bindings which look the same, using the same materials and decorative tools – as was often the case – the handcrafted nature of the process will inevitably lead to slight differences between the two.

Embellishing the covers was an important part of the process, and people have been making bindings which are decorative as well as functional for as long as they have been binding books. For many centuries the main way of doing this – although there were numerous other possibilities – was by impressing the leather, either in blind or in gold, using metal tools carrying an engraved pattern. Using these basic techniques, binders down the ages have created bindings of every kind of sophistication, from the simple to the luxurious. Each generation has had its master craftsmen who have been capable of producing highly elaborate and beautiful bindings, prized at the time as possessions for wealthy and discerning collectors, and subsequently admired as belonging to the artistic

Bookbinding, like printing, used to be a handmade process with every step of the operation carried out by individual craftsmen. It began with sewing the folded sheets together, included the lacing-on of boards, covering with leather and adding of endbands at head and foot, and concluded with the 'finishing', i.e. the decoration of the outer covers, commonly with heated metal tools

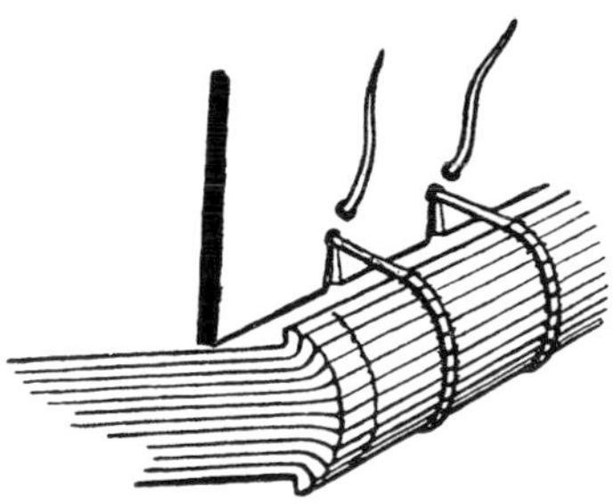

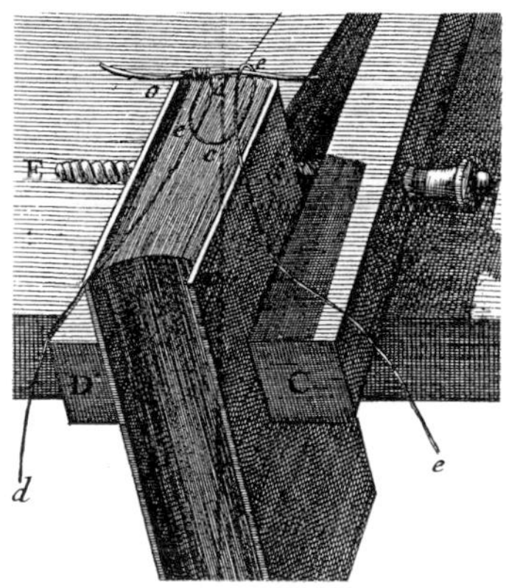

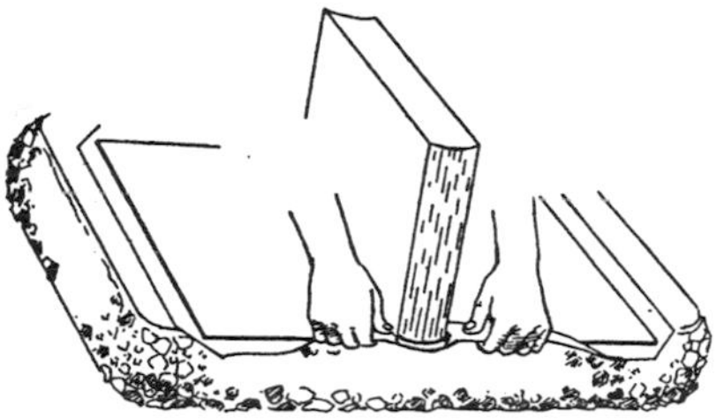

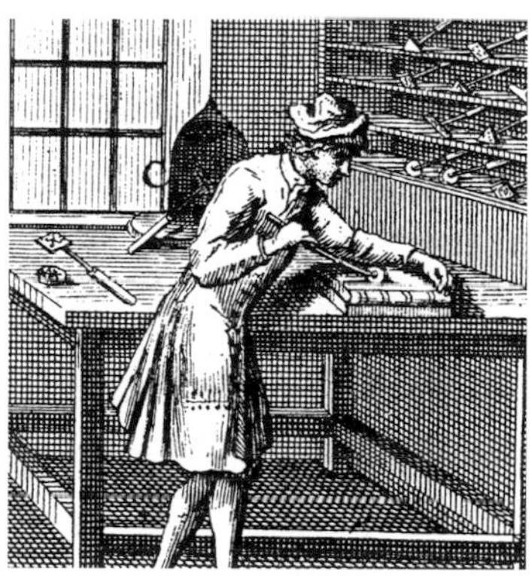

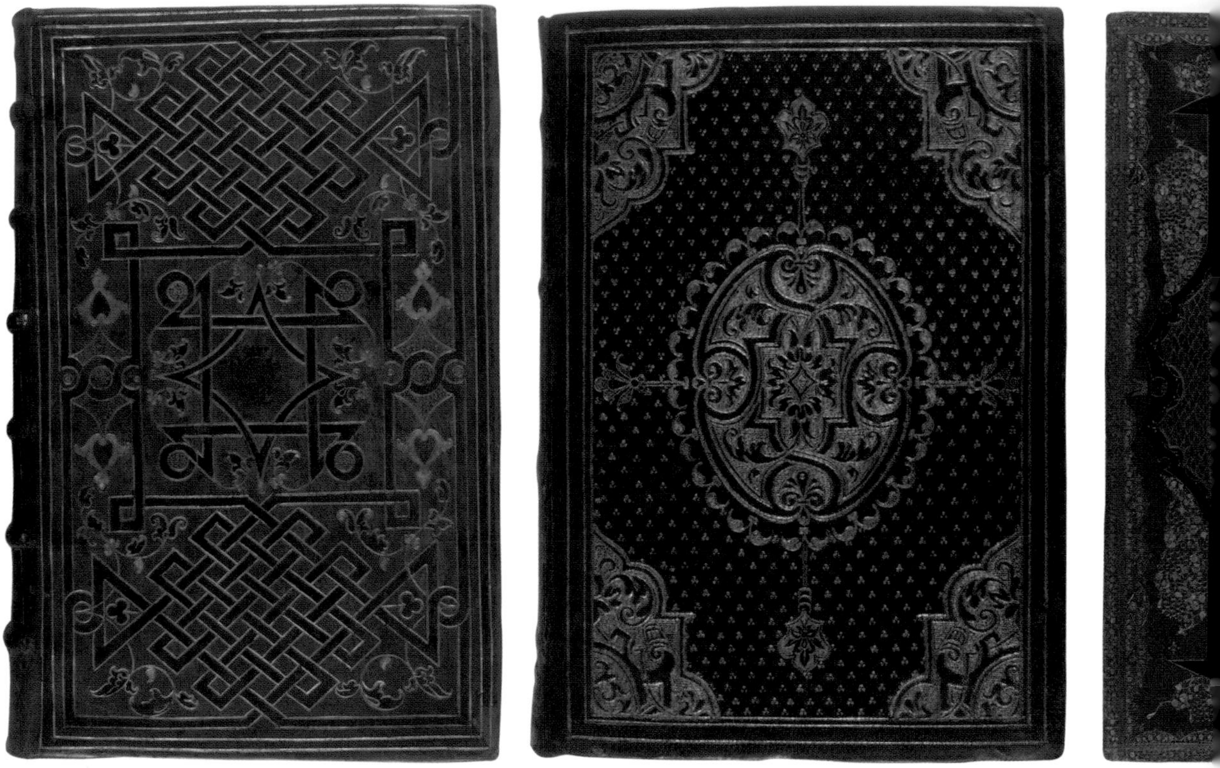

achievements of their age. For every binding like this that came into being, countless others were made that were less spectacular but which were nevertheless part of the historical fabric of their time.

Every binding tells a story, whether it is *de luxe* or humble. Binders offered their customers a choice, a spectrum of options from the simple to the elaborate, and the preferences they exercised can tell us something both about them and about their approach to the texts inside the books. These choices applied not only to external, decorative qualities but also to structural ones; there are various ways in which it is possible to cut corners in the sewing or other internal features of a handmade binding, leading to a cheaper but less hardwearing product. Early instructions from patrons to bookbinders are scarce, but where they do survive they often stress

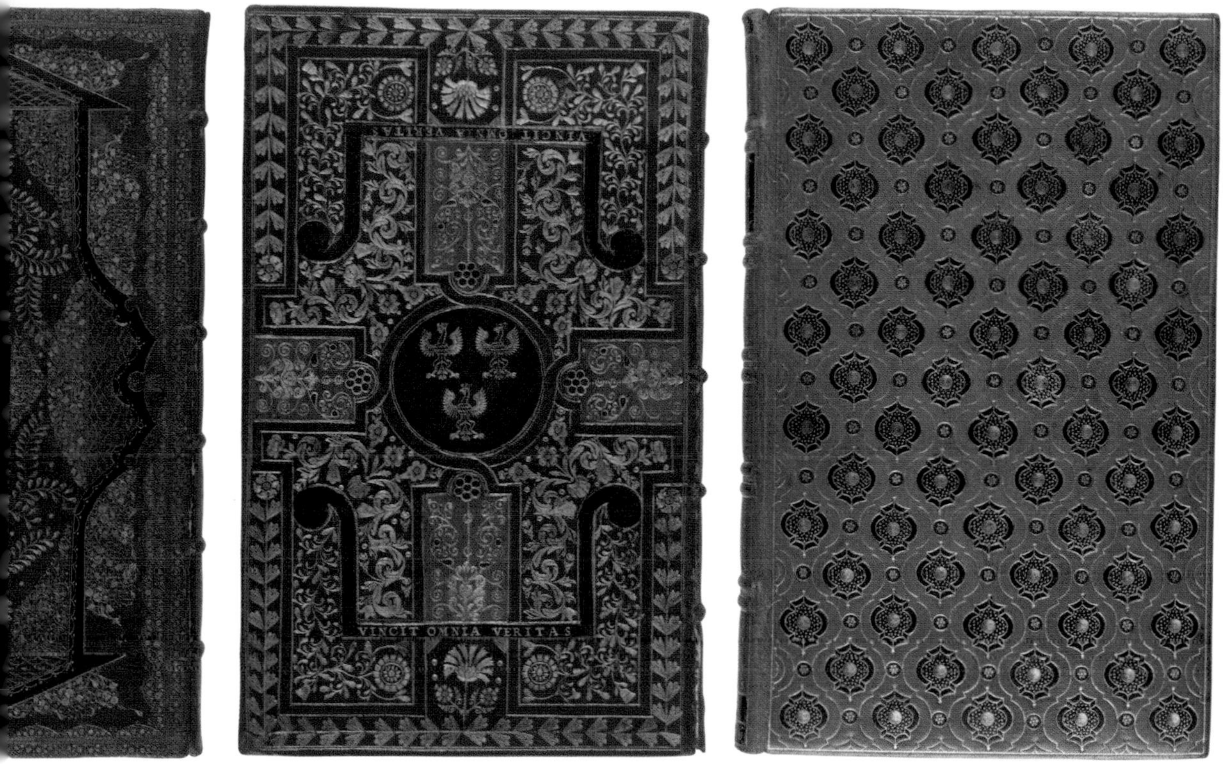

People have been using the outsides of books as a space for decoration for as long as they have been making them, as this selection of upmarket bindings from the 16th to the 18th century shows

the importance of sturdy sewing and good quality handiwork rather than handsome tooling.

Fancy bindings reveal owners who could afford to pay that bit extra, or perhaps people who wished to display their wealth or status on their bookshelves; or they may be covering books which were regarded as particularly important. Simpler bindings can be equally revealing of personal histories; many of the books owned by John Donne, when he was a struggling and impoverished poet, are bound in parchment wrappers rather than leather, the cheap (or softback) option of the time. Books have often been bound and rebound, or repaired, more than once during their history and those staging posts can indicate the changing regard for the texts inside. A book which has survived several centuries in pristine con-

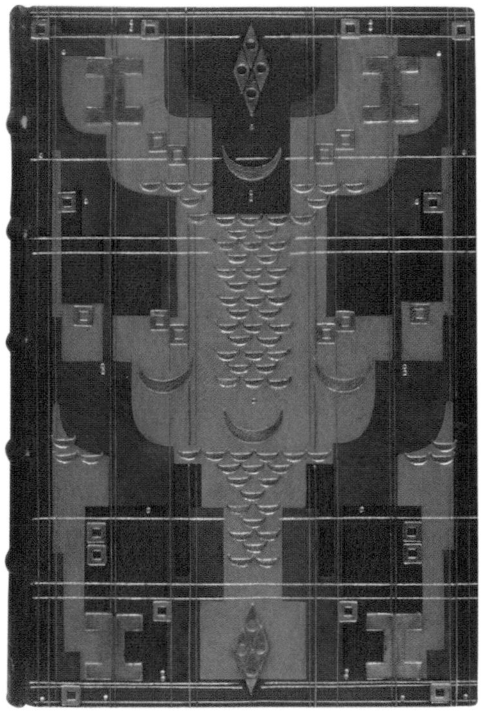

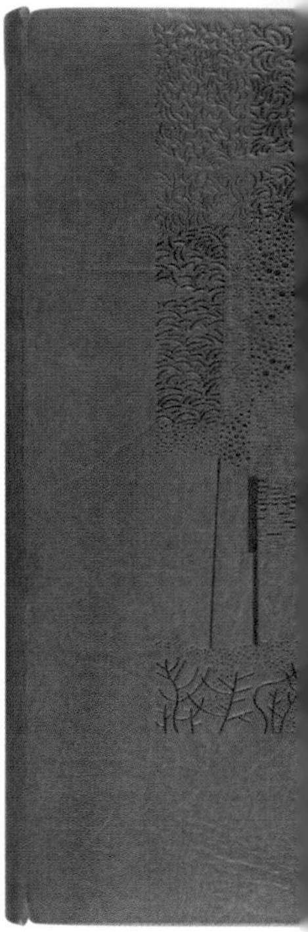

dition suggests a text which has not exactly been eagerly sought out. Many of the copies of Shakespeare's 1623 First Folio now found in libraries around the world are in top quality nineteenth-century bindings, reflecting the veneration in which that book then came to be held; the few copies (of more than 200 surviving) which retain contemporary bindings are mostly very plain. A seventeenth-century devotional text is much more likely to be found in a fine binding of its period than a literary one, in line with the values of that time, although we now consider literature to be far more important than theology.

A binding will not only carry these messages which we can interpret, but also more immediate information about where and when it was made. A wall of leather-bound books may at first glance look pretty uniform but although the basic materials and construction methods of bookbindings remained substantially unchanged

for many centuries, the decorative conventions underwent steady change from one generation to another, in line with the ever shifting more general currents of ornamental fashion. Just as sixteenth-century architecture or silverware are recognisably different from their eighteenth-century equivalents, so bookbindings are visually distinctive from one generation to another. This applies not only to handsomely decorated fine bindings, but also to much simpler ones; a sixpenny binding of 1600 is not the same as one of 1700, or even 1650. Unlike printers, bookbinders only rarely signed their work and we cannot often identify individual craftsmen; they worked within the stylistic conventions of their day and neither the binders, nor their customers, looked for individuality of design. What we can do, however, is place a particular binding within its time and place – we can recognise that it is English, or German, or French, and approximately when it was made – and also say

The tradition of making artistic and high quality bookbindings has continued throughout the 19th and 20th centuries, and has flourished in Britain since the middle of the 20th century under the aegis of the Designer Bookbinders movement

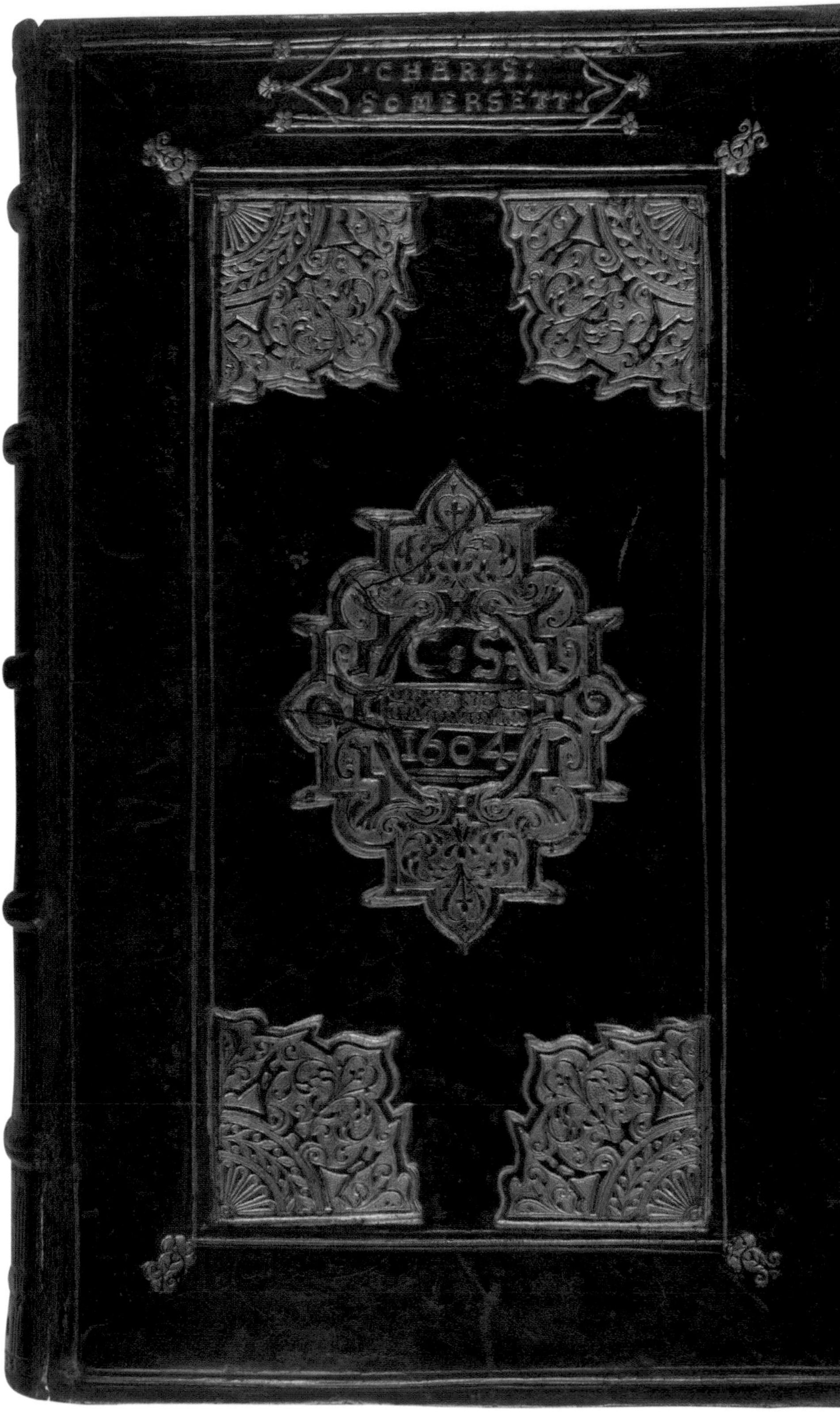
CHARLS:
SOMERSETT
C S
1604

While wealthy book owners could afford to have their bindings finely decorated, the less well-to-do had to accept something plainer. The book on the left was made in 1604 for Sir Charles Somerset, the one on the right was bought around the same time by the poet John Donne

Copies of Shakespeare's First Folio which retain contemporary bindings are typically very plainly and simply bound, like the Bodleian Library copy, (right) bound in Oxford in 1623. They are, however, more commonly found clothed in luxury bindings of the 19th and 20th centuries, reflecting the increased respect felt for the text in later times, and the tastes of the people who then owned them. The example shown here (opposite), from the Folger Shakespeare Library, is a 19th-century imitation of a binding in late 17th-century style

SHAKESPEARE
LONDON
1623

In the past, binders offered their customers more choice than we are used to today: these three books were all bound in the workshop of Daniel Boyse in Cambridge, around the same time in the early 17th century, to differing degrees of sophistication

whereabouts, within the range of options of its time, it sits.

Binders worked sometimes for individual book buyers, sometimes for booksellers. They sometimes produced quite distinctive bindings, and more often produced many bindings which looked very similar. This last point notwithstanding, the organisation of the book trade with its multiplicity of small workshops meant that any particular edition of a book – that set of 1000 copies of unbound sheets of a newly printed book mentioned earlier – would end up being put into a range of different bindings. Given that over time some copies would be bound again, the net result is that particular books come to survive in a wide variety of outer coverings. If you gather together twenty copies of a sixteenth-century book, or an eighteenth-century one, from different libraries and collections, the chances are that every one will have a different binding, with its own set of historical messages. Multiple copies of a twentieth-century book will probably be uniform as regards bindings (subject to wear and tear and the possible loss of the dust

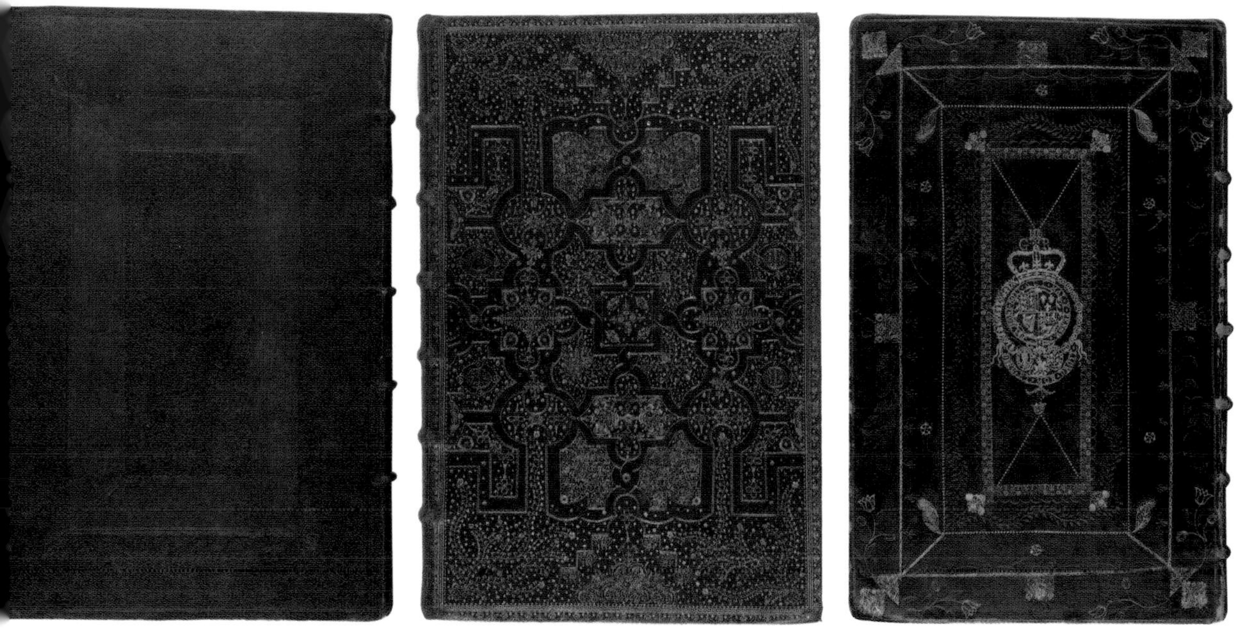

Three copies of the same late 17th-century book, all bound and sold around the same time, in bindings which look very different—the choice lay in how decorated (or otherwise) it was to be, and how much it would cost

jacket), but twenty copies of a nineteenth-century book are likely to show some variety. Until quite late in the century, books were still commonly issued in a range of binding choices, including different grades of quality and various colours and patterns of cloth.

GATHERING THE FRAGMENTS

A perhaps unexpected bonus of the historical bookbinding process is found in the use of fragments of older, discarded documentary materials. Despite an increasing exhortation to our consumer society to be less wasteful in discarding that which is reusable, we are very accustomed today to the idea that paper and packaging materials are plentiful, and that they can be used with a degree of abandon. Earlier generations did not have that luxury and the paper, boards and parchment which went into making bindings were relatively more expensive, and less expendable. In the sixteenth and seventeenth centuries particularly, when the

For much of the 19th century, after the introduction of edition binding in cloth, it remained common practice to offer new books in a variety of binding styles, as is clear from this advertisement from a book of 1881 (opposite). The first edition of Thomas Hardy's Poems of the Past and the Present *(1902) was issued simultaneously in a binding of green cloth, priced at 4s 6d, and in a superior option of cream cloth at 7s 6d*

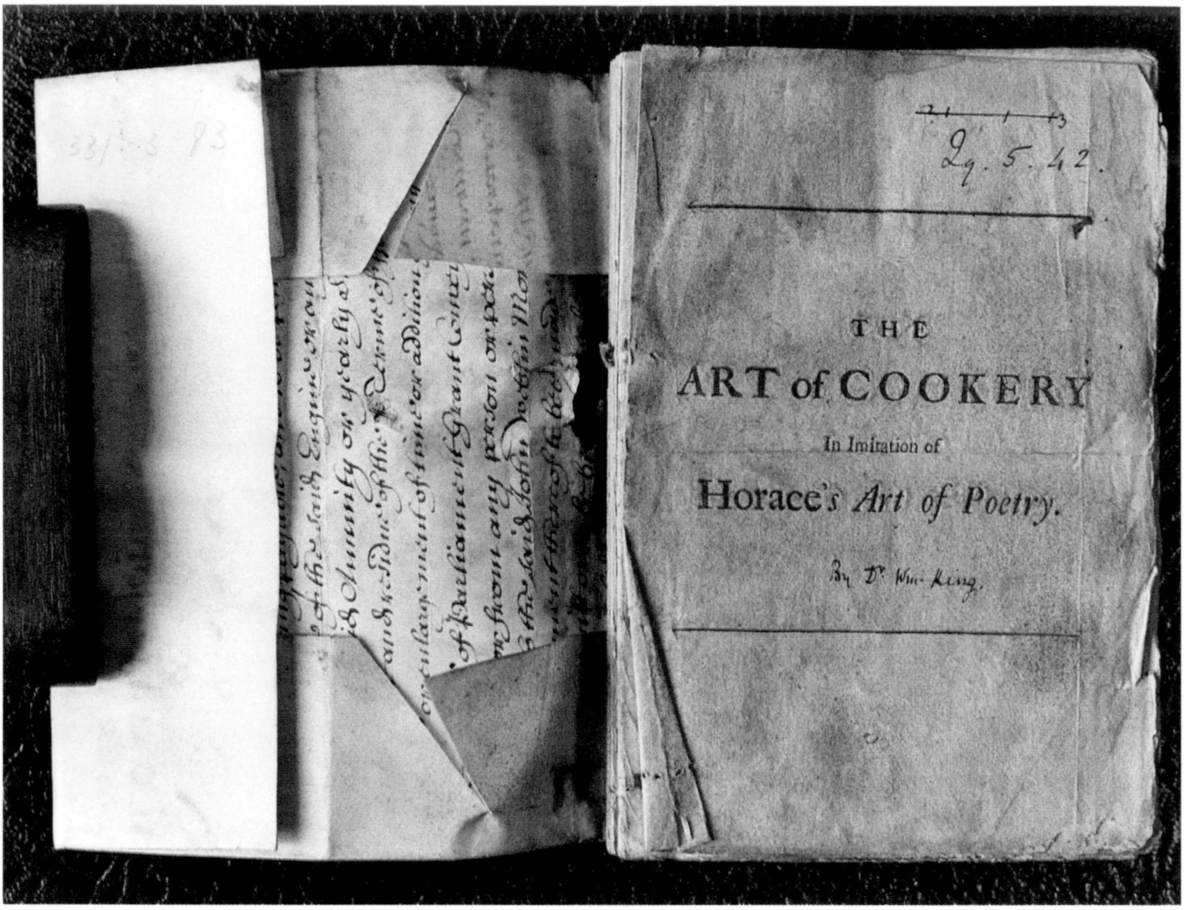

This early 18th-century pamphlet has been covered in a wrapper crudely cut from a contemporary legal deed

equation between rising book production and limited supplies of new materials made recycling economically sensible, bookbinders regularly quarried waste paper and parchment to put towards the construction of their bindings.

Such supplies were to be found in printing houses – discarded proof sheets, sheets damaged during printing, or sheets otherwise surplus to requirements – and even in a binder's own workshop, if he had old paper records of his business activities. They could be found in the offices of lawyers and others who had regular docu-

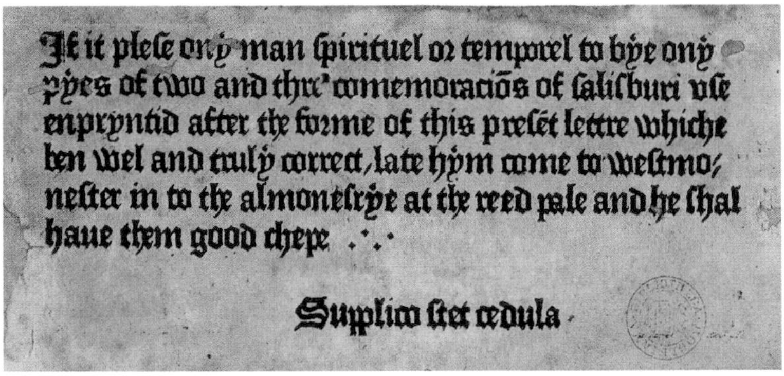

If it plese ony man spirituel or temporel to bye ony pyes of two and thre comemoraciõs of salisburi vse enpryntid after the forme of this presẽt lettre whiche ben wel and truly correct, late hym come to westmo/nester in to the almonesrye at the reed pale and he shal haue them good chepe.

Supplico stet cedula

This advertisement printed ca. 1477 by William Caxton, England's first printer, to announce his newly printed edition of a Church service book, is the earliest known printed English handbill. It survives today only because two copies were used as binders' waste, and thus preserved more by accident than design

mentary activities, and they could be found wherever people were discarding books and documents for which they had no further use. Just as medical or legal librarians today regularly weed their stock to throw away superseded editions, so book owners and library custodians in the past discarded texts which had become obsolete and could be replaced with more up-to-date material. The advent of printing led to considerable winnowing of old manuscript collections of books which became available in new versions, edited by contemporary scholars. This process was greatly accelerated by the political and religious upheavals of the sixteenth century, when the break with Rome in countries like England led to the deliberate destruction of countless books associated with Roman Catholic teaching or liturgy. Centres of learning like Oxford, with multiple old established libraries full of such works, became awash with discarded books, both manuscript and printed, which had become doctrinally unsound; a contemporary observer spoke of the quad of one of the Oxford colleges being full of the leaves of books, 'the wind blowing them into every corner'. Some of these dismembered books ended up as butter wrappers, pie cases, scarecrows, or were put to various other uses. Most of these paths led ultimately to complete destruction, but a small proportion of the total was rescued by bookbinders to use in a new generation of books.

Leaves from older books might be used as endleaves, as outer wrappers, or in more fragmentary form as spine linings, or cut into little strips to strengthen a book's hinges. They might also be compacted together to make a sheet of stiff card, which could be

BELOW & OVERLEAF

Fragments of earlier books can be found used, recycled, in a variety of ways. Cut up fragments of medieval manuscript books were commonly used in and around the 16th century to make endleaves (overleaf), or as strengthening strips in the spine hinges. Discarded leaves of parchment manuscripts were sometimes used to make the outer coverings of books

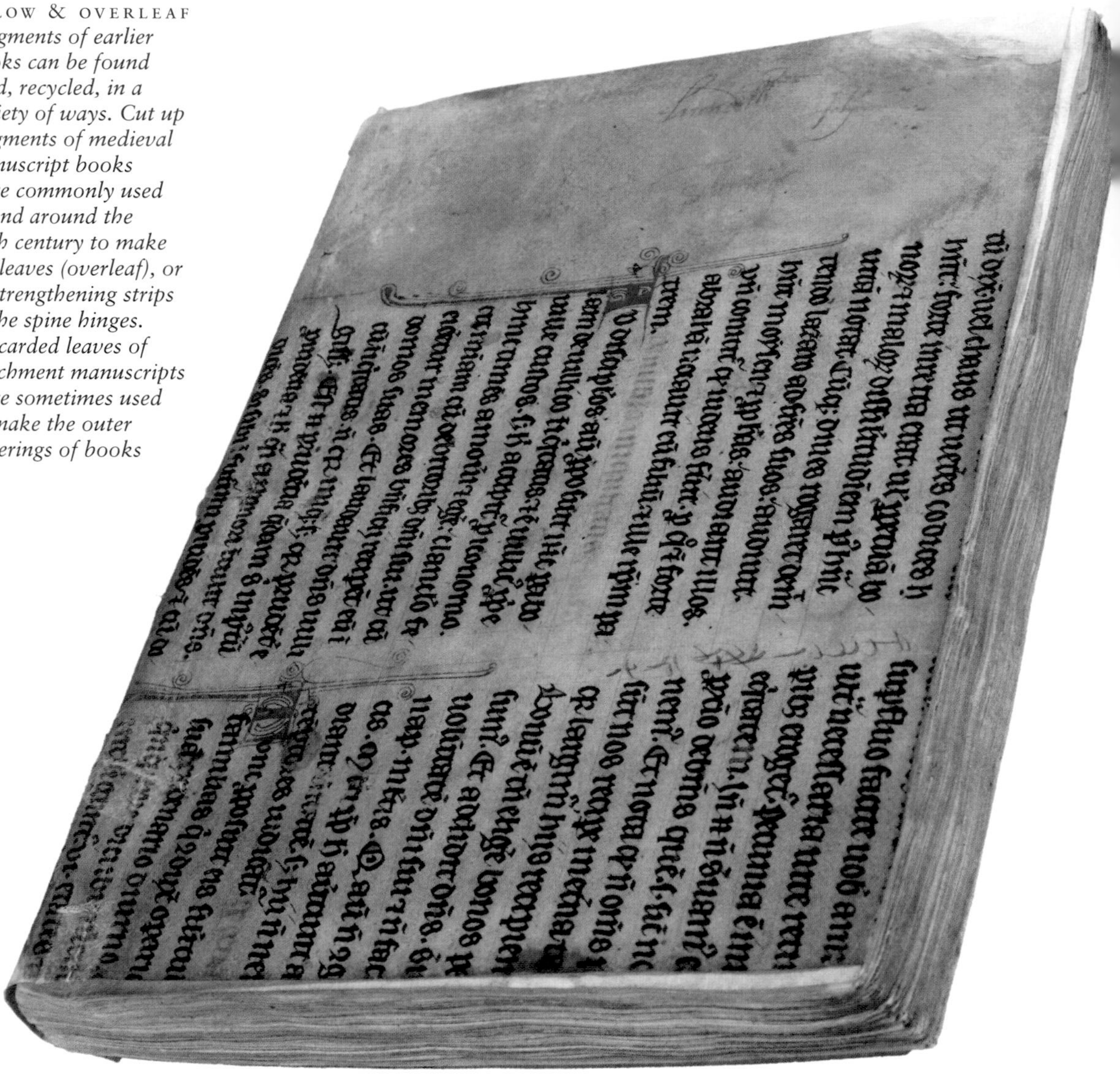

used as the boards of a book before being covered with leather; such sheets might contain forty or more separate leaves of printed waste, a potentially exciting find for bibliographical detectives. All kinds of things can be found as waste in bindings: fragments of Anglo-Saxon manuscripts, early business records, rare or unique printed materials, legal documents relating to otherwise unknown transactions. Numerous instances of works printed by William Caxton, England's first printer, are only known about today because scraps of the originals have been found recycled in bindings. Some early seventeenth-century bookseller's accounts discovered in a binding of the 1630s have a reference to 'Love's labours won', supporting the claims of some scholars that Shakespeare wrote a play of that title to complement *Love's labours lost*, although the text has never been found. Not all fragments are as significant as this, but it is not unusual to open a sixteenth-century book and be faced first of all with a piece of a twelfth- or thirteenth-century one. Towards the end of the sixteenth century, as the supply of unwanted manuscripts declined, printed waste from printers' shops or discarded printed books was increasingly used. Using material like this for endleaves became uncommon after the seventeenth century, but printed waste was regularly used for spine lining well into the nineteenth.

ABOVE
Spines were often lined with discarded fragments of printed material

Caseus dateue

Non nix, non argus. Methusale

Esau, aut Lazarus. Caseus ō bon

Optimus est caseus manibus quē dn

Caseus est uegnā nisi dixera ōra

Caseus insignis nō est dādus nisi dig

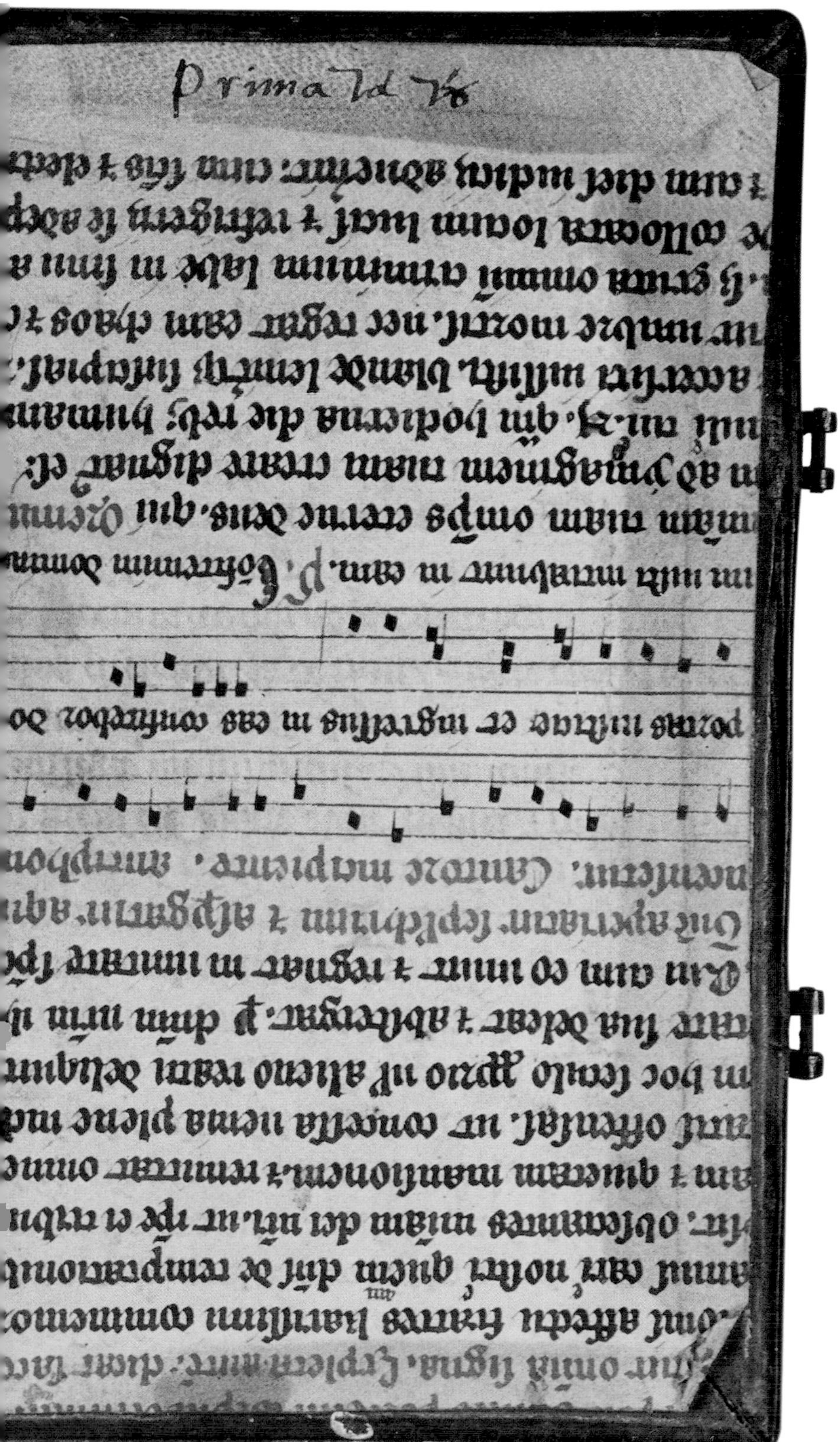

CHAPTER SIX

THE COLLECTIVE VALUE OF LIBRARIES

OPPOSITE
The King's Library, the collection of George III now in the British Library, which has been kept together since being given to the nation in 1823

OVERLEAF
The Bodleian Library, Oxford, in 1675, as engraved by David Loggan

The physical impact of books can be experienced collectively as well as individually; a library is more than the sum of the words it contains. Successful libraries, both old and new, combine functionality of access to resources with good working environments, to create a satisfying whole. Universities and public authorities continue to build libraries and extensions to libraries, despite the growing impact of offsite digital access, not only because bookstock continues to expand but also because people express a desire for libraries as workspaces and places to meet. Libraries offer a sense of connection with the past, and a connection with accumulated knowledge; people may remember the first day they visited their university library, or national library, impressed not only by the size and scale of the place but also by a feeling of privileged access to a major resource.

Libraries can be aesthetically rewarding places, beyond their value as quarries for information, as David Loggan recognised when he engraved his celebrated and much-reproduced late seventeenth-century views of the Bodleian Library, or as the *Illustrated London News* realised when it offered its readers interior views of the British Museum Library in 1851. The present-day production of colourful coffee-table books and calendars depicting great libraries of the world shows that this tradition lives on. The regular tread of tourists through picturesque historic libraries, like the chained library at Hereford or the Long Room at Trinity College, Dublin, is another example.

The focus of the preceding chapters has been very much on books at an individual level, looking at different ways in which they can bear witness to their past history, and yield up interesting messages about how they have been regarded and used. Historic libraries are full of such books but they are also, in aggregate, greater than the sum of their parts, as such a library which has

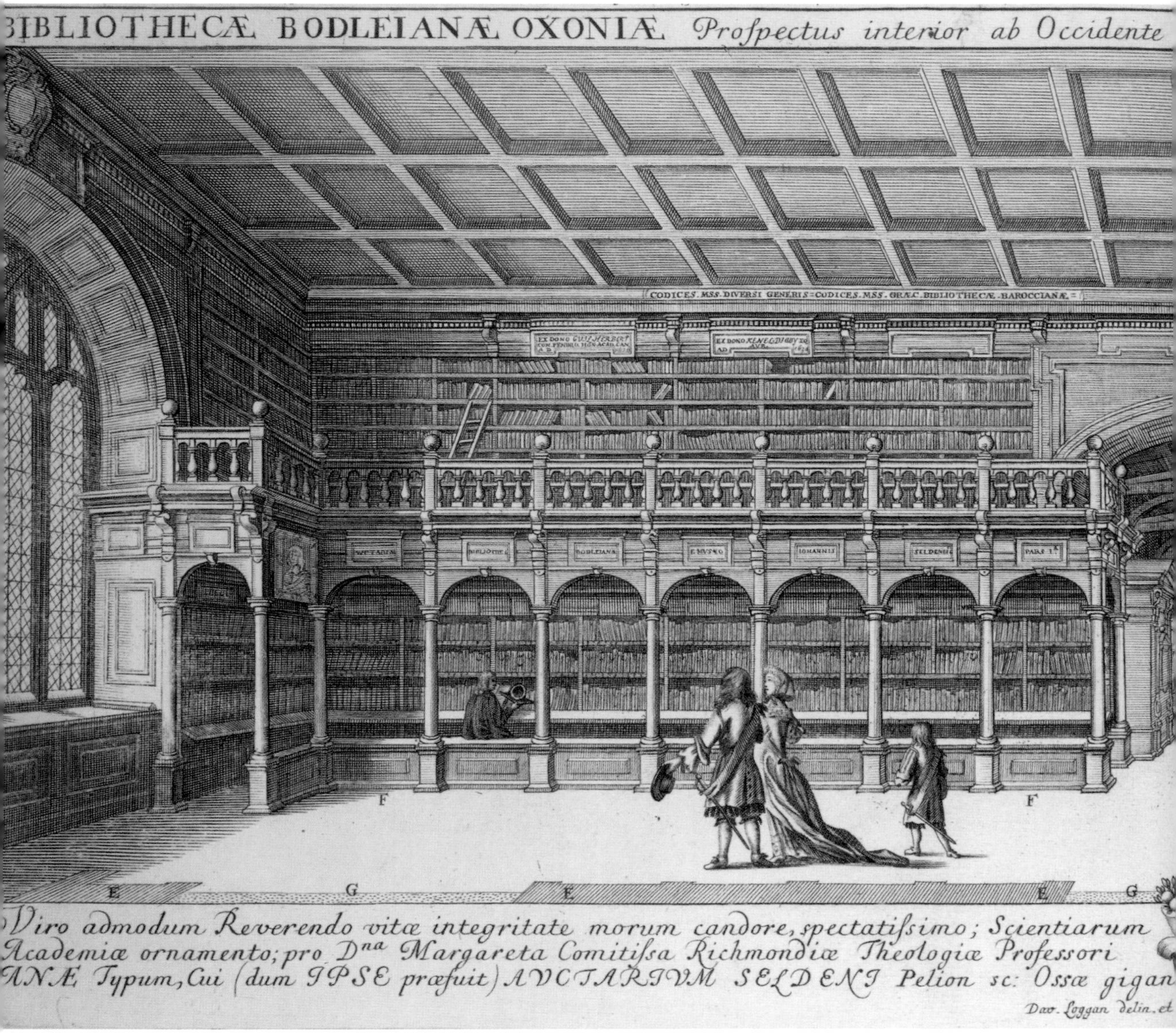
BIBLIOTHECÆ BODLEIANÆ OXONIÆ Prospectus interior ab Occidente
CODICES MSS DIVERSI GENERIS = CODICES MSS GRÆC BIBLIOTHECÆ BAROCCIANÆ
BODLEIANA
IOHANNIS
SELDENII
Viro admodum Reverendo vitæ integritate morum candore, spectatissimo; Scientiarum
Academiæ ornamento; pro Dna Margareta Comitissa Richmondiæ Theologiæ Professori
ANÆ Typum, Cui (dum IPSE præfuit) AUCTARIUM SELDENI Pelion sc: Ossæ gigan
Dav. Loggan delin. et

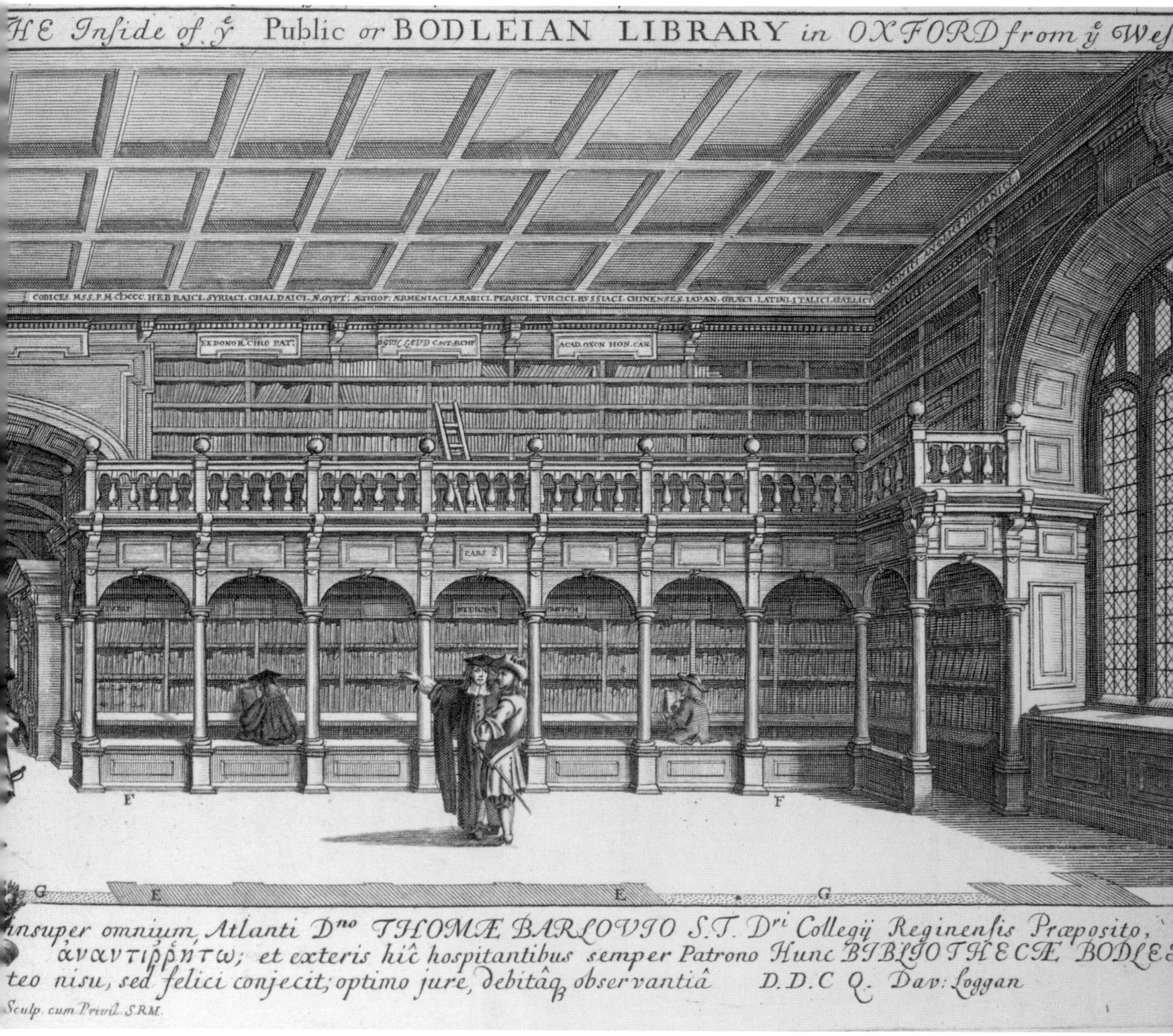
HE Inside of ye Public or BODLEIAN LIBRARY in OXFORD from ye Wes
CODICES MSS.P.M.CDCCC. HEBRAICI. SYRIACI. CHALDAICI. ÆGYPT. ÆTHIOP. ARMENIACI. ARABICI. PERSICI. TURCICI. RUSSIACI. CHINENSES. IAPAN. GRÆCI. LATINI. ITALICI. GALLICI
EX DONO R. CHRO PAT.
ACAD. OXON HON. CAN.
PARS 2
MEDICINA
F
F
G
E
E
G
nsuper omnium Atlanti Dno THOMÆ BARLOVIO S.T. Dri Collegij Reginensis Præposito,
ἀναντίρρητω; et exteris hîc hospitantibus semper Patrono Hunc BIBLIOTHECÆ BODLE
teo nisu, sed felici conjecit; optimo jure, debitâq observantiâ D.D.C Q. Dav: Loggan
Sculp. cum Privil. S.R.M.

The Arch Room of the British Museum Library in 1851, as reproduced in the Illustrated London News

been kept together captures an overview of individual or collective tastes and interests at different points in time. Knowing the contents of private and institutional libraries of the past allows us to compare them with other collections of their time, and to build up wider pictures of book ownership over the centuries, looking at average sizes, changing trends in language or subject, and in the place of origin of the books. We can see which books were popular and which were not; books have survived today in very uneven ways, and ones which are very rare today may once have

Samuel Pepys's library, which passed to Magdalene College, Cambridge after his death, preserves his personal collection of about 3,000 volumes in the bindings, bookcases and shelf arrangement of the owner's lifetime

been much more widely read than ones which have survived in relatively large quantities.

Samuel Pepys's celebrated collection, which is preserved intact in its original bookcases in Magdalene College, Cambridge, gives us a complete picture of the choices he made in building up his library of about 3,000 volumes, at his particular point in time in the late seventeenth century, and can be experienced or interpreted today at both an intellectual and an aesthetic level. Pepys (1633-1703) was an active bibliophile who delighted in the look of his books

as well as their contents, and had them bound so as to present a pleasing and uniform appearance. He often recorded the purchasing or reading of books in his diary, from which many of the boks on the shelves today can be identified.

The diocesan library founded by John Cosin, post-Restoration Bishop of Durham (1594-1672), stocked with his personal collection of five and a half thousand volumes, remains today in its purpose-designed library building between the Cathedral and the Castle in Durham. Inspired by contemporary French design (experienced by Cosin as an exile in Paris during the Interregnum), it was the first English library to be built with bookshelves around the room, departing from the traditional model of late medieval libraries with shelving jutting out from the walls. Its original bookcases still survive, decorated with painted roundels summarising the subject contents of each press; the illustrated book from which these pictures were copied also survives, with small paint splashes testifying to this use. The collection itself was accumulated throughout Cosin's life, including his time as a student and a don in Cambridge, as a pre-Civil War royalist cleric, as a continental fugitive during the 1650s and as a returned bishop. The physical characteristics of the books, as well as their textual contents, can be mapped onto the various stages of his career.

OPPOSITE
Cosin's Library in Durham, founded as a diocesan library by Bishop Cosin in 1669, preserves his donation in a purpose-designed library building, retaining the original shelving

The Victorian statesman William Gladstone (1809-98), four times Prime Minister, also acquired books throughout his life, from his time as an Eton schoolboy onwards. His collection of 32,000 volumes is another that survives today in a purpose-built library, at St Deiniol's in Hawarden, the result of Gladstone's personal bequest augmented by a public appeal after his death. Gladstone was a voracious reader and an active annotator, so his books capture not only his intellectual tastes but also his thoughts and reactions to what he read. The Library, designed as a residential facility with rooms and dining space built around the reading rooms, is also in its entirety an interesting chapter in the development of thinking about the use and value of libraries around the turn of the twentieth century.

Where personal libraries have not been preserved intact (the fate of the vast majority, over the centuries), it is sometimes possible to reconstruct their contents. Attempts have been made to estimate the libraries of Milton and Shakespeare, based on references in their writings, but this is a very inexact science. There are however many sale catalogues, or library catalogues made during owners' lifetimes, which make it possible to know what they had on their shelves. Personal collections of several hundred books were not unusual in the seventeenth century, or of thousands in the eighteenth and nineteenth. The library of the historian Edmund Gibbon, running to over 2000 books, has been pieced together from a variety of evidence, including his own catalogues (one of them written in the backs of playing cards), sale catalogues, and surviving volumes traced in libraries. Although few of the books can be traced today, we know that Sir Walter Ralegh had a library of about 500 volumes with him in the Tower of London, while he was imprisoned there in the early seventeenth century, because

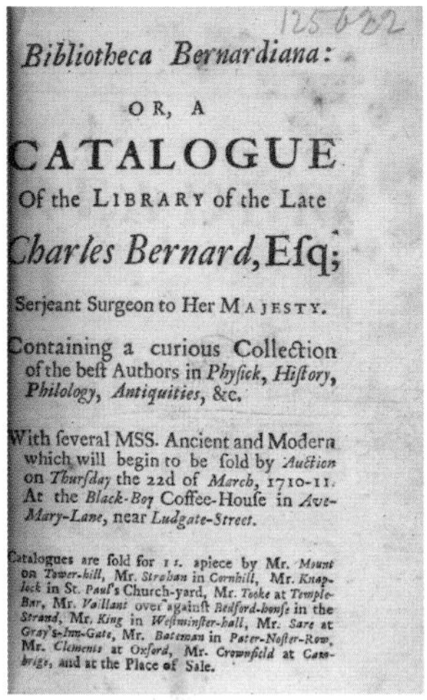
Bibliotheca Bernardiana:

OR, A

CATALOGUE

Of the LIBRARY of the Late

Charles Bernard, Esq;

Serjeant Surgeon to Her MAJESTY.

Containing a curious Collection of the best Authors in *Physick*, *History*, *Philology*, *Antiquities*, &c.

With several MSS. Ancient and Modern which will begin to be sold by *Auction* on *Thursday* the 22d of *March*, 1710-11. At the *Black-Boy* Coffee-House in *Ave-Mary-Lane*, near *Ludgate-Street*.

Catalogues are sold for 1 s. apiece by Mr. *Mount* on *Tower-hill*, Mr. *Strahan* in *Cornhill*, Mr. *Knaplock* in St. *Paul's* Church-yard, Mr. *Tooke* at *Temple-Bar*, Mr. *Vaillant* over against *Bedford-house* in the *Strand*, Mr. *King* in *Westminster-hall*, Mr. *Sare* at *Gray's-Inn-Gate*, Mr. *Bateman* in *Pater-Noster-Row*, Mr. *Clements* at *Oxford*, Mr. *Crownfield* at *Cambrige*, and at the Place of Sale.

a shelflist (which shows how he had them arranged on shelves) survives in a notebook now in the British Library. This collection formed his working library for writing his *History of the world*, first published in 1614 and much reprinted in the century that followed. The library of the surgeon Charles Bernard (1650-1711), with over 3000 volumes, is one of many known to us today from the sale catalogue produced shortly after his death, listing the titles in a classified sequence. Many institutional libraries include personal libraries swallowed in whole or in part over the centuries; the British Library, for example, was founded on a number of important private collections including those of Sir Hans Sloane, George Thomason, Joseph Banks, M.C. Cracherode and the manuscript collections of Sir Robert Cotton and Lord Robert Harley.

Cathedral libraries, town or parish libraries and the libraries of long-established universities and colleges, which have been built up over time, reveal the differing preferences and priorities of the educated sections of society over succeeding generations. The same applies to the family libraries preserved today in many country houses; although this part of our cultural heritage is much diminished by sales and dispersals, there are still many important collections which preserve the changing interests of owners over the centuries. These are not just the libraries of the rich and the aristocratic. There are splendid and spectacular collections like those of the Dukes of Devonshire at Chatsworth, or of the Earls of Leicester at Holkham Hall, but also more modest (though equally fascinating) family libraries like the one at Townend near Windermere in the Lake District. Here, the books accumulated by several generations of a yeoman family, far from cities or universities, still survive, together with original records of purchase through local auction sales. This collection can reveal all kinds of insights into the use, value and availability of books in rural Britain in the seventeenth and eighteenth centuries.

The introduction to a major exhibition of books from National Trust libraries mounted in 1999 recognised their value as collections – 'in their entirety the books that remain in the libraries offer a picture of intellectual and literary interests ... that is at least as vivid as the houses themselves', and drew attention to the importance of the bindings, bookplates and

OPPOSITE
St Deiniol's Library, at Hawarden in North Wales, was built at the beginning of the 20th century to house the library based on William Gladstone's collection

ABOVE
Early sale catalogues, of which many thousands survive, provide valuable knowledge about the contents of collections which are now dispersed

annotations that give individual significance to each book. It concluded by saying that 'the best and most important thing about books is that they can be read. That is how the country house library can still speak to us'. Perverse though it sounds, the time has come to turn this around; the primary value of these books as texts is debatable. Irrespective of the impact of facsimiles, digital or otherwise, the vast majority of the texts contained in country house libraries – and other kinds of small to medium historic libraries – are available in larger research collections whose contents are easily discoverable via increasingly joined up online catalogues. Few people will now journey to these libraries to read the books as texts, when they are accessible in a university or national library, or via a computer screen. They will, however, want to study and experience them for their unique qualities as historic artefacts, and as collections, within an integral, broader historic whole.

It is worth adding that books which have lived in cathedral, parish, college or country house libraries are far more likely to have preserved their layers of historic evidence than those which have suffered the ravages of generations of readers, and restorers, in large research libraries. Discarding original bindings, replacing

The library at Townend in the Lake District, built up by successive generations of yeomen farmers, shows us how books were acquired and used by people far away from the traditional centres of learning and the book trade

endleaves, removing fragments, washing away or cropping off inscriptions and marginal notes are all processes which have been carried out with ruthless efficiency (and the best of intentions) by previous generations of library custodians, whose primary concern has been to keep the books in a fit state to be read. Conservators are now much more aware of the importance of preserving original evidence but a great deal has disappeared for ever. Rare (and fortunate) indeed is the historic collection, of any kind, which has not been subjected to some extent to these programmes of rebacking, rebinding, or repairing but smaller historic libraries are more likely to have been spared the worst. A seventeenth-century book called up from the stacks of a major research library is quite likely to be in a twentieth-century binding, which may in turn have replaced a nineteenth-century one, and its current physical state may have no clues at all about earlier layers of evidence which have been completely lost. The same book in a country house library will probably be in a contemporary binding, in a condition which gets us close to what it looked and felt like on the day it was bought, and will testify to the ways in which it has or has not been used and regarded during succeeding generations.

BY:
The Book of Nails
Floating Concrete Octopus
1992

CHAPTER SEVEN

VALUES FOR THE FUTURE

OPPOSITE
An image for the future? The Book of Nails, *a piece of book art made by the artists' collective Floating Concrete Octopus, 1992*

OVERLEAF
Literature saving the past from destruction by Time, by Louis du Guernier, ca.1700

The essential theme of this book – that books may be interesting, historically significant objects, above and beyond their textual content – is a worthy thesis in its own right, but it is a particularly important one at a time when the world of books is undergoing the major changes outlined in Chapter I. The fast moving developments which new technology is bringing about promise to transform the way we access texts. It is easy to foresee a future in which books have ceased to be the primary medium for transmitting ideas and information; in some areas, that time is already here. To take a negative view of these developments is not only ostrich-like but also quite wrong-headed in failing to grasp the opportunities and benefits which electronic communication can bring. The coming changes will affect not only the ways in which we transmit and read the kind of information which was traditionally contained in books, but also our whole framework of values around them. They will affect our relationships with books individually, and collectively in libraries. There will be choices to be made over the preservation of our existing printed heritage: what is worth saving, and why, if texts are readily available in other ways? What is it about a book that makes it worth cataloguing and storing, or makes it worth adding to a private or institutional collection?

Many libraries exist not only to provide access to content, but also to look after that content for the future; different libraries put varying degrees of emphasis on these themes, depending on their particular missions. All over the world, they currently preserve a vital part of our literary and cultural heritage as books on shelves. This long-respected role of libraries is nicely summarised iconographically in an etching by Louis du Guernier, made around 1700, which represents Literature saving the past from destruction by Time; her cherubs store away documents on shelves to preserve them for future generations. Once new texts normally circulate

L. du Guernier sculp.

Protesters against the disposal of material from New York Public Library towards the end of the 20th century likened it to military tactics during the Vietnam War

electronically, and the printed heritage is largely accessible via digital surrogacy, the preservation of that heritage will be harder to champion. Books, in the popular imagination, and in the minds of those who fund libraries, will be in danger of being regarded merely as an obsolete technology of questionable long-term value.

We might reflect, here, on the changes which took place after the last great breakthrough in the technology of textual communication, following the invention of printing. Countless medieval manuscripts were destroyed in the sixteenth century once the new process was established and accepted, and older books came to be perceived as textually, philosophically and physically superseded. The Reformation was a period of well attested activity in the winnowing of libraries but it is actually only a peak in a graph which has always registered activity; there is nothing unusual about libraries or private owners discarding books, and they have been doing so for centuries. Most libraries need to have some kind of collection management policy in place to allow for the deaccessioning of books which have become superseded, like out-of-date textbooks or reference books, or books which no longer fit with their mission and purpose. A degree of recycling of ownership is arguably a good thing for books, especially if we are interested in the historical veneers which different custodians create.

The emptying out of library shelves is nevertheless a topic which stimulates heat and debate. One of the trends in library history during the last hundred years or so has been a great shift of books from private to institutional ownership, as academic and major publicly-funded libraries have actively developed broad and deep collections, and the prospect of undoing all that has typically rung alarm bells. The sale of a small number of incunabula and other valuable books from the John Rylands Library in Manchester in the late 1980s, to raise funds to help develop the Library's activities, created a degree of excitement in the national press, and library sales like this continue to attract attention when they are detected. The growing trend towards discarding more general stock from public and academic libraries, as electronic resources become increasingly used instead of books, can also generate headlines.

What are the grounds for objection? In early twenty-first century Britain, public libraries are widely felt to be in decline, with an

"It became necessary to destroy the town in order to save it."

- attributed to an American officer firing on Ben Tre, Vietnam, February 8, 1968.

Beginning in 1978, the New York Public Library trashed these collections along with 100,000 other pamphlets. They are, lamentably, still saving their town.

A melancholy greeting for the holiday season, A.D. MCMXCVII, from Michael Zinman.

Libraries dum

A rush to liberate space for e-learnin suites is blamed for disposal of print material. **Rebecca Attwood** report

Universities dispose of more than 1.8 million books and journals a year, according to official figures.

Statistics obtained by *The Times Higher* show that 36 institutions got rid of more books and printed volumes than they acquired. In 2005-06, ten universities disposed of more than 40,000 items. Dundee University disposed of 100,035 items and acquired 18,067 hard-copy texts in the year. Bangor University withdrew 55,500 items from reader use, Ulster University withdrew 50,493, and Imperial College London 48,911,

ety of College, National, and University Libraries (Sconul).

With an increase in the use of online resources and with students demanding virtual learning environments and more study space, the number of books removed from university libraries is on the increase. In 1997, the average number was just over 7,000 per institute, compared with

Toby Bainton, secretar Sconul, said researchers reg printed resources as less than electronic ones. "The av number of e-books availabl library has risen by more th per cent since last year and than half of serials acquire now in electronic form," he s

But others are not convi "These national figures

intertwined downward spiral of reduced budgets, diminishing user numbers and the de-professionalising of the services. The relatively low proportion of their spend on putting books on shelves (as opposed to investing in new technology, other media and making different use of space) is much commented on. Battle lines have been drawn between those who argue for radical reinvention of such libraries to meet changed social trends, and those who think their decline is closely linked to the growing failure to buy enough books. The issues were prefigured in the debate generated by Bill West's 1991 book *The strange rise of semi-literate England*, when he took public libraries to task for the dispersal of collections, often acquired or bequeathed in earlier generations but now re-

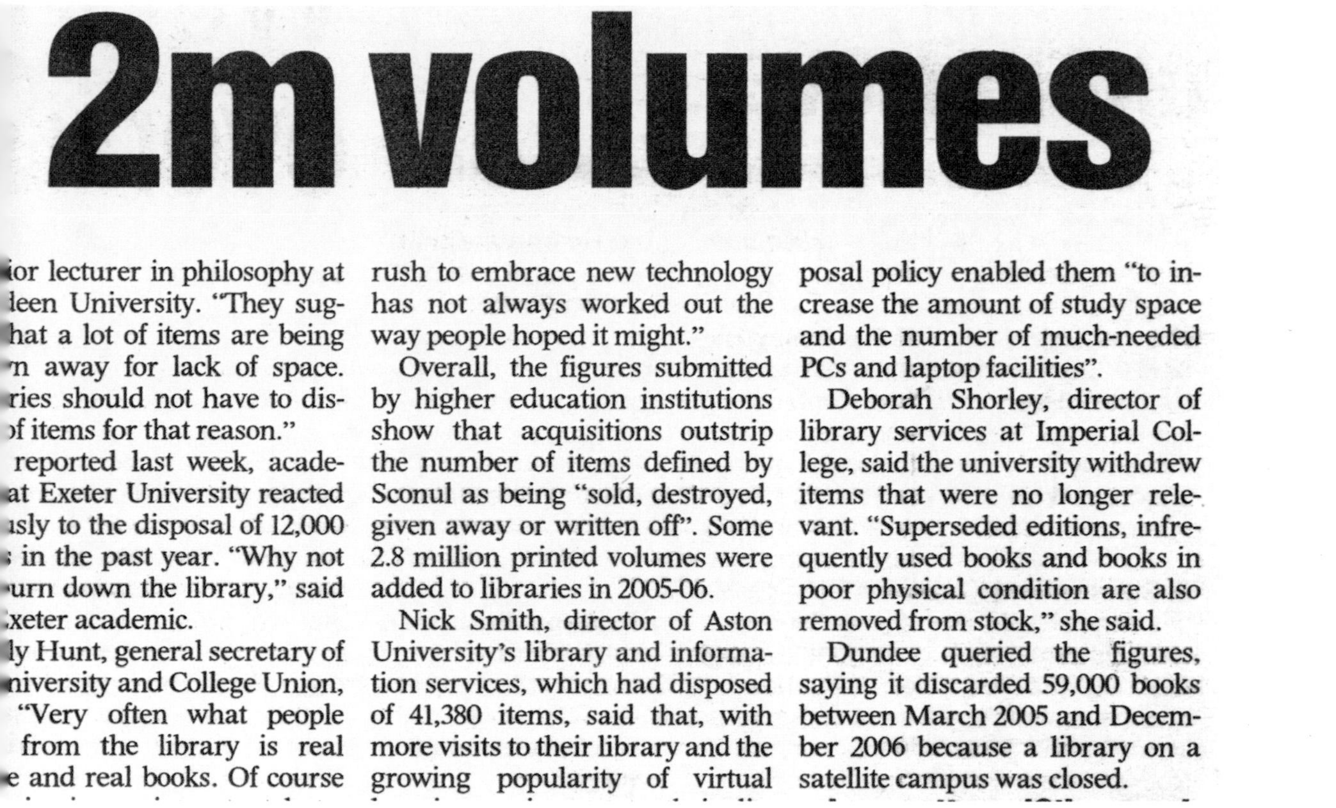

2m volumes

ior lecturer in philosophy at leen University. "They sug-hat a lot of items are being 'n away for lack of space. ries should not have to dis-of items for that reason."

reported last week, acade-at Exeter University reacted ısly to the disposal of 12,000 ; in the past year. "Why not ·urn down the library," said ;xeter academic.

ly Hunt, general secretary of niversity and College Union, "Very often what people from the library is real e and real books. Of course

rush to embrace new technology has not always worked out the way people hoped it might."

Overall, the figures submitted by higher education institutions show that acquisitions outstrip the number of items defined by Sconul as being "sold, destroyed, given away or written off". Some 2.8 million printed volumes were added to libraries in 2005-06.

Nick Smith, director of Aston University's library and information services, which had disposed of 41,380 items, said that, with more visits to their library and the growing popularity of virtual

posal policy enabled them "to increase the amount of study space and the number of much-needed PCs and laptop facilities".

Deborah Shorley, director of library services at Imperial College, said the university withdrew items that were no longer relevant. "Superseded editions, infrequently used books and books in poor physical condition are also removed from stock," she said.

Dundee queried the figures, saying it discarded 59,000 books between March 2005 and December 2006 because a library on a satellite campus was closed.

The growing takeup of electronic resources for teaching and research will inevitably increase the pressure on libraries to liberate expensive space used for the storage of physical volumes

garded with bafflement or distaste by custodians and audiences whose cultural values have changed. His criticisms were essentially focused around the importance of retaining good books whose textual value should be better respected, and which people ought to be wanting to read. This is clearly unrealistic: the evolving behaviour patterns of recent decades, in a society with widened access to higher education and multimedia communications, and more money to buy books rather than borrow them, is an inevitable driver of change. Quite what the public library sector has lost in terms of interesting collections formed by previous generations, and historic evidence of the kind described in this book, is another matter which would merit separate attention, although it rarely features in the ongoing debates about the nature and purpose of public libraries.

More recently, Nicholson Baker stirred up some excitement with his *Double fold* (2001), an extended polemic against research libraries in America and Britain, for replacing runs of newspapers with microfilm copies and discarding the originals. Baker's extreme and one-sided position, dismissing those who have to manage limited resources as 'cost-sphinctering coneheads' with little attempt to understand the difficulties they face, weakens his case but his discovery that many newspapers are simply no longer available within the library system other than as surrogates demonstrates a genuine collective failure. Where and when is it right to draw the line, and why? Baker argued that 'a great research library must keep its duplicates, even its triplicates, for a number of reasons, the most basic ones being that books become worn with use, lost, stolen, or misshelved'. If we reach the point at which books – i.e. texts – are primarily stored and circulated electronically, and the world has confidence in the permanence of the electronic media, these arguments will become irrelevant. Others have made the more persuasive point that understanding the history of communication via newspapers involves their physical form as well as the words on their pages, and that surrogates are not necessarily equals.

Barring some kind of natural or man-made disaster which renders international computer networking, and the electricity needed to power it, impossible, it seems inevitable that mass digitization of the printed heritage will gather momentum, and the value of books will come under closer questioning as time passes. In which case, what are the criteria that should be applied to decide whether or not a book is a valuable object worthy of preservation? The extent to which it possesses interesting characteristics of its own, which are not replicated in whatever surrogate or alternative is proposed, is surely a vital consideration. Printed books, unlike archives, are by their very nature not meant to be unique; mass replication of an identical original was at the heart of Gutenberg's invention. This book should at the very least have demonstrated that things are not quite that simple, and that there are various ways in which books may possess unique qualities as a result of the way they were made, or the historic evidence they have accumulated. In assessing the value of a book, we should focus not solely on its text but also on the other things it has to offer researchers.

Highlighting the interest of books beyond their texts is important not only in order to inspire the present generation to look at books in a wider way, but also to encourage the development of a groundwork of cultural values which will guard against the taking of bad decisions in the future. As books become history, let us recognise that this is not just history as a synonym for quaint but obsolescent, but may be history in the sense of unique artefacts within the fabric of cultural heritage. The aim of this particular book is to stimulate ideas, broaden horizons, and raise awareness of the multifaceted interest of books. Reader, write your thoughts in the margins of this copy – if it is yours to write in - and turn it into a unique object for posterity.

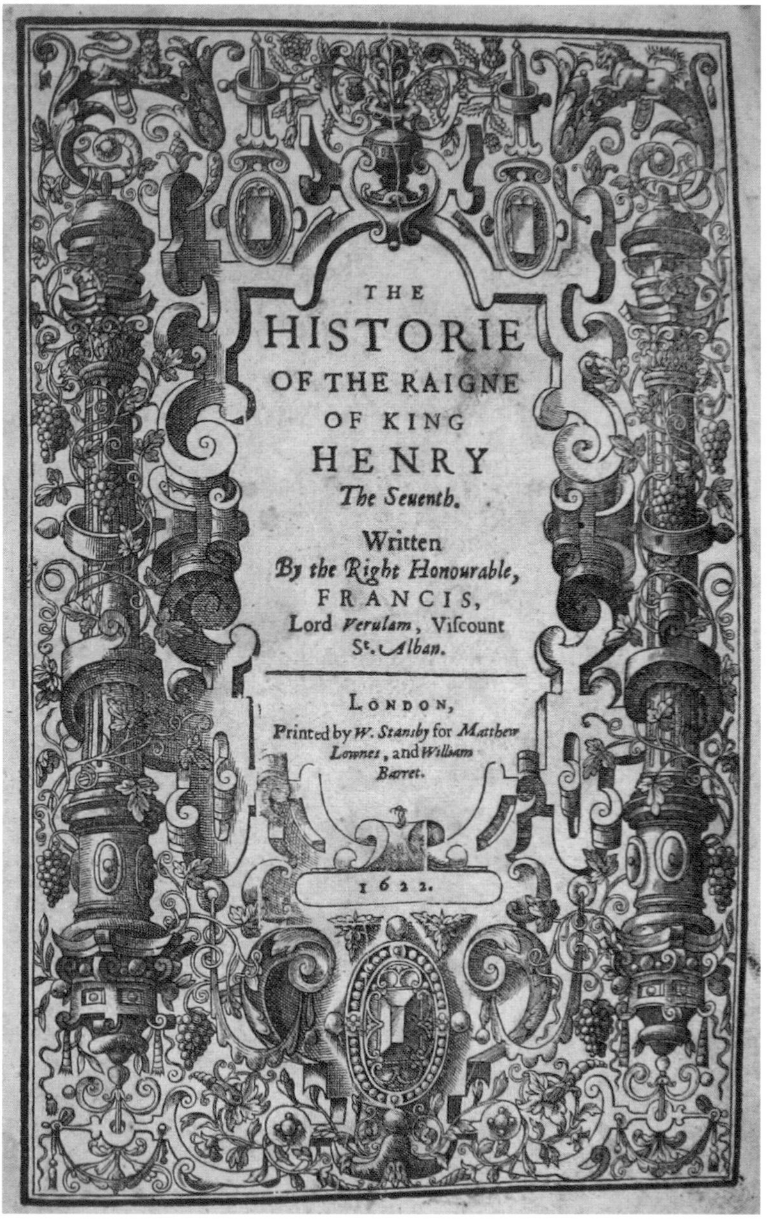

THE
HISTORIE
OF THE RAIGNE
OF KING
HENRY
The Seuenth.

Written
By the Right Honourable,
FRANCIS,
Lord *Verulam*, Viſcount
S^t. *Alban.*

LONDON,
Printed by *W. Stansby* for *Matthew Lownes*, and *William Barret.*

1622.

Francis Bacon (1561-1626) is most commonly remembered for his philosophical and scientific writings, and as someone who helped to lay the foundations for the flowering of scientific discoveries in later 17th-century England. He also had an important, if turbulent, political career which ended in impeachment in 1621 for his involvement with the granting of monopolies. His Historie of the Raigne of King Henry VII *was one of the first works to come from his later years of enforced retirement, and was written partly in the hope of effecting a rapprochement with James I. It was well received by his contemporaries and has since been regarded as a valuable example of the development of English historiography in the early 17th century*

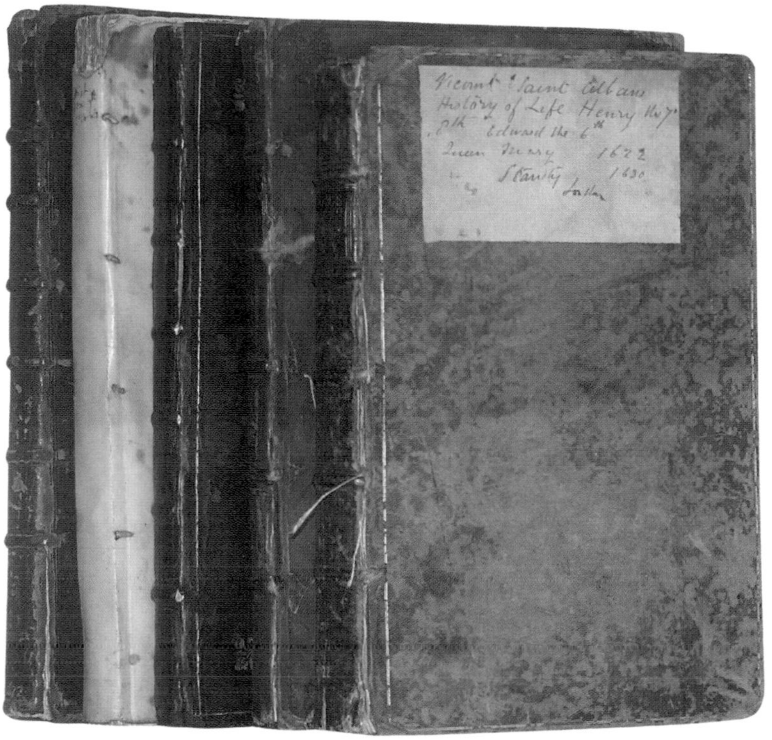

VARIETY BETWEEN COPIES

A CASE STUDY

Much of this book has been devoted to setting out the various ways in which the historical evidence to be found in books, beyond the words on the pages, distinguishes particular copies and provides information about the ways in which they have been used and regarded. By way of example, here are five copies of the same book – Francis Bacon's account of the reign of Henry VII, published in 1622 – with their individual histories and differentiating features.

Copy 1 is bound in a contemporary plain binding of calf leather over pasteboards, undecorated save for simple blind lines round the border – this was the standard option of the time for a solid binding, something meant to last, but without unnecessary frills

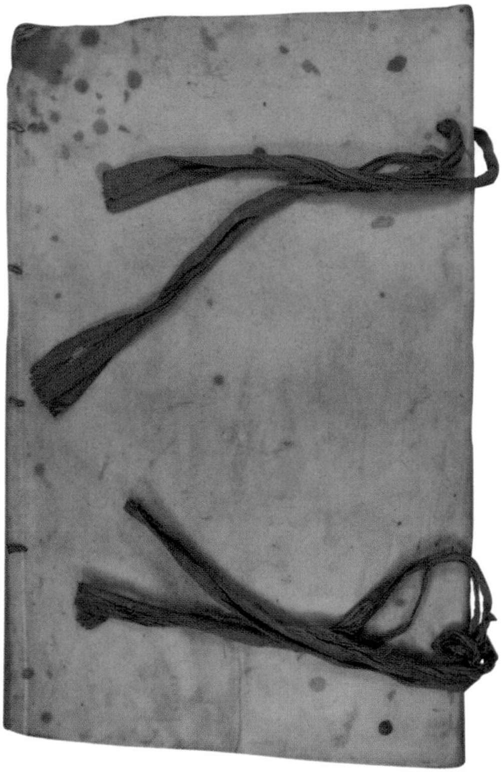

Copy 2 is bound in contemporary undecorated limp vellum, a cheaper option than leather over boards. By way of analogy with modern binding styles, this is the paperback option for the early 17th century

Copy 3 is also contemporary, but is a much more upmarket binding with a gilt-tooled centrepiece and other gilt decoration on calf leather. The first owner of this book – probably the man who inscribed the titlepage – wanted something more handsome (and expensive) than the kind of binding represented by copy 1

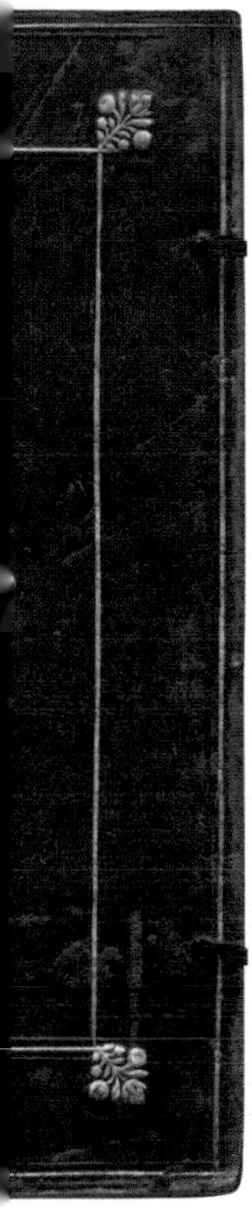

Copy 4 has a blind-tooled calf binding whose decorative style shows that it dates from the late 17th or early 18th century. An owner of that time chose to have it rebound; internal evidence suggests that it originally lacked a solid binding (see next page)

Copy 5 is also in a later binding, from the middle or second half of the 18th century, of sheep leather over boards (a cheaper option than calf). It is bound up with another book, Francis Godwin's Annales of England *(1630), a logical adjunct to Bacon's book as it covers English history from the reign of Henry VIII though to Mary. The front cover has a paper label stuck on, noting the contents of the volume in an 18th-century hand*

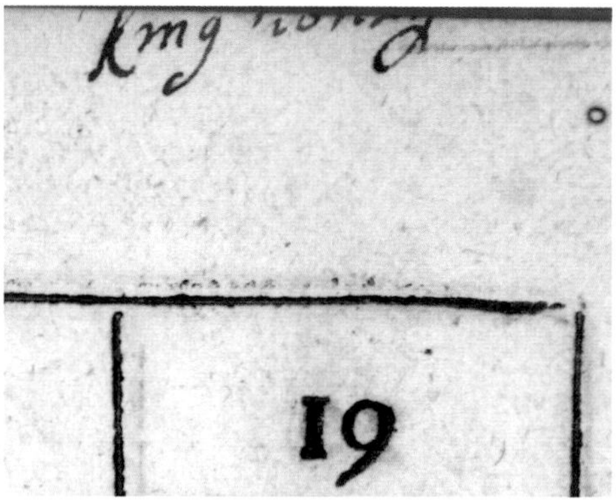

The fact that copy 5 (now in an 18th-century binding) had an earlier existence in a different binding can be seen from the cropping of early manuscript notes in some of the margins – the 18th-century binder trimmed the edges down further, in line with standard practice

The binding of copy 3 made use of small fragments from a contemporary discarded manuscript, on parchment, to strengthen the spine hinges; small stubs are visible between the flyleaves and the textblock

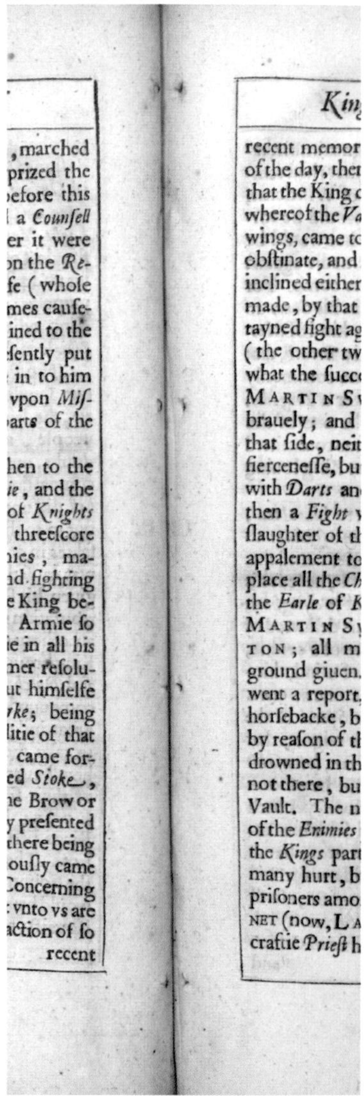

The inner margins of copy 4, also in a non-contemporary binding, provide evidence of the form in which it was originally used. These holes at intervals down the spine edge, which run through the book, show that it was first held together in a temporary binding, perhaps with paper or vellum covers, and stab-stitched rather than properly sewn and bound

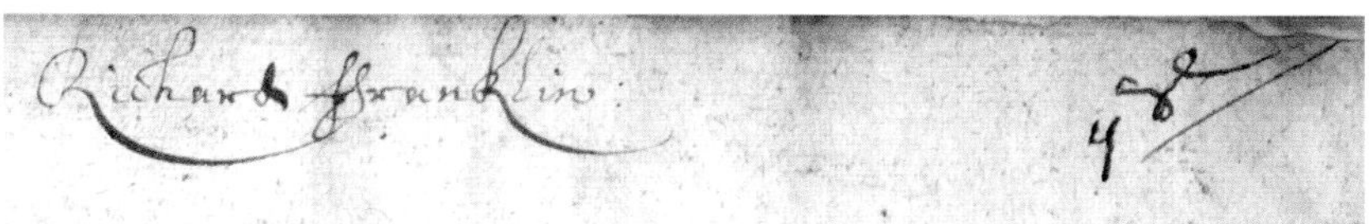

Copy 3 has on its pastedown the bookplate of Viscount Birkenhead (Frederick Smith, 1872-1930, lawyer and statesman; Lord Chancellor 1919-22, Secretary of State for India 1924-28). On the facing flyleaf a 17th-century owner, Richard Franklin, has written his name and the price he paid for the book (4 shillings); his [wife?] Marie added her name and the date 1636 on the back pastedown

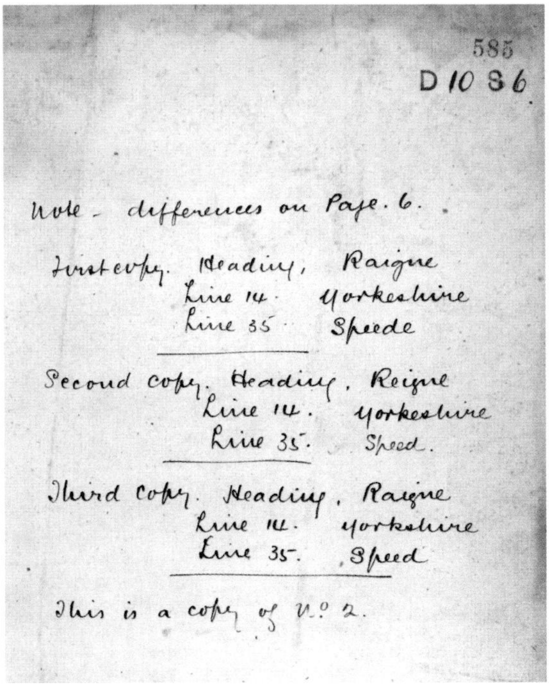
585
D 10 S 6

Note - differences on Page. 6.

First copy. Heading, Raigne
Line 14. Yorkeshire
Line 35 Speede

Second copy. Heading, Reigne
Line 14. Yorkeshire
Line 35. Speed.

Third copy. Heading, Raigne
Line 14. Yorkshire
Line 35. Speed

This is a copy of No 2.

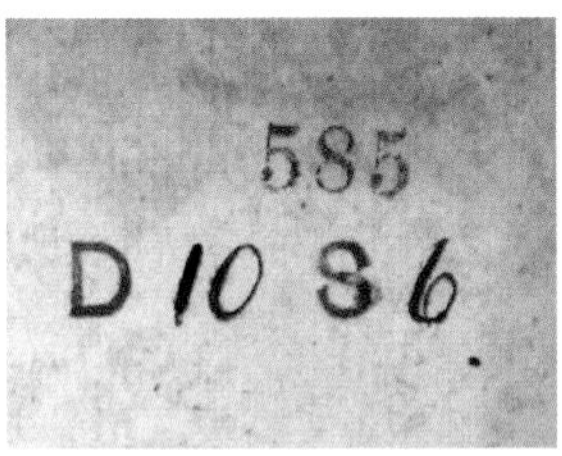
585
D 10 S 6

Copy 1 was previously in the collection of Sir Edwin Durning-Lawrence (1837-1914), MP and ardent champion of the cause to prove that Bacon wrote Shakespeare's plays. The flyleaf is inscribed with his distinctive library shelfmark and also has notes in his hand showing that he had carefully collated his several copies of the book, noting variations in the printing

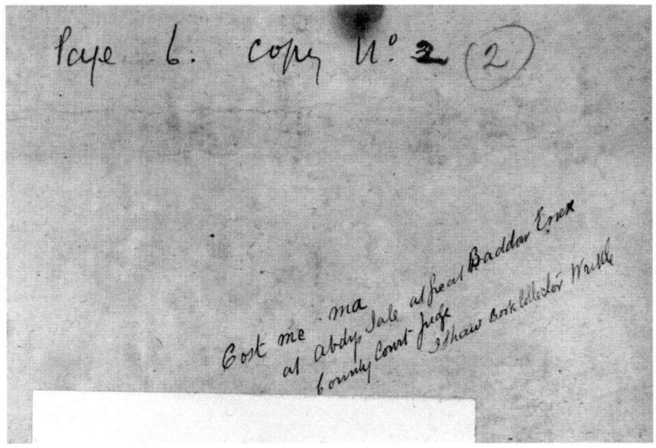
Page 6. copy No 2 (2)

Cost me ma
at Abdy sale at Great Baddow Essex
County Court Judge
J Shaw book collector Writtle

Copy 5 also belonged to Durning-Lawrence but its immediately preceding pedigree can be traced from a note on the flyleaf, written ca.1900, 'Cost me ma at Abdys sale at Great Baddow Essex ... J Shaw book collector Writtle'. Abdy is John Thomas Abdy (1822-99), Regius Professor of Civil Law at Cambridge. 'ma' is Shaw's private code; he evidently wanted to keep the actual price secret

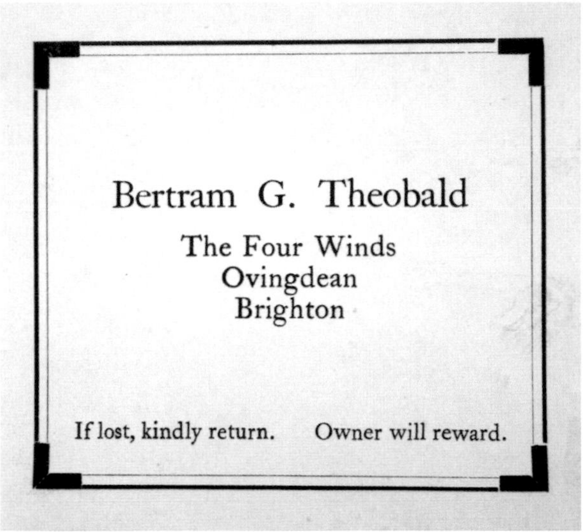

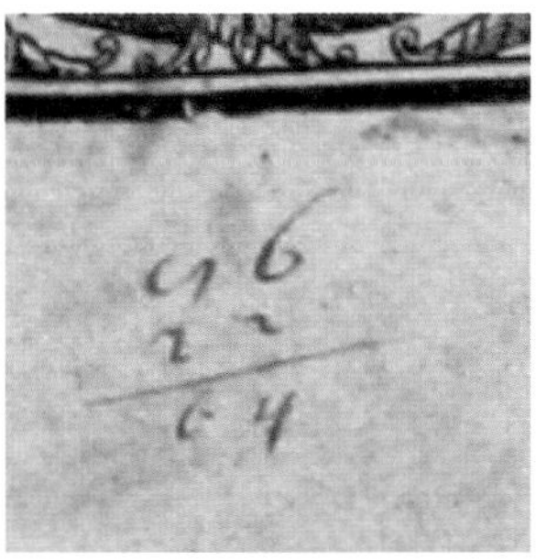

The bookplate on the front pastedown of copy 4 shows that it belonged to Bertram Theobald (1871-1940), another enthusiast for the theory (much debated around the turn of the 20th century) that Shakespeare's works were actually written by Francis Bacon. Earlier owners of this copy remained anonymous but one of them at the end of the 17th century was evidently interested in the age of the book at that time – he wrote a sum at the bottom of the titlepage, in 1696, calculating that it was then 64 years old

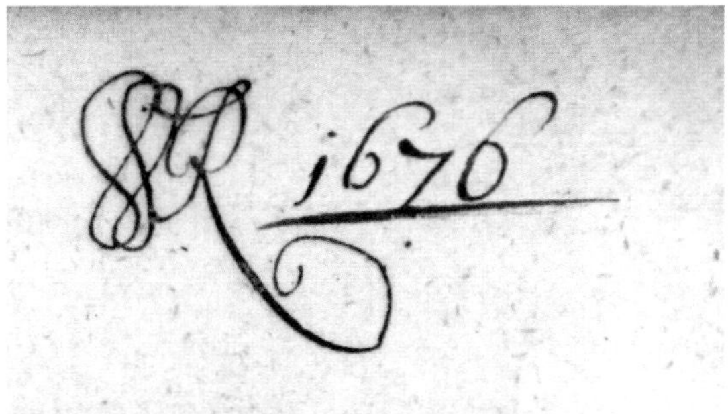

Copy 3 illustrates some of the frustrations and difficulties which can beset book historians. A 17th-century owner has inscribed the flyleaf with his initials and the date of acquisition—'WR 1676' - but we have no clues as to what the initials stand for. The titlepage has a different owner's inscription in the top corner, together with a motto, but these have been subsequently crossed out. The motto can be deciphered ('Que sera, sera') but not the name above

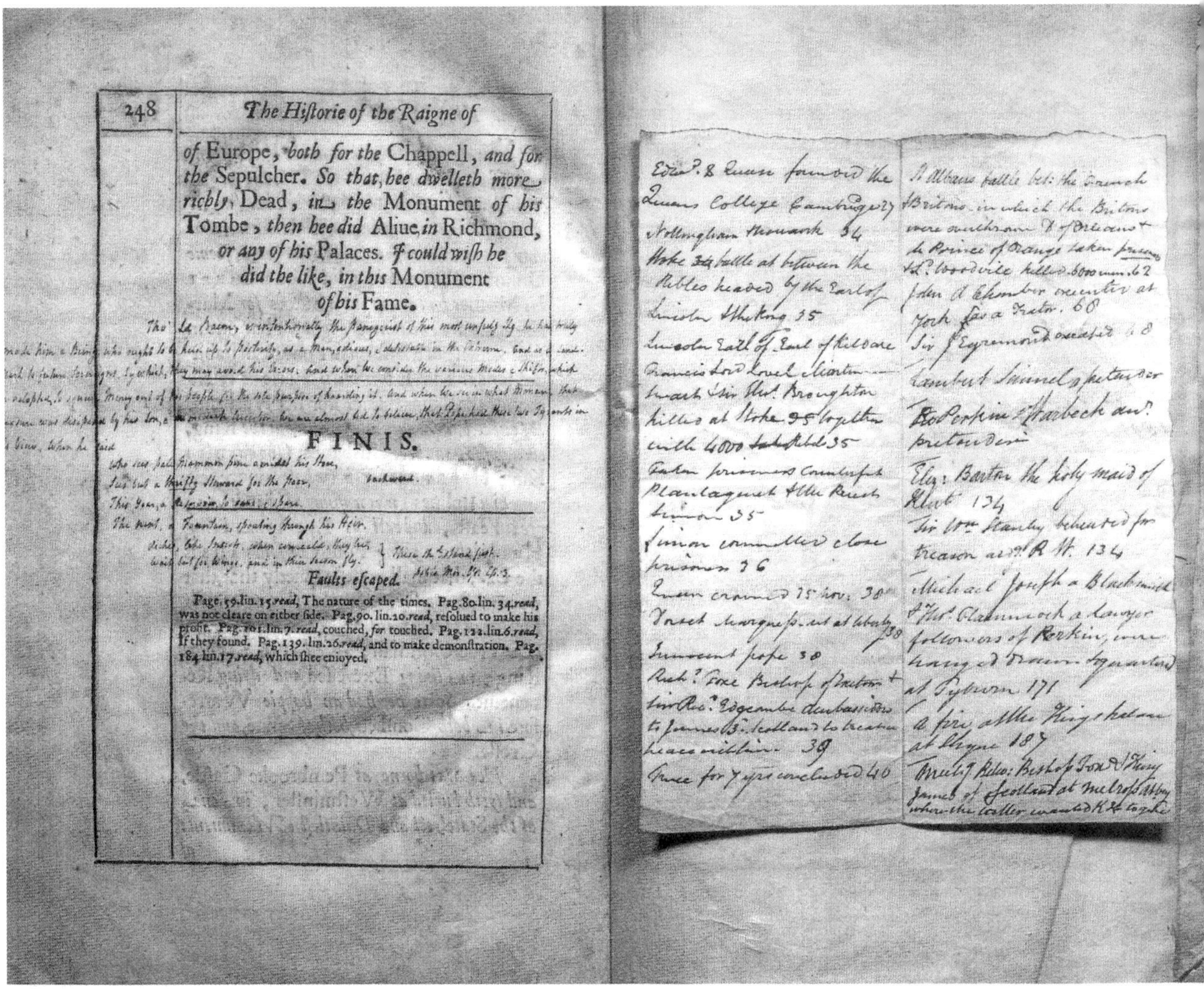

248 *The Historie of the Raigne of*

of Europe, *both for the* Chappell, *and for the* Sepulcher. *So that, hee dwelleth more richly,* Dead, *in the* Monument *of his* Tombe, *then hee did* Aliue, *in* Richmond, *or any of his* Palaces. *I could wish he did the like, in this* Monument *of his* Fame.

FINIS.

Faults escaped.

Page.59.lin.15.*read,* The nature of the times. Pag.80.lin.34.*read,* was not cleare on either side. Pag.90.lin.10.*read,* resolued to make his profit. Pag.101.lin.7.*read,* couched, *for* touched. Pag.122.lin.6.*read,* If they found. Pag.139.lin.26.*read,* and to make demonstration. Pag.184.lin.17.*read,* which shee enioyed.

Copy 1 has annotations on the text in a 19th-century hand, and a folded sheet of page references loosely inserted. This owner summarised his assessment of Bacon's biography, and his views on Henry VII: 'Tho Lord Bacon, is intentionally the panegyrist of this most unfeeling King, he has truly made him a being who ought to be held up to posterity, as a man, odious, & detestable in the extreme ...'

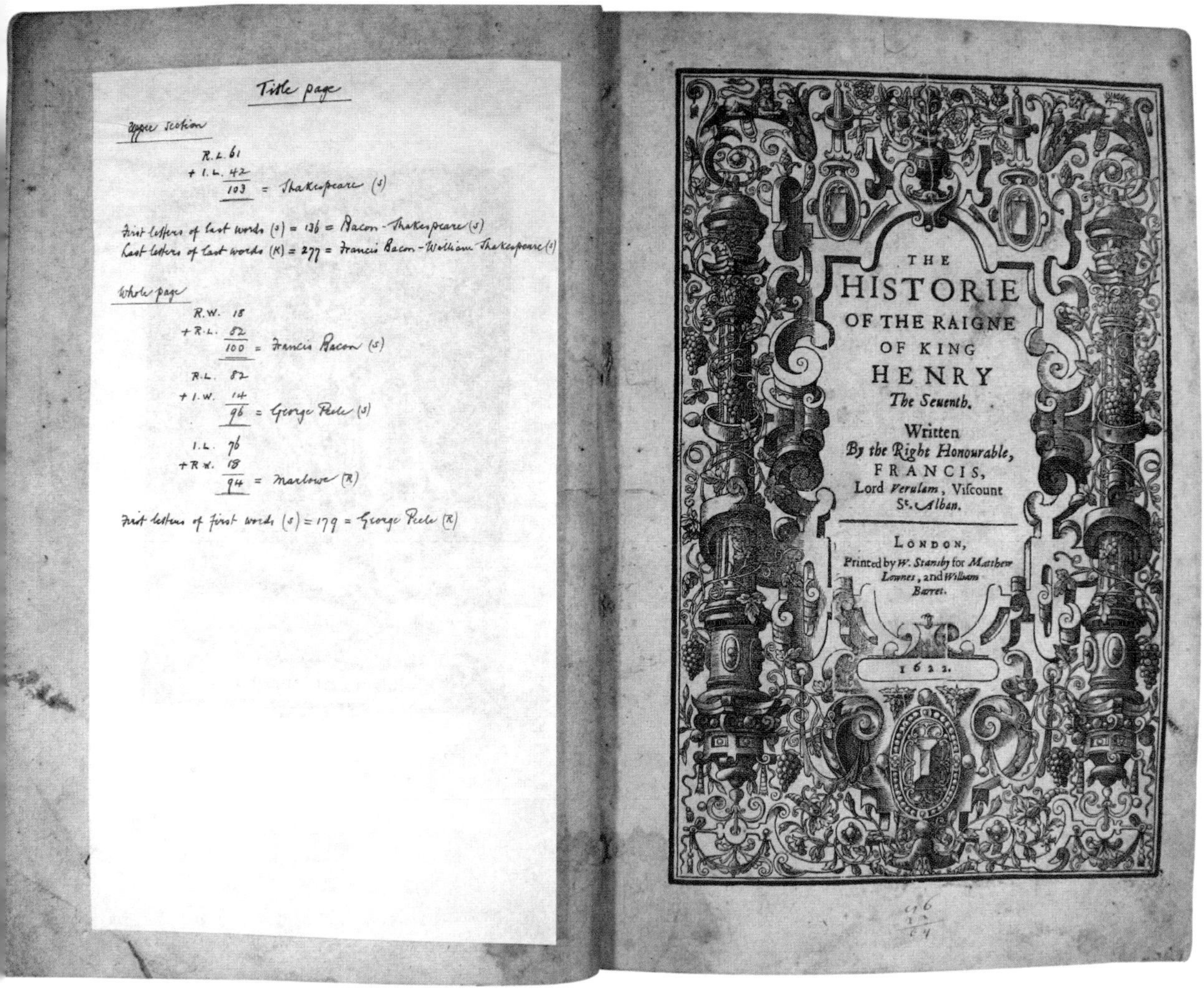

opy 4 shows a later
id rather different way
which an interest
as taken in the text
numerous leaves
ave sheets of notes
isted over them, in
ertram Theobald's
ind, with elaborate
ts of workings, based
i letters in words and
imerical codings, to
veal hidden messages
pposedly linking
acon with Shakespeare

The book has a complex publishing history and two editions, with different typesettings and variant readings, were both published in 1622 with the same titlepage. Individual copies may have mixed sheets from the two editions; although all 5 copies in this sample are technically from the same edition, some differences are found in some of the gatherings. Compare the spellings of 'Raigne/Reigne' in the headline here, and the spellings of 'Yorkshire/Yorkeshire' in line 14 of the text (these pages come from copy 1, and copy 2)

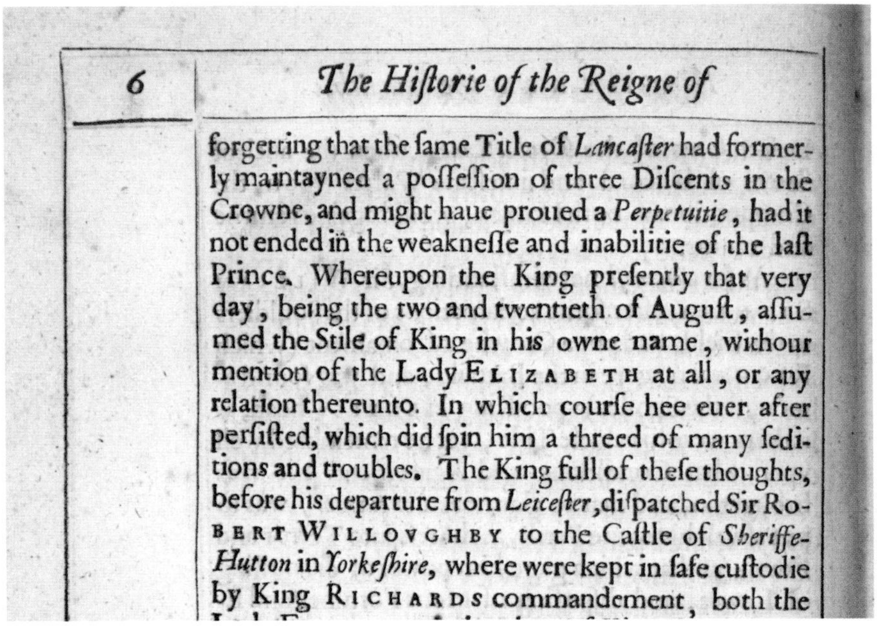

6 *The Hiſtorie of the Reigne of*

forgetting that the ſame Title of *Lancaſter* had formerly maintayned a poſſeſſion of three Diſcents in the Crowne, and might haue proued a *Perpetuitie*, had it not ended in the weakneſſe and inabilitie of the laſt Prince. Whereupon the King preſently that very day, being the two and twentieth of Auguſt, aſſumed the Stile of King in his owne name, without mention of the Lady ELIZABETH at all, or any relation thereunto. In which courſe hee euer after perſiſted, which did ſpin him a threed of many ſeditions and troubles. The King full of theſe thoughts, before his departure from *Leiceſter*, diſpatched Sir ROBERT WILLOVGHBY to the Caſtle of *Sheriffe-Hutton* in *Yorkeſhire*, where were kept in ſafe cuſtodie by King RICHARDS commandement, both the

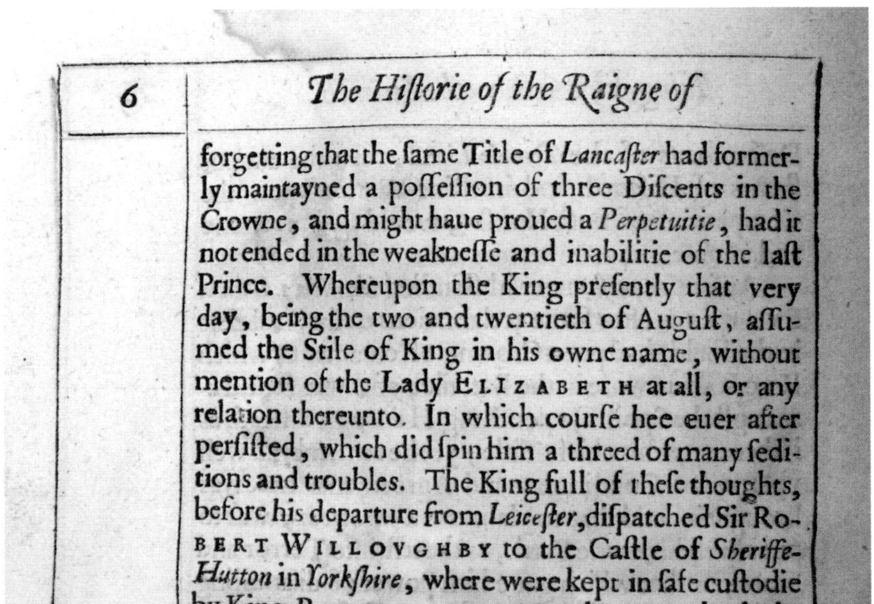

6 *The Hiſtorie of the Raigne of*

forgetting that the ſame Title of *Lancaſter* had formerly maintayned a poſſeſſion of three Diſcents in the Crowne, and might haue proued a *Perpetuitie*, had it not ended in the weakneſſe and inabilitie of the laſt Prince. Whereupon the King preſently that very day, being the two and twentieth of Auguſt, aſſumed the Stile of King in his owne name, without mention of the Lady ELIZABETH at all, or any relation thereunto. In which courſe hee euer after perſiſted, which did ſpin him a threed of many ſeditions and troubles. The King full of theſe thoughts, before his departure from *Leiceſter*, diſpatched Sir ROBERT WILLOVGHBY to the Caſtle of *Sheriffe-Hutton* in *Yorkſhire*, where were kept in ſafe cuſtodie by King RICHARDS commandement, both the

FURTHER READING

If you would like to pursue further some of the topics and lines of inquiry raised in this book, the following (and the further leads they contain) are good places to start.

THE FUTURE OF BOOKS AND LIBRARIES

S. Birkets: *The Gutenberg elegies: the fate of reading in an electronic age.* Boston (Faber and Faber) 1994.

Bill Cope and Angus Phillips (eds): *The future of the book in the digital age.* Oxford (Chandos Publishing), 2006.

J. Gomez: *Print is dead: books in our digital age.* London (Macmillan), 2007.

G. Sapp: *A brief history of the future of libraries: an annotated bibliography.* Lanham (Scarecrow Press), 2002.

R. Wendorf (ed.): *Rare book and manuscript libraries in the twenty-first century.* Cambridge, Mass. (Harvard University Library), 1993.

J. Yellowlees Douglas: *The end of books – or books without end? Reading interactive narratives.* Ann Arbor (University of Michigan Press), 2000.

BIBLIOGRAPHY AND BOOK HISTORY AS A DISCIPLINE: CURRENT DIRECTIONS

S. Eliot and J. Rose (eds): *A companion to the history of the book.* Oxford (Blackwell), 2007.

D. Finkelstein & A.McCleery (eds.): *The book history reader.* London (Routledge), 2002.

L. Howsam: *Old books and new histories: an orientation to studies in book and print culture.* Toronto (University of Toronto Press), 2006.

D. F. McKenzie: *Bibliography and the sociology of texts.* Cambridge (Cambridge University Press), 1999.

D. McKitterick: *Print, manuscript and the search for order 1450-1830.* Cambridge (Cambridge University Press), 2003.

BOOK DESIGN, TYPE, AND ITS HISTORY

A. Bartram: *Five hundred years of book design*. London (The British Library), 2001.

G. Dowding: *Introduction to the history of printing types*. London (Wace), 1961, reprinted London (The British Library), 1998.

N. Drew: *By its cover: modern American book cover design*. New York (Princeton Architectural Press), 2005.

R. Hendel: *On book design*. New Haven and London (Yale University Press), 1998.

S. Loxley: *Type: the secret history of letters*. London and New York (I. B. Tauris), 2005.

D. Martin: *An outline of book design*. London (Blueprint), 1989.

A. Powers: *Front cover: great book jackets and cover design*. London (Mitchell Beazley), 2001.

H. Williamson: *Methods of book design*. 3rd edn. New Haven and London (Yale University Press), 1983.

BOOKS AS ART, BOOK ILLUSTRATION, AND THE ART OF THE BOOK

Art of the printed book 1455-1955: masterpieces of typography ... from the collections of the Pierpont Morgan Library New York. New York (Pierpont Morgan Library), 1973.

J. Bettley (ed): *The art of the book: from medieval manuscript to graphic novel*. London (V&A Publications), 2001.

D. Bland: *A history of book illustration*. London (Faber and Faber), 1958.

S. Bury: *Artists' books: the book as a work of art, 1963-1995*. Brookfield (Scolar Press), 1995.

C. de Hamel: *A history of illuminated manuscripts*. London (Phaidon Press), 1986.

D. Diringer: *The illuminated book: its history and production*. London (Faber abd Faber), 1958.

J. Harthan: *The history of the illustrated book: the western tradition*. London (Thames and Hudson), 1981.

C. Hogben & R. Watson (eds.): *From Manet to Hockney: modern artists' illustrated books*. London (V&A Museum), 1985.

S. Morison: *Four centuries of fine printing*. London (Ernest Benn), 1924, and later editions.

K. Wasserman: *The book as art: artists' books from the National Museum of Women in the Arts*. New York (Princeton Architectural Press), 2007.

PRINTING HISTORY

P. Gaskell: *A new introduction to bibliography*. Oxford (Clarendon Press), 1972.

C. Clair: *A history of printing in Britain*. London (Cassell), 1965

S. Steinberg: *Five hundred years of printing*. London (Faber & Faber), 1955.

M. Twyman: *Printing 1770-1970*. London (The British Library), 1998.

OWNERS' MARKS, MARGINALIA, OWNERS AND THE HISTORY OF READING

J. Andersen and E. Sauer (eds): *Books and readers in early modern England: material studies*. Philadelphia (University of Pennsylvania Press), 2002.

S. A. Baron: *The reader revealed*. Seattle and London (University of Washington Press), 2001.

E. Duffy: *Marking the hours: English people and their prayers, 1240-1570*. New Haven and London (Yale University Press), 2006.

S. Fischer: *A history of reading*. London (Reaktion Books), 2003.

O. Gingerich: *An Annotated Census of Copernicus'* De revolutionibus *(Nuremberg, 1543 and Basel, 1566)*. Leiden (Brill), 2002.

H. Jackson: *Marginalia: readers writing in books*. New Haven and London (Yale University Press), 2001.

R. Myers et al (eds.), *Owners, annotators and the signs of reading*. New Castle and London (Oak Knoll Press and the British Library), 2005.

D. Pearson: *Provenance research in book history: a handbook*. London (The British Library), 1994.

K. Sharpe: *Reading revolutions: the politics of reading in early modern England*. New Haven and London (Yale University Press), 2000.

R. Stoddard: *Marks in books*. Cambridge, Massachusetts (The Houghton Library), 1985.

BOOKBINDING

M. Foot: *The history of bookbinding as a mirror of society*. London (The British Library), 1998.

R. Lewis: *Fine bookbinding in the twentieth century*. Newton Abbot (David & Charles), 1984.

P. Marks: *The British Library guide to bookbinding: history and techniques*. London (The British Library), 1998.

H. Nixon & M. Foot: *The history of decorated bookbinding in England*. Oxford (Clarendon Press), 1992.

D. Pearson: *English bookbinding styles, 1450-1800*. London (The British Library), 2005.

FRAGMENTS IN BINDINGS

L. Brownrigg & M. Smith (eds.): *Interpreting and collecting fragments of medieval books*. Los Altos Hills and London (The Red Gull Press), 2000.

THE HISTORY AND AESTHETICS OF LIBRARIES

N. Barker: *Treasures from the libraries of National Trust country houses*. New York (The Royal Oak Foundation and the Grolier Club), 1999.

J. Bosser and G. de Laubier, *The most beautiful libraries of the world*. London (Thames and Hudson), 2003.

P. Hoare (ed): *The Cambridge history of libraries in Britain and Ireland*. 3v. Cambridge (Cambridge University Press), 2006.

C. Höfer: *Libraries*. London (Thames and Hudson), 2005.

D. H. Stam (ed): *International dictionary of library histories*. 2v. Chicago and London (Fitzroy Dearborn), 2001.

DISPOSAL AND DESTRUCTION OF BOOKS

N. Baker: *Double fold: libraries and the assault on paper*. New York (Random House), 2001.

K. W. Humphreys, 'The loss of books in sixteenth-century England', *Libri* 36 (1986), pp.249-258.

R. Knuth: *Libricide: the regime-sponsored destruction of books and libraries in the twentieth century*. Westport (Praeger), 2003.

D. McKitterick: *Do we want to keep our newspapers?* London (Office for Humanities Communication), 2002.

L. X. Polastron: *Books on fire*. London (Thames and Hudson), 2007.

J. Raven (ed): *Lost libraries: the destruction of great book collections since antiquity*. Basingstoke (Palgrave Macmillan), 2004.

W. West: *The strange rise of semi-literate England: the dissolution of the libraries*. London (Duckworth), 1991.

PICTURE SOURCES

Books and manuscripts used as picture sources for this book are listed here (BL = British Library; NAL = National Art Library, Victoria & Albert Museum, SHL = Senate House Library, University of London).

p.8: BL 11765.h.21, *Cassell's Illustrated Shakespeare*, London, 1864; BL C.39.c.26, C. Marlowe, *The Tragicall History of the Life and Death of Doctor Faustus*, London, 1620.

p.9: BL Or.74.d.45, *A Mirror for Emperors*, 1604; BL H.91/3364, R. Bradbury, *Fahrenheit 451*, London, 1990.

p.10: United States National Archives photo no. 208-N-39840.

p.13: *The Guardian* Saturday Review, 31 July 1999.

p.14: BL Cup.407.c.13, B. Warde, *Quotations*, New Jersey, 1953; billhead of Henry Atkinson, bookseller in Appleby, 1829.

p.24: SHL [DeM] M1 [Copernicus] fol SSR, N. Copernicus, *De Revolutionibus Orbium Coelestium*, Nuremberg, 1543.

p.26: BL MS Royal 14.E.V, G. Boccaccio (tr. L du Premierfait), *Las cas des nobles homes et femmes*, written 1470-83.

p.28 : BL MS Royal 1.E.IX, *Biblia*, written ca.1405-15 ; BL MS Royal 2.A.XVI, *Psalterium*, written ca.1530-47; BL C.23.e.6, E. Castell, *Lexicon Heptaglotton*, London, 1669; BL C.84.d.2, J. Morgagni, *De Sedibus et Causis Morborum*, Venice, 1761. The image of Richard Lucy is taken from a painting at Charlecote House, Warwickshire.

p.30: BL G.2371, G. Heresbach, *Foure Bookes of Husbandrie*, London, 1586.

p.35: BL C.21.c.44, W. Shakespeare, *Sonnets*, London, 1609; BL 011761.ee.23, W. Shakespeare, *Sonnets*, New York, 1933.

p.36-7: BL 11686.ee.35, E. A. Poe, *The poetical works*, Edinburgh, 1869; BL 11686.dd.18, E. A. Poe, *The complete poems*, New York, 1908; X.958/4749 E. A. Poe, *Tales, poems, essays*, London, 1981.

p.38: BL 2708.e.452, H. Williamson, *Methods of Book Design*, 3rd edn, London, 1983.

p.40: J. Motley, *The Rise of the Dutch Republic*, London, 1906, author's collection.

p.41: G. Heyer, *Regency Buck*, London, 1959 (this printing 1972), author's collection; BL H.2005/2066, G. Heyer, *Regency Buck*, London, 2004.

p.42: A. Giberne, *Won at Last*, London, 1892; H. Batsford and C. Fry, *The English Cottage*,

London, 1938; J. Hubback, *Wives who went to College*, London, 1957; E. Showalter, *Hystories*, London, 1997, all author's collection.

p.44-5: BL YA.1992.a.7247, YA.1997.b.4119, X.998/3288, YK.1989.b.1762, H.2000/2255, and RF.2002.a.68: L. Carroll, *Alice's Adventures in Wonderland*, in editions of 1888, 1922, 1973, 1984, 1998 and 1999.

p.46: BL C.14.c.2, Eusebius, [*Evangelica praeparatio*], Venice, 1470.

p.47: BL C.9.d.3, [*Biblia*, Mainz, 1455?]; 60.e.14, G. Tory, *Champ Fleury*, Paris, 1532.

p.48: BL 937.g.80, [Collection of newscuttings and playbills].

p.50: Herzog August Bibliothek, Wolfenbüttel 16.1.Eth.20, U. Boner, *Der Edelstein*, Bamberg, 1461.

p.51: Vatican Library MS lat.3867, Virgil, *Aeneid*, written ca.500.

p.52-3: BL IA.7997, S. Brant, *Narrenschiff*, Nuremberg, 1494; BL Maps C.10.a.14, D. King, *The Cathedrall and Conventuall Churches*, London, 1656; BL C.70. h.5, G. Wither, *Emblemes*, London, 1635.

p.54-5: BL C.30.b.3, H. Humphreys, *The Miracles of our Lord*, London, 1848.

p.56: BL C.119.g.1, W. Fox Talbot, *The Pencil of Nature*, London, 1844.

p.57: BL MS Cotton Domitian A.XVII, *Psalterium*, written ca.1400-20.

p.58-9: BL C.27.e.14, *Horae*, Paris, 1549; BL 12835.b.9, *Gammer Gurton's Story Books*, London, 1845.

p.60-1: BL 681.k.13, W. Hamilton, *Campi Phlegraei*, Naples, 1776.

p.62-3: BL Cup.510.ac.100, S. Johnson, *The Vanity of Human Wishes*, Cambridge, 1984.

p.64: BL C.102.l.5, *The Four Gospels*, Waltham St Laurence, 1931.

p.66-7: BL C.43.h.19, G. Chaucer, *The Works*, Hammersmith, 1896.

p.68-9: BL 1076.i.25, G. Herbert, *The Temple*, Cambridge, 1633; BL Cup.503.p.5, P. van Ostaijen, *Bezette Stad*, Antwerp, 1921; BL MS Harley 647, Aratus (tr. Cicero), written ca.820-840; BL Ch.790/224, *A Curious Hieroglyphick Bible*, London, 1793.

p.70: BL RF.2003.a.233, N. Parra, *The Antibook*, London, 2002.

p.72-3: NAL Safe 1.A.1, P. Verlaine, *Parallèlement*, Paris, 1900.

p.74-5: BL Cup.936/836, M. Kaufman, *Aunt Sallie's Lament*, West Burke, 1988; NAL X901035, K. Smith, *Book 91*, Barrytown, 1982; NAL X920105, J. Christie, *Mirror Book*, Guildford, 1985; NAL X930043, A. Norris, *Lijepa naša domovina*, 1993; NAL X920025, G. Seillé, *Mapa ed Veneiis*, Burton on Trent, 1990.

p.80: Cambridge University Library Keynes B.4.3, J. Donne, *The First Anniuersarie*, London, 1612.

p.81: BL Cup.410.f.742, G. Greene, *Stamboul Train*, London, 1932.

p.82: Harvard University, Houghton Library 2003J-SJ497, S. Johnson, *A Journey to the Western Isles*, London, 1775.

p.83: BL 8530.aaa.32, J. Randall, *An Introduction to ... Arts and Sciences*, London, 1765; BL RB.23.a.25203, *The New Book of Knowledge*, London, 1787.

p.84: BL G.12088(1) and 468. b.10(4), *The Book of Common Prayer*, Edinburgh, 1637.

p.86-7: *The Holy Bible*, London, 1649, author's collection.

p.88-9: BL Cup.404.b.49 and 135. b.9, C. Middleton, *The History of ... Cicero*, London, 1741.

p.90-1: BL C.42.b.12, G. Herbert, *The Temple*, London, 1844.

p.92: BL Add. MS. 42518, G. Chaucer, *Workes*, London, 1598.

p.99: BL C.67.f.3, F. Mason, *Of the Consecration of the Bishops*, London, 1613; BL C.65.l.10, J. Alsted, *Elementale Mathematicarum*, Frankfurt, 1611; BL C.65.k.12, M. Madan, *A Collection of Psalms*, London, 1767; BL C.65.g.15, J. Randall, *Saint Paul's Triumph*, London, 1626.

p.100: BL C.126.g.4, E. Swedenborg, *True Christian Religion*, London, 1519.

p.102-3: BL 577.k.21(6), J. Jekyll, *Facts and Observations Relating to the Temple Church*, London, 1811.

p.104-5: BL 1411.e.13, *The Holy Bible*, London, 1671.

p.106-7: BL 1142.h.21, W. Wollaston, *A Plan of a Course of Chemical Lectures*, Cambridge, 1794.

p.108-9: BL C.28.g.7, M. de Montaigne, *Les essais*, Paris 1602.

p.110-1: BL C.45.e.18, J. Reynolds, *Works*, London, 1798.

p.112: BL 3913.k.4, D. Erasmus, *Paraphrasin in Evangelium Matthaei*, Basle, 1522.

p.113: BL 3623.e.18, Prosper of Aquitaine, *Opera*, Lyons, 1539.

p.115: BL 548.l.3, E. Rudius, *De Affectib. Externarum Corporis Humani*, Venice, 1606.

p.116: BL C.28.g.9, I. Watts, *Logick*, London, 1745.

p.117: Lanhydrock House, Cornwall B.7.7, W. Camden, *Anglica, Normannica ... a veteribus scripta*, Frankfurt, 1603.

p.118-9: BL C.45.a.19, *Introduction to the Latin Tongue*, Eton, 1775.

p.120: BL IA.3420, St Augustine, *Sermones*, Cologne, 1475?

p.121: BL G.11548, G. Puttenham, *The Arte of English Poesie*, London, 1589.

p.122: BL C.60.k.8, O. Wilde, *Vera*, New York, 1882.

p.123: BL E.592(1), *The Life and Death of Philip Herbert*, London, 1649.

p.124-5: *The Holy Bible*, Cambridge, 1810, author's collection.

p.126: BL 104.c.44, C. Morton, *A Discourse Concerning a Lumber-Office*, London, 1696.

p.127: BL C.45.d.23, James I, *Triplici Nodo, Triplex Cuneus*, London, 1607.

p.128: BL C.35.a.14, *This Prymer*, Paris, 1532.

p.129: *The Book of Common Prayer*, Cambridge, 1763, author's collection.

p.130-1: BL C.41.e.31, *Horae*, Paris, 1527; SHL [DeM] M1 [Copernicus] fol SSR, N. Copernicus, *De Revolutionibus Orbium Coelestium*, Nuremberg, 1543.

p.132: BL 573.k.4, N. Serarius, *Moguntiacarum Rerum ... libri quinque*, Mainz, 1604.

p.133: Fulda Landesbibliothek, MS Bonifatianus 2, Leo, *Epistolae* and other texts, written ca.700-750.

p.134: Corpus Christi College, Cambridge, MS 286, Gospels, written in the 6th century.

p.135: Trinity Hall, Cambridge MS 1, Thomas of Elmham, *Chronicles of St Augustine's Abbey*, written ca.1414-18.

p.136-7: BL C.12.e.17, B. Jonson, *Volpone*, London, 1607; SHL [S.L.] I [Wilde – 1893], O. Wilde, *Salomé*, Paris, 1893.

p.138-9: BL MS Harley 2342, Prayer Book of Lady Jane Grey, written in the first half of the 16th century.

p.140: BL C.109.c.4, L. M. Budgen, *Episodes of Insect Life*, London, 1849-51.

p.142: BL 1568/4414, *The life ... of Robinson Crusoe*, Edinburgh, 1769; BL 1607/618, D. Defoe, *Life and Adventures of Robinson Crusoe*, London, 1864; BL X.990/18823, D. Defoe, *Robinson Crusoe*, Toronto, 1981.

p.144-5: BL C.19.g.2, Pliny, *Naturalis Historia*, Lyons, 1548; BL C.25.h.3, *The Second Tome of Homelyes*, London, 1563; BL 7.f.13, *Book of Common Prayer*, London, 1674; BL C.27.f.10, J. Theobald, *Albion*, Oxford, 1720; BL Davis 172, *Novelle Otto*, London, 1790.

p.146-7: BL C.68.i.10, P. Shelley, *The Revolt of Islam*, London,

1818 (bound by Thomas Cobden-Sanderson); BL C.108.bbb.6, F. Villon, *Les Ballades*, London, 1900 (bound by Sybil Pye); BL C.128. f.10, H. Bates, *Through the Woods*, London, 1936 (bound by Edgar Mansfield); BL C.188.c.1, W. Shakespeare, *Macbeth*, Guildford, 1970 (bound by Philip Smith); BL C.183.b.8, L. Clark, *An Intimate Landscape*, London, 1981 (bound by Angela James).

p.148: BL C.128.k.3, D. Erasmus, *Adagiorum Chiliades*, Frankfurt, 1599.

p.149: Cambridge University Library Q*.11.56(D), A. Gentilis, *In Titulum Digestorum*, Hanau, 1614.

p.150-1: Bodleian Library, Oxford Arch G.e.7, and Folger Shakespeare Library, Washington STC 22273 fo.1 no.60: W. Shakespeare, [*Works*], London, 1623.

p.152: R. Cock, *Censura Quorundam Scriptorum*, London, 1623, author's collection; BL Davis 38, *The Booke of Common Prayer*, London, 1622; BL Davis 180, E. Spenser, *The Faerie Queene*, London, 1609.

p.153: BL 206.g.2, Eve.b.52, and Davis 191: L. Eachard, *A General Ecclesiastical history*, London, 1702.

p.154: Advertisement from the end of *Foxe's Book of Martyrs*, London, 1881, author's collection.

p.155: BL X20/6991 and 012624. h.25/20, T. Hardy, *Poems of the Past and the Present*, London, 1902.

p.156: Emmanuel College, Cambridge 331.3.83, W. King, *The Art of Cookery*, [London, 1705].

p.157: Bodleian Library, Oxford Douce fragm.e.1, advertisement by William Caxton, Westminster, ca.1477.

p.158: BL C.69.aa.11, N. Hemmingsen, *The Epistle of the Blessed Apostle*, London, 1581.

p.159: Canterbury Cathedral Library W2/B-9-15, D. de Coetlogon, *An Universal History*, London, 1745.

p.160-1 Durham University Library Kellett 331, Galen, *De Sanitate Tuenda*, Tübingen, 1541.

p.164-5: BL 128.h.10, D. Loggan, *Oxonia Illustrata*, Oxford, 1675.

p.166: BL P.P.7611, *The Illustrated London News*, 7 June 1851.

p.171: BL 125.b.22, *Bibliotheca Bernardiana*, London, [1711].

p.174: NAL X930037, Floating Concrete Octopus, *The Book of Nails*, Madison, 1992.

p.180 *Times Higher Education Supplement*, 16 November 2007

Case study: copy 1, SHL [D-L.L.] (XVII) [Bacon] copy 1; copy 2, SHL [S.L.] I [Bacon] copy 2; copy 3, SHL [S.L.] I [Bacon] copy 1; copy 4, SHL Bacon Society 1208; copy 5, SHL [D-L.L.] (XVII) [Bacon] copy 3.

INDEX

ACKNOWLEDGMENTS

All photographs of British Library materials are reproduced by permission of the British Library Board: the permission of the following institutions is gratefully acknowledged for others (noted by their page numbers in this book):

The Astrup Fearnley Collection, Oslo, Norway, p.32-3; The Trustees of the British Museum, p.21; The Syndics of Cambridge University Library, pp. 80, 149; the Master and Fellows of Corpus Christi College, Cambridge, p.134; the Master and Fellows of Emmanuel College, Cambridge, p. 156; the Pepys Library, Magdalene College, Cambridge, p.167; the Master and Fellows of Trinity Hall, Cambridge, p.135; the Dean and Chapter of Canterbury Cathedral, p.159; Circle Press, p.75; Corbis, p.6, 29, 76; Durham University Library, p.160-1; the Folger Shakespeare Library, p.151; Harvard College Library, p.82; the University of London, p.24, 131, 137, 184-204; Lucasfilm Ltd, p.16-17; the National Archives, Washington, p.10-11; the National Trust, p.28, 117, 173; the Curators of the Bodleian Library, Oxford, p.150, 157; St Deiniol's Library, Hawarden, p.170; the Trustees of the Victoria & Albert Museum, p.72-3, 74-5, 174; the Wellcome Trust, p.176-7; the Herzog August Bibliothek, Wolfenbüttel, p.50.

The writing of books involves much assistance and kindness along the way from colleagues, friends and library custodians who help with finding things, reading drafts, and suggesting ways of steering a better course. I cannot mention everyone who has contributed like this during the time that this book has been in preparation but I would particularly like to thank Karen Attar, Giles Mandelbrote, Richard Ovenden and Mark Purcell for commenting on various drafts along the way. Christopher de Hamel, Kathleen Houghton, Dave Jackson, Elizabeth James, Barry McKay, Sally Nicholls and Julia Walworth have all helped in various ways in obtaining pictures. The design and layout of the book involved considerable trial, error and discussion, and the creative input of Phil Cleaver and David Way should be appreciatively recognized. My wife and my son have each played their parts in stimulating ideas and making suggestions, and I hope that they like the outcome of a project they have heard much discussed. I also hope that the world at large finds something worthwhile in the book's contents, but if not, the responsibility lies with the author alone.